# UNIX® System V
# Performance Management

Edited by
## Phyllis Eve Bregman
## Sally A. Browning

**P T R Prentice Hall**
Englewood Cliffs, New Jersey 07632

Library of Congress Cataloging-in-Publication Data

Bregman, Phyllis Eve.
    UNIX System V performance management/[edited by] Phyllis Eve Bregman,
Sally A. Browning
        p.  cm -- (Prentice Hall open systems library)
    Includes bibliographical references and index.
    ISBN 0-13-016429-1
    1. UNIX System V (Computer file)  I. Browning, Sally A.
II. Title.  III. Series.
QA76.76.063B74    1993
005.4'3--dc20                                                        93-8174
                                                                       CIP

Editorial/production supervision: *Harriet Tellem*
Cover design: *Eloise Starkweather*
Manufacturing buyer: *Mary E. McCartney*
Acquisitons editor: *Phyllis Eve Bregman*
Cover art: *Carnival of Harlequin* (Miro) 1924-25. (From Albright-Knrox Art Gallery, Buffalo, New York)

Published by P T R Prentice-Hall, Inc.
A Simon & Schuster Company
Englewood Cliffs, New Jersey 07632

The publisher offers discounts on this book when ordered in bulk quantities. For more information contact:

        Corporate Sales Department
        P T R Prentice Hall
        113 Sylvan Avenue
        Enlgewood Cliffs, NJ 07632

        Phone: 201-592-2863
        Fax: 201-592-2249

Printed in the United States of America
10 9 8 7 6 5 4 3 2 1


ISBN 0-13-016429-1


Prentice-Hall International (UK) Limited, *London*
Prentice-Hall of Australia Pty. Limited, *Sydney*
Prentice-Hall Canada  Inc., *Toronto*
Prentice-Hall Hispanoamericana, S.A.,
Prentice-Hall of India Private Limited, *New Delhi*
Prentice-Hall of Japan, Inc., *Tokyo*
Simon & Schuster Asia Pte. Ltd., *Singapore*
Editora  Prentice-Hall do Brasil, Ltda., *Rio de Janeiro*

# Table of Contents

**List of Figures and Tables**                                    ix

**Preface**                                                      xiii

**Chapter 1:   Improving System Performance**                      1

Overview                                                           1
Investigating Performance Problems                                 2
Processes, Scheduling, and Workloads                               5
File Systems and Storage Device Performance                        7
Communication Issues                                              10
Monitoring System Performance                                     11
Reconfiguring UNIX                                                12

**Chapter 2:   Users, Processes, and Workloads**                  15

Overview                                                          15
Streamlining the Work Environment: System and User Profiles       16
Process Structure                                                 21
Scheduling Processes                                              25
Configuring the Scheduler                                         28
Changing Scheduler Parameters with `dispadmin`                    37
Paging Behavior                                                   41
Process Accounting                                                44

## Chapter 3:    The File System                                        53

Overview                                                                  53
File System Organization                                                  55
The s5 File System Type                                                   57
The ufs File System Type                                                  60
The bfs File System Type                                                  63
Selecting a File System Type                                             66
Creating a File System                                                    67
Using mkfs to Create an s5 File System                                   69
Using mkfs to Create a ufs File System                                   72
Using mkfs to Create a bfs File System                                   74
The vfstab File                                                           75
Maintaining a File System                                                 76
Improving and Controlling File System Usage                              79
Assigning Disk Quotas                                                     82
Checking a File System for Consistency                                   84
Checking s5 File Systems                                                  86
Checking ufs File Systems                                                 92
Checking bfs File Systems                                                 95

## Chapter 4:    Storage Devices                                        97

Overview                                                                  97
Properties of Devices                                                    101
Suggestions for Managing Storage Devices                                103
Formatting Disks                                                         104
Bad Block Handling                                                       104
Bad Block Recovery                                                       107
Dealing with Data Loss                                                   116
Partitioning a Hard Disk                                                 116
The boot and stand Partitions                                           119
Changing Default Boot Parameters                                        125
Making New Bootable Disks                                               127
Managing Device Attributes                                              132
Managing Device Groups                                                  140
Managing Device Reservations                                            145

# Chapter 5:   Communications                                   149

| | |
|---|---|
| Overview | 149 |
| STREAMS | 149 |
| The Benefits of STREAMS | 151 |
| Basic Network Utilities | 152 |
| BNU Database Support Files | 155 |
| BNU Log Files | 157 |
| Detecting BNU Problems | 160 |
| System V File Sharing | 160 |
| RFS vs. NFS | 162 |
| Remote File Sharing | 166 |
| Sharing Resources on RFS | 167 |
| RFS Troubleshooting Techniques | 168 |
| Network File System | 170 |
| NFS Administration | 172 |
| Monitoring NFS Performance | 173 |
| NFS Troubleshooting Techniques | 175 |
| Using the Automounter | 184 |

## Chapter 6:   Monitoring System Activity                189

Overview                                                              189
Automatically Collecting System Activity Data                         190
Collecting System Activity Data on Demand                             192
Monitoring File Access                                                194
Monitoring Buffer Activity                                            195
Monitoring System Calls                                               196
Monitoring Disk Activity                                              199
Monitoring Page-Out Activity                                          201
Monitoring Kernel Memory Usage                                        202
Monitoring Interprocess Communication                                 204
Monitoring Page-In Activity                                           205
Monitoring Scheduling Queue Activity                                  206
Monitoring Unused Memory Status                                       207
Monitoring CPU Utilization                                            208
Monitoring System Table Status                                        210
Monitoring Swapping Activity                                          211
Monitoring RFS Operations                                             212
Monitoring Terminal Activity                                          213
Monitoring Overall System Performance                                 214
Monitoring RFS Client Caching                                         218
Monitoring RFS Server Activity                                        220
Displaying System Activity Data                                       221
Summary: Using System Monitoring To Detect And Correct Performance
        Problems.                                                     223

# Chapter 7:    Performance Tools                      227

Overview                                                         227
Timing Application Program Execution                             228
Monitoring Resource Usage by Remote Clients                      231
Kernel Profiling                                                 232
Reporting Disk Access Location and Seek Distance                 236
Recovering from System Trouble                                   240
Performing a System Dump                                         242

# Chapter 8:    Configuring UNIX                      245

Overview                                                         245
Configuration Scenarios                                          247
Reconfiguring the System Through a Reboot                        248
Recovering from an Unbootable Operating System                   253
User-Level Configuration of the UNIX System                      254
Configuring a New mUNIX                                          255
Tunable Parameters                                               256
General Kernel Tunables                                          262
System Information                                               264
Hardware Information                                             264
Buffer Cache                                                     265
Paging                                                           266
Per Process Limits                                               267
File Access Features                                             269
STREAMS                                                          270
Scheduler Information                                            271
XENIX Shared Data                                                272
High Resolution Timers                                           272
Ports Board                                                      273
Time Sharing Scheduler                                           273
s5 File System Type                                              273
ufs File System Type                                             274
Profiler                                                         275
Interprocess Communication                                       275
RFS Parameters                                                   278

**Quick Reference  Guide to Performance Management**          **281**

**Chapter 9:**   `Checking s5` **File Systems**          **287**

Initialization Phase                                      288
General Errors                                            288
Phase 1: Check Blocks and Sizes                          289
Phase 1B: Rescan for More DUPS                           292
Phase 2: Check Pathnames                                 293
Phase 3: Check Connectivity                              295
Phase 4: Check Reference Counts                          297
Phase 5: Check Free List                                 300
Phase 6: Salvage Free List                              303
Cleanup Phase                                            303

**Chapter 10:**   **Checking** `ufs` **File Systems**          **305**

Initialization Phase                                      305
Phase 1: Check Blocks and Sizes                          311
Phase 1B: Rescan for More DUPS                           315
Phase 2: Check Pathnames                                 315
Phase 3: Check Connectivity                              323
Phase 4: Check Reference Counts                          326
Phase 5: Check Cylinder Groups                           330
Cleanup Phase                                            332

**Glossary**          **333**

**Index**          **347**

# List of Figures and Tables

**1-1**  Potential Performance Problems.                                        3
**1-2**  Outline of typical troubleshooting procedures.                         4
**1-3**  SPAU commands.                                                        13

**2-1**  A Sample System Profile.                                              17
**2-2**  Additional Shell Script for the System Profile.                       18
**2-3**  A Sample User's Profile.                                              19
**2-4**  Executing User Commands.                                             22
**2-5**  State diagram for user processes.                                    24
**2-6**  The System V Release 4 Process Scheduler.                            26
**2-7**  Tunable scheduler parameters.                                        30
**2-8**  A Simplified Scheduling Example.                                     32
**2-9**  Part of a simple real-time dispatch table.                           34
**2-10**  Output from dispadmin -l.                                           37
**2-11**  Output from dispadmin -g.                                           39
**2-12**  Setting scheduler parameters with dispadmin -s                      40
**2-13**  State diagram for LRU paging algorithm.                             42
**2-14**  Holiday List                                                        46
**2-15**  A Daily Usage Report                                                49
**2-16**  A Daily Command Summary Report.                                     49
**2-17**  A Total Command Summary Report.                                     52

**3-1**  Mountable file systems.                                              56
**3-2**  Accessing storage blocks in an s5 file system.                       59
**3-3**  Maximum addressability for s5 file systems.                          59
**3-4**  Accessing storage blocks in a ufs file system.                       62
**3-5**  Maximum addressability for ufs file systems.                         62
**3-6**  Accessing storage blocks in a bfs file system.                       65
**3-7**  Inter-record Gap and Blocks/Cylinder Recommendations for s5          71
**3-8**  Files that grow through normal use.                                  77
**3-9**  An fsck example.                                                     86
**3-10**  fsck options.                                                       87

**4-1**   Directory listings for a user's directory and /dev.          99
**4-2**   Sample disk address conversion                              112
**4-3**   Default disk partitions for a 72MB drive.                   117
**4-4**   Physical layout of disk partitions.                         118
**4-5**   The /stand file system.                                     120
**4-6**   Recommended device attribute values.                        133
**4-7**   Standard device attributes.                                 133

**5-1**   Streams and pipes.                                          151
**5-2**   Making a connection through BNU.                            154
**5-3**   Format of an entry in the command log.                     157
**5-4**   Format of an error log entry.                               158
**5-5**   Format of conn entries in perflog.                          159
**5-6**   Format of xfer entries in perflog.                          159
**5-7**   File sharing.                                                161
**5-8**   Sharing resources in RFS networks.                          168
**5-9**   Mounting a remote resource.                                 171

**6-1**   Automatically collecting system activity data.              192
**6-2**   sar options.                                                 193
**6-3**   Output from sar -a.                                          194
**6-4**   Output from sar -b.                                          196
**6-5**   Output from sar -Db.                                         196
**6-6**   Output from sar -c.                                          198
**6-7**   Output from sar -Dc.                                         198
**6-8**   Output from sar -d.                                          200
**6-9**   Output from sar -d.                                          200
**6-10**  Output from sar -g.                                          202
**6-11**  Output from sar -k.                                          204
**6-12**  Output from sar -m.                                          204
**6-13**  Output from sar -p.                                          206
**6-14**  Output from sar -q.                                          207

**6-15** Output from sar -r.                                                    208
**6-16** Output from sar -u.                                                    209
**6-17** sar -u output on a co-processor system.                                209
**6-18** Output from sar -Du.                                                   210
**6-19** Output from sar -v.                                                    211
**6-20** Output from sar -w.                                                    212
**6-21** Output from sar -x.                                                    213
**6-22** Output from sar -y.                                                    214
**6-23** Output from sar -A.                                                    216
**6-24** Output from sar -C.                                                    220
**6-25** Output from sar -S.                                                    221
**6-26** Example of sag Output.                                                 222
**6-27** Using sar reports to detect performance problems.                      224

**7-1**  A timex example.                                                       228
**7-2**  Output from fusage.                                                    232
**7-3**  Output from prfpr.                                                     235
**7-4**  Output from sadp: A Cylinder Access Histogram                          237
**7-5**  Output from sadp: A Seek Distance Histogram                            238
**7-6**  Using errdump.                                                         241
**7-7**  Using sysdump.                                                         244

**8-1**  A sample system reconfiguration.                                       251
**8-2**  Suggested Parameter Values.                                            258
**8-3**  Suggested RFS tunable parameter settings.                              280

**9-1**  Abbreviations used in fsck error messages.                             287

# Preface

This book discusses performance management techniques and tools for UNIX System V Release 4.

▲ Chapter 1, *Improving System Performance*, gives an overview of performance management. It discusses the major system components, the problems that can arise in each area, and the kinds of detection and solution techniques that can be applied. It includes a general plan of attack for finding the causes of system degradation and gives some examples of common problems.

▲ Chapter 2, *Users, Processes, and Workloads*, describes user environments, process structure, process scheduling, the paging algorithm, and process accounting. As a system administrator, you can head off some of the potential performance problems by constructing suitable .profile scripts and by keeping stack of system use patterns. You can tune scheduler and paging parameters to better suit your computational mix as well.

▲ Chapter 3, *The File System*, presents the notion of file system type and describes three that are used to organize space on secondary storage: s5, ufs, and bfs. Guidelines are given for choosing a file system type and administrative tasks that can prevent, detect, and correct file system problems are described.

▲ Chapter 4, Storage Devices, describes how to format and partition hard disk drives and diskettes, including bad block handling. It also discusses the /stand and /boot partitions, making bootable disks, and managing device properties and usage.

▲ Chapter 5, Communications, discusses four mechanisms in UNIX to support communication between processes, between user applications and the kernel, and between computers: STREAMS, the Basic Network Utilities (BNU), Remote File Sharing (RFS), and the Network File System (NFS). The four mechanisms are described with a focus on performance monitoring and tuning.

▲ Chapter 6, *Monitoring System Activity*, presents a set of tools for monitoring system performance both automatically and on demand. The primary tool is sar(1), which collects a wide variety of statistics about system behavior selected by a collection of more than 20(!) options. The chapter ends with a table listing some common performance concerns, the `sar` options that apply, and the threshold values to look for.

▲  Chapter 7, *Performance Tools*, introduces the rest of the SPAU (System Performance Analysis Utilities) toolkit. `timex` will time application program execution. `fusage` will give RFS performance information. `prfdc`, `prfld`, `prfpr`, `prfsnap`, and `prfstat` are used for to profile and tune your kernel. `sadp` measures disk seek distances. `errdump` and `sysdump` can help you track down system failures.

▲  Chapter 8, *Configuring UNIX*, gives procedures for reconfiguring your UNIX system. It included information about the tunable parameters that were introduced in preceding chapters.

▲  *The Quick Reference Guide* lists more than sixty tasks a system administrator might undertake to identify and correct a performance problem. Each task is accompanied by a procedure to follow or a reference to an appropriate tool, and a pointer to the chapter in this book that addresses the problem.

▲  A *Glossary* that defines some terms associated with UNIX and performance management that may be new to you.

▲  A comprehensive *Index*.

## Related Reading

*UNIX System V Release 4 Programmer's Guide: Networking Interfaces*, UNIX System Laboratories, Prentice Hall, Englewood Cliffs, NJ, ISBN: 0-13-947078-6.

*UNIX System V Release 4 Programmer's Reference Manual: Operating System API* UNIX System Laboratories, Prentice Hall, Englewood Cliffs, NJ, ISBN: 0-13-951294-2.

*UNIX System V Release 4 System Administrator's Guide*, UNIX System Laboratories, Prentice Hall, Englewood Cliffs, NJ: ISBN: 0-13-947086-7.

*UNIX System V Release 4 User's Reference Manual/ System Administrator's Reference Manual* (two volumes), UNIX System Laboratories, Prentice Hall, Englewood Cliffs, NJ: ISBN: Commands a-l: 0-13-951310-8; Commands m-z: 0-13-9511328-0.

*UNIX System V Release 4 System Files and Devices Reference Manual*, UNIX System Laboratories, Prentice Hall, Englewood Cliffs, NJ: ISBN: 0-13-951302-7.

*UNIX System V Release 4 Programmer's Guide*: STREAMS, UNIX System Laboratories, Prentice Hall, Englewood Cliffs, N, ISBN: 0-13-947003-4.

*UNIX System V Release 4 Device Driver Interface/Driver-Kernel Interface (DDI/DKI) Reference Manual*, UNIX System Laboratories, Prentice Hall, Englewood Cliffs, NJ: ISBN:

*UNIX System V Release 4 Programmer's Guide: SCSI Driver Interface*, UNIX System Laboratories, Prentice Hall, Englewood Cliffs, NJ: ISBN: 0-13-957556-1.

Maurice J. Bach, *The Design of the UNIX Operating System,* Prentice Hall, Englewood Cliffs, NJ.

## Conventions

The following notational conventions are used in the text:

*Italics*                              represent placeholders in commands and options for context-sensitive values like files names, device types and names, numeric values, etc. Chapter and section names are italicized when referenced in the text as well.

`Courier`                          is used for literal commands and options, and output from the computer. Names of menus in the menu interface are also set in `Courier` type.

◆ *Note*                Notes contain remarks slightly off the subject at hand but still pertinent to the discussion.

▼ Caution            Cautions are used to warn you of potential quicksand.

## Acknowledgments

This book is derived from information in the UNIX System V Release 4 and
SV/386 Release 3.4 System Administrator's Guides and Programmers Reference Manuals, and on-line manual pages. While the material has been rear-
ranged and re-worked, expanded here and contracted there, it retains much
of the flavor and many of the words of the original material.

Our thanks to Dorothy Chang, Elka Grisham, Dick Hamilton, and Bill Klinger
from UNIX System Laboratories for their continuous support during this
project. Thanks also to Mary Fox and John Van Dyk for reviewing the manu-
script, and Sally would like to thank her husband, Bart N. Locanthi, Jr. and
her three children, Jennifer, John, and David, for their patience and understanding when I disappear into my office for a few weeks. Phyllis would like
to thank Ron and her children Nicole and Rebecca. Someday I'll be home for
dinner!

Phyllis Eve Bregman and Sally A. Browning

April, 1993

# 1

# *Improving System Performance*

## ❑ Overview

System performance is a measure of how a computer system executes its tasks: its timeliness or responsiveness and availability. This book describes ways to monitor and enhance the performance of your UNIX system. It suggests ways to find and fix performance problems by highlighting areas of the system that affect performance, by providing examples of how to improve performance, and by listing tools that monitor performance. These activities are collectively called performance management.

Performance management, like all administrative tasks, is a continual process. Paying attention to performance on a routine basis, such as automatically collecting and examining usage statistics, will help you identify and correct potential problems before they seriously impact your users.

The default UNIX configuration is satisfactory for many work environments, but may not take into consideration the traffic patterns and the behavior of specific applications on your system. For this reason, you may need to reconfigure your system to provide the service required by your users and their applications. You can use the default configuration as a starting point and as you gain experience with your users and their demands on system resources, you can tune the system to their needs.

Just as a car performs best when properly tuned, your system will perform best when *it* is properly tuned. A collection of tools that monitor performance can help you pinpoint performance problems and determine whether they require user training, application tuning, system maintenance, or system configuration solutions.

## ❑ Investigating Performance Problems

Locating the source of the problem can require some careful detective work. There is no canned procedure to follow, but rather an approach and a shopping list of potential problem areas. The list is shown in Figure 1-1 and covers basic areas where problems usually surface. Figure 1-2 lays out an approach for tracking down a problem and suggests some actions that may alleviate the problem. It uses the performance monitoring tools, principally the sar program, as well some familiar tools like du and ps. The most common indication that a problem exists is consistently poor response time.

The search path in Figure 1-2 serves as an outline for the rest of the book as well. The next four chapters focus on large sections of UNIX that can develop performance problems and that can be configured with your system and user community in mind: the scheduler and process handling capabilities, the file system, the storage device parameters, and the networking capabilities. Following those are chapters on the performance monitoring tools and a guide to reconfiguring UNIX to meet your system performance goals.

The rest of this chapter gives the flavor of what kind of problems can be identified and solved in each of the system areas given above: process handling, file systems, disk drive performance, and networking. It also previews the tools that will help you identify problems.

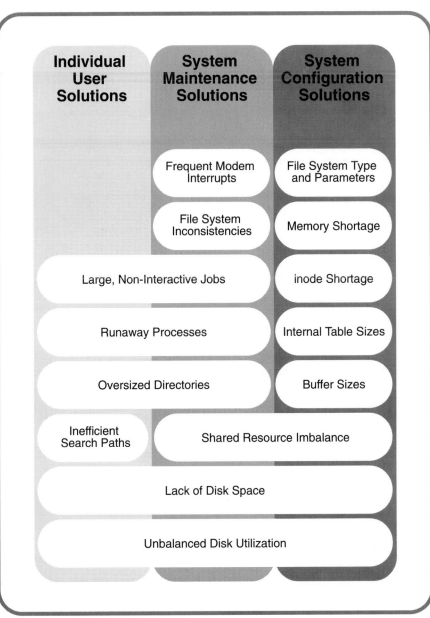

**Figure 1-1**
*Potential Performance Problems.*
Performance bottlenecks can occur because the system is not configured optimally, because routine maintenance activities have been overlooked, or due to characteristics of an individual user or process.

**Figure 1-2**
*Outline of typi-*
*cal trouble-*
*shooting*
*procedures.*
*The flowchart sug-*
*gests a possible*
*approach to take to*
*identify a perfor-*
*mance problem.*
*You will want to*
*widen the search*
*or tailor it differ-*
*ently, depending*
*on your system*
*configuration,*
*usage, nd symp-*
*toms.*

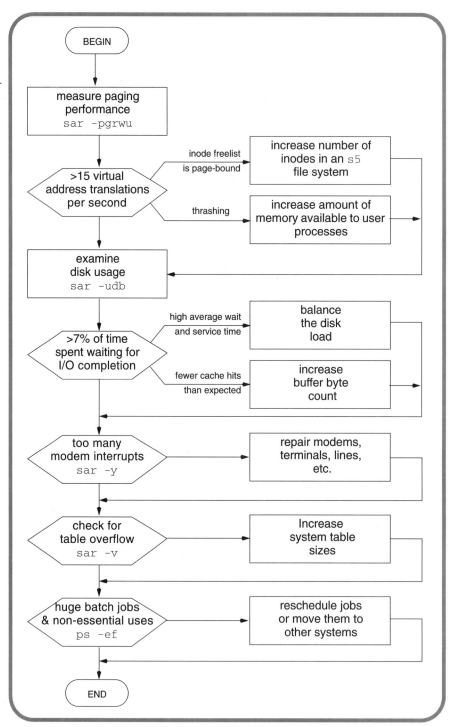

# ❏ Processes, Scheduling, and Workloads

Chapter 2, *Users, Processes, and Workloads*, looks at user processes and the system code that supports them with performance issues in mind. It describes the process structure in UNIX, the scheduling algorithm and parameters, and paging behavior. Performance concerns like these are discussed:

▲ system configuration issues like

  • paging behavior and memory size

  • process, inode, file, and shared memory tables in the kernel that are improperly sized for your system

▲ user -specific bottlenecks like

  • poorly constructed PATH variables

  • runaway processes

  • large noninteractive jobs running during peak hours.

## Paging Performance and Memory Size

The first thing to look at is the paging activity, since page faults are costly in both disk and CPU overhead. Get the `sar -pgrwu` report. By using this information you can reasonably determine whether more memory is needed or if the excess paging activity is due to too few inodes which indirectly causes reusable pages to be discarded.

If memory shortage occurs frequently then memory should be increased in some way. Removing optional kernel utilities that are not needed by your applications increases the amount of memory available to user applications. And additional memory can be added to the hardware configuration.

## Examining Kernel Table Sizes

To check for potential table overflows, get the `sar -v` report. It will report any table overflows in the process or inode tables. Overflows in these tables are avoided by increasing `NPROC` and `NINODES` in the `/etc/master.d/kernel` and `/etc/master.d/s5` files. If the tables never seem to fill up, perhaps you can reduce their size, thereby freeing up some memory by reducing the size of the kernel.

## Controlling User `PATH` Variables

User `PATH` variables are difficult to control. Regular mail should be sent to users informing them of how poorly formed search paths can cause system problems, and reminding them of the guidelines to use when defining or modifying their `$PATH` definition.

`$PATH` is a command line in the user's `.profile` file that is searched each time a command is executed. Before outputting the `not found` error message, the system must search every directory in `$PATH`. These searches require both processor and disk time. If you notice a disk or processor slowdown, changes here can help performance.

Some things that should be checked for in user `PATH` variables are:

▲   `$PATH` is read left to right, so the most likely places to find the command should be first in the path. Make sure that a directory is not searched more than once per command.

▲   Users may prefer to have the current directory listed first in the path (`:/usr/bin`).

▲   In general, `$PATH` should have the least number of required entries.

▲   Searches of large directories should be avoided if possible. Put any large directories at the end of `$PATH`.

▲   Directories that are actually a symbolic link to another directory should not appear in `$PATH`.

## Controlling Runaway Processes

The `ps` command is used to obtain information about active processes. This command gives a "snapshot" of what is going on at a given point in time and can tell you which processes are loading the system. The pertinent entries are TIME (minutes and seconds of CPU time used by processes) and STIME (time when the process first started).

When you spot a runaway process (one that uses progressively more system resources over a period of time while you are monitoring it), you should check with the owner. It is possible that such a process should be terminated immediately via the `kill -9` shell command. When you have a real runaway, it continues to eat up system resources until everything comes to a grinding halt.

When you spot processes that take a very long time to execute you should consider using the `cron` or `at` command to execute the job during off-hours.

## Shifting the Workload to Off-Peak Hours

Examine the files in `/var/spool/cron/crontabs` to see if jobs are queued up for peak periods that might better be run at times when the system is idle. Use the `ps` command to determine what processes are heavily loading the system. Encourage users to run large, noninteractive commands (such as `nroff` or `troff`) at off-peak hours. You may also want to run such commands with a low priority by using the `nice` or `batch` shell commands.

# ❑ File Systems and Storage Device Performance

Chapter 3, *The File System*, and Chapter 4, *Storage Devices*, look at file systems and disk drives, focusing on features and conditions that can influence system performance. Some problem areas to investigate are

▲   user-related issues like

- directories that are too large
- controlling greedy use of file system resources by enforcing a disk quota system

▲ system maintenance issues like

- providing working room in critical file system
- balancing file system use
- detecting and repairing inconsistencies in the file system with `fsck`

▲ system configuration issues like

- creating more file system space by changing disk partitions
- creating and mounting new files systems
- selecting an appropriate file system type

## Lack of Disk Space

Making files is easy under the UNIX operating system. Therefore, users tend to create numerous files using large amounts of space. The file systems containing the following directories should maintain, at the very least, the following start-of-day counts.

| | | |
|---|---|---|
| `/tmp` | 2000 to 4000 | 512-byte blocks |
| `/usr` | 500 to 1000 | 512-byte blocks |
| `/home` | 3000 to 6000 | 512-byte blocks |
| `/var` | 4000 to 8000 | 512-byte blocks |

Other file systems should have 6 to 10 percent of their capacity available.

## Balancing File System Space

You can also control file system space by balancing the load between file systems. To do this, user directories often need to be moved. Users should be notified of moves well enough in advance so that they can program around the expected change. Make sure that users with common interests are in the same file system.

## Selecting a File System Type

The default file system type is the s5 file system type with a logical block size of 2K bytes. For most applications this should be best. Depending on the average size of the file, however, you may want to change either the logical block size or even the file system type of the file system. There are three logical block sizes of s5 file systems: 512 byte, 1K bytes, and 2K bytes (the default). The ufs file system has two logical block sizes: 4K and 8K bytes. Each has its advantages and disadvantages in terms of performance.

The UNIX kernel uses the logical block size when reading and writing files. If the logical block size of the file system is 2K, whenever I/O is done between a file and memory, 2K chunks of the file are read into or out of memory.

Large logical block size improves disk I/O performance by reducing seek time and also decreases CPU I/O overhead. On the other hand, if the logical block size is too large then disk space is wasted. The extra space is lost because even if only a portion of a block is needed the entire block is allocated. For example, if files are stored in 1K (1024 bytes) logical blocks, then a 24-byte file wastes 1000 bytes. If the same 24-byte file is stored on a file system with a 2K (2048 bytes) logical block size, then 2024 bytes are wasted. However, if most files on the file system are very large this waste is reduced considerably.

For a file system with mostly small files, small logical block sizes (512 byte and 1K) have the advantage of less wasted space on disk. However, CPU overhead may be increased for files larger than the block size.

The sar -u command can help determine if large I/O transfers are slowing the system down.

## Controlling Directory Size

Very large directories are extremely inefficient and can affect performance. Two directories in particular, /var/mail and /var/spool/uucp, tend to get very large and should be monitored periodically. If a directory becomes bigger than 10 logical blocks (forty, 512-byte blocks or 1280 entries for a 2K logical block size) or 2560 entries, whichever is smaller, then directory searches are likely causing performance problems. The find command, as shown below, can ferret out such problem directories.

```
find / -type d -size +40 -print
```

◆ *Note*      find thinks in terms of 512-byte blocks.

Another important thing to remember is that removing files from directories *does not* make those directories any smaller. When a file is removed from a directory, the inode (file header) number is set to null, leaving an unused slot in the directory. Over time the number of empty slots may become quite large. For example, if you have a directory with 100 files in it and you remove the first 99 files, the directory still contains 100 inodes, with 99 empty slots, at 16 bytes per slot, preceding the active slot. Unless a directory is reorganized on the disk, it will retain the largest size it has ever achieved.

## ❏ Communication Issues

Chapter 5, *Communications*, addresses network performance, taking a very broad definition of what constitutes a network. It covers the Basic Network Utilities (BNU) to control modems, STREAMS to support interprocess communication, and both Remote File Sharing (RFS) and the Network File System (NFS) to provide shared resources across a network, all of which can affect system performance. We discuss:

▲   system configuration issues like

  •   client caching performance and parameters

▲   system maintenance issues like

  •   excessive interrupts from faulty modems, terminals, and lines

  •   shared resources that reside on an inappropriate server

  •   dead servers, down hosts, and so on

# ❑ Monitoring System Performance

The need to improve and control system usage may not be evident unless you monitor your system regularly. For example, it may not be obvious that a system is degraded. Just as a driver might not notice the difference between 48 and 50 miles per hour without the aid of a speedometer, you might not notice a 4 percent degradation without performance monitoring. Chapter 6, *Monitoring System Activity*, shows you how to measure many of the statistics that reflect system performance and how to interpret the numbers and tune system parameters and configurations accordingly.

Chapter 7, *Performance Tools*, describes other applications and commands that provide performance information. For example, you can monitor your file system usage by executing the df command regularly during the day. The df command prints out the number of free file blocks and inodes.

The du command can be executed daily after hours. It summarizes file system usage, giving a total for each directory. Note that if there are links between files in different directories that are on separate branches of the file system hierarchy, du will count the excess files more than once.

The output from these commands can be kept for later comparison. In this way, directories which rapidly increase their space usage can be spotted. However, these reports may not provide the amount of detail that you need to pinpoint exact performance problems.

The System Performance Analysis Utilities (SPAU) tools provide commands for collecting and examining system usage data. These reports can be used to analyze the current performance of the computer and determine load-balancing and system-tuning strategies that will improve performance. SPAU contains ten commands and two shell scripts, listed in Figure 1-3. They are described in detail in Chapter 6, *Monitoring System Activity*, and Chapter 7, *Performance Tools*.

# ❑ Reconfiguring UNIX

The system configuration is defined by a set of parameters that can be altered by a system administrator to fit a given configuration and usage pattern. This procedure is usually referred to as tuning the kernel, as you are adjusting the essential control structures at the heart of the system (the kernel). Use the `/usr/sbin/sysdef` shell command to see what the current parameter values are. These parameters, their default values, and how to tune them are described in detail in Chapter 8, *Configuring UNIX*.

| Command | Function |
|---------|----------|
| `prfdc` | Performs the data collection function of the profiler by copying the current value of all the text address counters to a file where the data can be analyzed. |
| `prfld` | Used to initialize the recording mechanism in the system. |
| `prfpr` | Formats the data collected by `prfdc` or `prfsnap`. |
| `prfsnap` | Collects data (like `prfdc`) at the time of invocation only. |
| `prfstat` | Used to enable, disable, or check the status of the sampling mechanism. |
| `sadc` | Used to sample and save the system activity data. Reports disk access location and seek distance in tabular form. |
| `sadp` | Calls `sadc` or uses files created by `sadc` to sample cumulative activity counters internal to the UNIX system and provides reports on various system-wide activities. Results are saved in binary format. |
| `sag` | Graphically displays the information collected by `sar`. |
| `sar` | Calls `sadc` or uses files created by `sadc` to sample cumulative activity counters internal to the UNIX system and provides reports on various system-wide activities. Results are saved in binary format. |
| `sa1` | Shell script used to collect and store data in binary file `/var/adm/sa/sa`*dd* where *dd* is the current day. |
| `sa2` | Shell script that writes a daily report in file `/var/adm/sa/sar`*dd* where *dd* is the current day. To use any of the commands beginning with `prf`, you must be logged in as `root`. The same is true for both `sa1` and `sa2`. |
| `timex` | When `timex` is used to execute another command, the elapsed time, user time, and system time spent in execution of the command are reported in seconds. |

**Figure 1-3**
*SPAU commands.*
*The tools comprise the SPAU package. They are described in detail in Chapters 6 and 7.*

# 2

# *Users, Processes, and Workloads*

## ❑ Overview

This chapter looks at performance issues that surround your user community and the work they expect to accomplish on your computer system. Much of the material is tutorial in nature: it helps to understand a little about the UNIX kernel and its view of users and processes before you attempt to improve your system's scheduling or paging performance by adjusting the configurable parameters.

In this chapter you will read about:

▲ *streamlining your environment to suit the particular needs of your users.* For example, you may want to organize system resources differently, depending on whether your users are programmers or writers.

▲ *configuring your scheduler to match your workload.* Process structure and the scheduling algorithm are discussed, along with the configurable scheduler parameters.

▲  *establishing paging policy parameters that reduce thrashing*. Tools that can help you determine whether you need more physical memory to improve paging performance are also described.

▲  *understanding system use by examining accounting reports*. You can characterize your users and workload by looking at the daily and monthly usage reports.

# ❏ Streamlining the Work Environment: System and User Profiles

Your computer performs several routines between the time a user logs in and the time a shell prompt appears. These routines are listed in the two files that are executed during the login sequence: the *system profile* (/etc/profile) and the *user profile* ($HOME/.profile). This section describes these files and explains how you can change them to enhance the performance of your system so it best serves the needs of your users.

### The System Profile

When a user enters a valid login name and password, the computer runs a program called the system profile (/etc/profile). This program is an executable ASCII file that performs several important actions:

▲  it defines and exports some environment variables

▲  it displays the message of the day (/etc/motd).

▲  it displays a list of news items if the user is not root

▲  it displays a message about mail items if the user has mail

▲  it defines the default user mask

A sample /etc/profile is shown in Figure 2-1.

**Figure 2-1**
*A Sample System Profile.*
*The system profile is executed each time a user successfully logs in to the system. This one defines some environment variables, displays the message of the day, alerts the user to new news items and electronic mail, and sets up a default system mask.*

```
#ident"@(#)nsadmin:profile1.3"
# The profile that all logins get before using their own .profile.

trap ""  2 3
export LOGNAME

. /etc/TIMEZONE

# Login and -su shells get /etc/profile services.
# -rsh is given its environment in its .profile.
case "$0" in
-su )
  export PATH

 ;;
-sh )
   export PATH

   #  Allow the user to break the Message-Of-The-Day only.
   trap "trap '' 2"  2
   cat -s /etc/motd
   trap "" 2

   if mail -e
   then
      echo "you have mail"
   fi


   if [ "${LOGNAME}" != "root" ]
   then
      news -n
   fi


 ;;
esac

umask 022
trap  2 3
```

You can edit the system profile to change existing definitions. For example, you may want to change the value assigned to your system mask from 022 to 077 to make files and directories created by users more secure. (See chmod(1) in the *User's Reference Manual* for information on file permissions.) Or you may want to change the default PATH to provide access to locally developed commands.

You can also edit the contents of the system profile to automate certain routines. For example, you can add shell commands to this file to display the current time and date and tell a user the number of people logged in on the computer, as shown in Figure 2-2.

**Figure 2-2**
*Additional Shell Script for the System Profile.*
*You should change the system profile only when the change you make will be beneficial to all users of the computer.*

```
...
echo `date`

   if mail -e
   then
       echo "you have mail"
   fi
if [ "${LOGNAME}" != "root" ]
   then
       news -n
   fi

n=`who | wc -l`
echo "There are $n users on `uname -n`."
...
```

## The User's Profile

For new users, System V provides a directory called /etc/skel that contains the standard user profile, .profile. If you want to provide new users with other directories and files (such as an rje directory or a .mailrc file), you can add them to the skel directory. If you prefer, you can create a new "skeletal" directory with a customized .profile. Then, whenever you add a new user login name to your system, you can provide a set of directories and files for the new user immediately by having the contents of skel (or your own version of it) copied into the user's home directory.

To have this copy made, specify the -k option with the useradd command, as follows:

    useradd -k *pathname*

*pathname* is either /etc/skel or the pathname of your customized skel directory. This mechanism obviates the need to add standard directories and files by hand to each new home directory.

After executing the system profile, the computer executes the user's profile. The user's profile executes commands and shell scripts in the same way that the system profile does. Figure 2-3 shows a sample .profile file.

```
PS1="Yes? "
HOME=/home/jean
LOGNAME=jean
PATH=:/bin:/usr/bin:/usr/lbin:$HOME/bin
CDPATH=`for i in $HOME $HOME/* $HOME/junk/* ; \
 do if test -d $i ; \
 then echo ":$i\c" ; fi ; \
 done`
TERMINFO=/home/jean/terminfo
TERM=630
export PS1 HOME LOGNAME PATH CDPATH TERMINFO TERM
umask 022
11 mail
```

**Figure 2-3**
*A Sample User's Profile.*
*It sets the prompt, search path, terminal type, and other environment variables.*

An individual user can redefine some of the environment variables in the .profile to customize his or her environment (to suit factors such as the type of terminal being used, and the type of work being done). If you want to change the environment for your users, you can redefine the environment variables in the standard user profile (/etc/skel/.profile). The environment variables set in the user profile are defined below. If you want to change the environment for your users, you can modify this file to include some or all of the environment variables shown in Figure 2-3. These environment variables are defined below.

## Environment Variables

This section describes the seven environment variables defined in the sample user profile shown in Figure 2-3.

PS1   The user's shell-level prompt

HOME   The user's home directory. Scripts and system programs that need to reference the user's home directory use this environment variable to find it.

If a user is moved to another file system, the only change in his or her profile needed to simulate the original working environment is a change in the definition of $HOME. For example, if a user whose login name is jean is moved from the /home file system to the /home2 file system, the only change needed in her user profile is a change in the definition of $HOME from /home/jean to /home2/jean. Once this environment variable has been changed, the user will have complete access to all the files and commands that were available in the environment defined by the previous value of PATH.

LOGNAME    The user's login name. Scripts and system programs that need to reference the user's login name use this environment variable to find it.

PATH       The list of directories and the order in which these directories are searched for a command requested by a user. This order may be important. When identically named commands exist in different locations, the first command found with that name is used. For example, in Figure 2-3, PATH is defined as

PATH=/bin:/usr/bin:/usr/lbin:$HOME/bin

/usr/bin is defined before /home/jean/bin. If a user invokes a command called sample without specifying its full path name, and this command resides in both /usr/bin and /home/jean/bin, the version found in /usr/bin will be used.

CDPATH     Specifies the directories searched when a unique directory name is typed without a full path name. This environment variable is used as an argument to the cd command. For example, two directories exist under /home/jean: bin and rje. If you are in the /home/jean/bin directory and type cd rje, you will change directories to /home/jean/rje even though a full path is not specified.

TERMINFO   Supported terminal definitions are found in /usr/share/lib/terminfo. When using an unsupported terminal, a user can create a definition for it in another ter-minfo directory and define TERMINFO as a path to this directory in his or her profile (such as /home/jean/terminfo). The system first checks the TERMINFO path defined by the user. If no definition is found, the computer searches the default directory, /usr/share/lib/terminfo, for a definition. If no definition for the terminal is found in either location, the computer identifies the terminal as "dumb." (Refer to tic(1M) in the *System Administrator's Reference Manual* and to curses(3X), term(4), and terminfo(4) in the *Programmer's Reference Manual* for more information about the commands used with this directory.)

TERM      The terminal used by this user. When the user invokes an editor, the computer looks for a file with the same name as the definition of this environment variable (in Figure 2-3, a 630 terminal). The system searches the directory referenced by TERMINFO (in Figure 2-3, /home/jean/terminfo) to determine the characteristics of the terminal.

New environment variables can be defined in a user's profile at any time. By convention, environment variables are defined as follows:

*VARIABLE_NAME*=value.

The variable name appears in uppercase, followed by an equals sign and the value. Once an environment variable is defined, it can be used globally by executing the export command with the environment variable as an argument to it.

# ❏ Process Structure

A process is a specific execution of a program. It consists of a self-contained code or text section, a data section with both initialized and un-initialized storage, and an execution stack whose size is adjusted dynamically by the kernel at runtime. Processes execute by following the instructions in their text segment; they cannot jump into the text of another process. A process reads and writes its own data and stack sections and cannot access the data and stack of other processes.

Processes communicate with the operating system and with other processes via system calls. A new process is created by the fork(2) system call and is assigned a process ID, or PID. PID 0 belongs to a special process created at boot time, called the *swapper*, which is responsible for swapping processes in and out of memory. The swapper creates *init*, with PID 1, which is the ancestor of every other process on the system. Both the swapper and init exist throughout the lifetime of the system.

init reads the file /etc/inittab for a list of processes to spawn. The list typically includes a *getty* process for each terminal line on the system; getty monitors activity on the line, waiting for a user to login in. A logged in user has a shell process that accepts and executes commands from the terminal, most likely by creating child processes. When the user logs out, the shell process exits and control returns to its parent, the getty, which continues monitoring the line.

**Figure 2-4**
*Executing User Commands.*
*When the system is booted, process 0, the* swapper, *is created. It in turn forks an* init *process which starts up a* getty *on each terminal line. When a user starts typing on the line, the* getty execs login, *and if the user succeeds in logging in, a login shell which persists until the user logs off. The command* ls -l | wc *creates two processes that are linked with a pipe.*

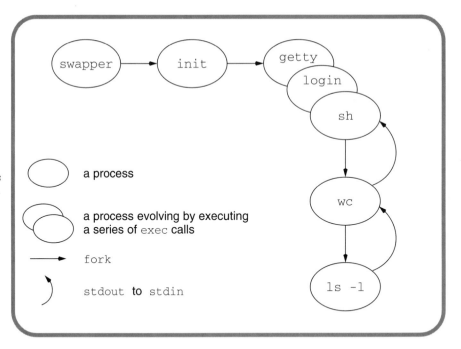

Most processes are *user processes*, associated with a user on a terminal, like the sh, wc, and lc processes in Figure 2-4. Some are *kernel processes* that provide system-wide services like pageout, the page reclaimer. They are part of the kernel and can be changed only by rebuilding the operating system. Still others are *daemon processes* that also provide system wide services like network control, print spooling, and accounting functions, but are compiled from application programs and can be modified like any user program.

Figure 2-5 shows the states a process passes through in its lifetime, and the transitions that move it from state to state. The parent process executes a fork to create the process, shown as state C in Figure 2-5. The process moves to one of the "ready to run" states, $R_m$ or $R_s$, depending on the availability of memory. Once it is chosen to run, it will execute until either it exhausts its time slice or it sleeps until some condition is satisfied or an event occurs (when input or output is completed, for example, or when another page is loaded). System calls cause the process to run in kernel mode (state $E_k$) and interrupt handling may preempt the process (state P) for brief periods. When the process exits, it enters a zombie state, Z, until the parent process takes note.

**Figure 2-5**
*State diagram
for user pro-
cesses.*

*A process is cre-
ated as the result
of a* `fork` *system
call. If there is suf-
ficient available
memory, the pro-
cess will be load-
ing into memory
and added to the
run queue. Other-
wise, it must wait.
A process runs
until it is pre-
empted by higher
priority job or
until its time slice
is exhausted.*

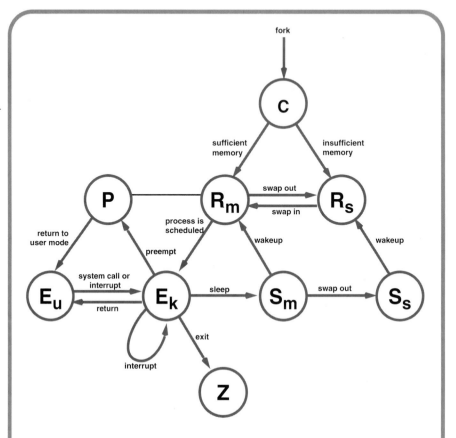

**KEY**

**C**    the process is newly created, and is neither ready to run nor asleep

$E_u$    the process is executing in user mode

$E_k$    the process is executing in kernel mode

**P**    the process is preempted in favor of another process while switching
from kernel to user mode.

$R_m$    the process is in memory and ready to run

$R_s$    the process is ready to run but swapped out

$S_m$    the process is in memory and asleep

$S_s$    the process is asleep and swapped out

**Z**    the process has exited but the parent process has not yet noticed

# ❑ Scheduling Processes

The scheduler determines when processes run. It maintains process priorities based on configuration parameters, process behavior, and user requests; it uses these priorities to assign processes to the CPU. System V Release 4 gives users absolute control over the order in which certain processes run and the amount of time each process may use the CPU before another process gets a chance.

By default, the Release 4 scheduler uses a time-sharing policy that adjusts process priorities dynamically to provide good response time to interactive processes and good throughput to processes that use a lot of CPU time. It offers a real-time scheduling policy as well. Real-time scheduling allows users to set fixed priorities on a per-process basis. The highest-priority real-time user process always gets the CPU as soon as it is runnable, even if system processes are runnable.

The default scheduler configuration works well in most UNIX environments, and real-time processes are not necessary. However, when the requirements for an application include strict timing constraints, real-time processes may provide the only means to satisfy those constraints.

◆ *Note*    Real-time processes used carelessly can have a dramatic negative effect on the performance of time-sharing processes.

The scheduler has an overriding effect on the performance and perceived performance of a system. The default scheduler is tuned to perform well in representative work environments, but you must understand how it operates to know whether you can reconfigure it to better suit local needs.

Figure 2-6 is a conceptual picture of the System V Release 4 process scheduler. Each process belongs to a scheduler class and has an associated priority. Processes are grouped by class and priority into queues.

**Figure 2-6**
*The System V
Release 4 Pro-
cess Scheduler.
The default sched-
uler configuration
has sixty user and
real time priority
levels and forty
system priority
levels. User prior-
ity 0 has lowest
priority while
real-time priority
159 is the highest
priority scheduler
class. Jobs are
scheduled from
highest to lowest
priority, so real-
time processes
always take prior-
ity over system
processes, which
always take prior-
ity over time-shar-
ing processes.*

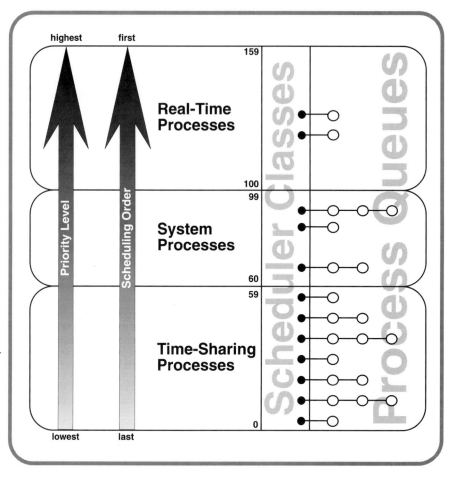

When a process is created, it inherits its scheduler parameters from its parent process, including scheduler class and a priority within that class. A process changes class only as a result of a user request. The system manages the priority of a process based on user requests and a policy associated with the scheduler class of the process.

In the default configuration, there are three scheduler classes:

▲ *the time-sharing class.* The goal of the time-sharing policy is to provide good response time to interactive processes and good throughput to CPU-bound processes. The scheduler switches CPU allocation frequently enough to provide good response time, but not so frequently that it spends too much time doing the switching. Time slices are typically on the order of a few hundred milliseconds.

The time-sharing policy changes priorities dynamically and assigns time slices of different lengths. The scheduler raises the priority of a process that sleeps after only a little CPU use (a process sleeps, for example, when it starts an I/O operation such as a terminal read or a disk read); frequent sleeps are characteristic of interactive tasks such as editing and running simple shell commands. On the other hand, the time-sharing policy lowers the priority of a process that uses the CPU for long periods without sleeping.

The default time-sharing policy gives larger time slices to processes with lower priorities. A process with a low priority is likely to be CPU-bound. Other processes get the CPU first, but when a low-priority process finally gets the CPU, it gets a bigger chunk of time. If a higher-priority process becomes runnable during a time slice, however, it preempts the running process.

▲  *the system class.* The system class uses a fixed-priority policy to run kernel processes such as servers and housekeeping processes like the paging daemon. The system class is reserved for use by the kernel; users may neither add nor remove a process from the system class. Priorities for system class processes are set up in the kernel code for those processes; once established, the priorities of system processes do not change. (User processes running in kernel mode are not in the system class.)

▲  *the real-time class.* The real-time class uses a fixed-priority scheduling policy so that critical processes can run in predetermined order. Real-time priorities never change except when a user requests a change. Contrast this fixed-priority policy with the time-sharing policy, in which the system changes priorities in order to provide good interactive response time.

In the default configuration, the initialization process `init` belongs to the time-sharing class. Because processes inherit their scheduler parameters, all user login shells begin as time-sharing processes.

The scheduler converts class-specific priorities into global priorities. The global priority of a process determines when it runs—the scheduler always runs the runnable process with highest global priority. Numerically higher priorities run first. Once the scheduler assigns a process to the CPU, the process runs until it uses up its time slice, sleeps, or is preempted by a higher-priority process. Processes with the same priority run round-robin.

Administrators specify default time slices in the configuration tables, but users may assign per-process time slices to real-time processes.

By default, all real-time processes have higher priorities than any kernel process, and all kernel processes have higher priorities than any time-sharing process. Privileged users can use the `priocntl`(1) command or the `priocntl`(2) system call to assign real-time priorities.

◆ *Note*     As long as there is a runnable real-time process, no kernel process and no time-sharing process runs.

# ❑ Configuring the Scheduler

The default configuration includes both the time-sharing and the real-time scheduler classes. The time-sharing class is tuned for representative UNIX system workloads. Such workloads have a high proportion of interactive processes, which sleep early and often. The real-time class is configured for applications that need it.

For traditional time-sharing uses such as software development, office applications, and document production, real-time processes may be unnecessary. In addition, they may be undesirable:

▲ *they consume memory that cannot be paged*: the u-blocks of real-time processes are never paged out.

▲ *they introduce new ways to cause performance problems*: a high-priority real-time process can block out all other processing.

In a computing environment where only time-sharing is needed, you may want to remove the real-time scheduler class from your configuration. On the other hand, if a machine is running an application that has strict requirements on the order in which processes must run, then the real-time scheduler class provides the only way to guarantee that those requirements are met.

This section describes the parameters and tables that control scheduler configuration, and tells how to reconfigure the scheduler, assuming your workload is reasonable for your system resources, such as CPU power, primary memory, and I/O capacity. If your workload overtaxes your hardware, reconfiguring the scheduler won't help.

## Default Global Priorities

Figure 2-6 shows the scheduling order and global priorities for each scheduler class. When your system is built, it constructs this information from the tunable parameters and scheduler parameter tables described in Figure 2-7. Although you are not required to define scheduler classes with consecutive, non-overlapping global priorities, like the default priorities, we recommend that you do so for the sake of simplicity. Likewise, we recommend that you make all real-time global priorities greater than the global priorities of all other classes.

Kernel processes such as the swapper and the paging daemon run in the system scheduler class, and compete with user processes for CPU time. If you reconfigure the scheduler, make sure that the system class gets enough priority over the time-sharing class to give kernel processes the CPU time they need. Any real-time applications must be written carefully to ensure that the kernel gets the processing time it needs.

## Tunable Parameters

Figure 2-7 describes the tunable parameters that control scheduler configuration. These parameters are specified in files in the /etc/master.d directory.

**Figure 2-7**
*Tunable sched-*
*uler parameters.*
*These system con-*
*figuration parame-*
*ters determine the*
*number, name, and*
*priority of up to*
*three scheduler*
*classes, and the*
*class membership*
*for the* init *pro-*
*cess.*

| master.d Parameter File | Parameter | Description | Default Value |
|---|---|---|---|
| kernel | MAXCLSYSPRI | The maximum global priority of processes in the system class. When the kernel starts system processes, it assigns their priorities using MAXCLSYSPRI as a reference point. | 99 |
| | | MAXCLSYSPRI must be 39 or greater, because the kernel assumes it has at least that great a range of priorities below MAXCLSYSPRI. If you request a MAXCLSYSPRI below 39, it is changed to 39. | |
| | | The most important system processes get global priorities at or near MAXCLSYSPRI; the least important system processes get global priorities at or near (MAXCLSYSPRI-39). | |
| | INITCLASS | The scheduler class assigned to the init process. This scheduler class is inherited by all descendants of init, which normally include all user login shells. | TS |
| | SYS_NAME | The character string name of the system scheduler class. | SYS |
| ts | TSMAXUPRI | The range within which users may adjust the priority of a time-sharing process using the priocntl system call: the valid range is -TSMAXUPRI to +TSMAXUPRI. | 20 |
| | NAMETS | The character string name of the time-sharing scheduler class. This name is returned by the priocntl system call and it is assigned to the tunable parameter INITCLASS to specify the default scheduler class for user processes. | TS |
| rt | NAMERT | The character string name of the real-time scheduler class. | RT |

# The Time-Sharing Parameter Table `ts_dptbl`

The scheduler uses `ts_dptbl`(4), the time-sharing scheduler (or dispatcher) parameter table, to manage time-sharing processes. A default version of `ts_dptbl` is delivered with the system, and an administrator may change it to suit local needs. Save a backup of the default version of `ts_dptbl`. `ts_dptbl` is specified in the `ts` file in the `master.d` directory. It is automatically built into the kernel as part of system configuration.

You may change the size and values of `ts_dptbl` depending on your local needs, but only experienced administrators should make such changes. The default values have a long history of good performance over a wide range of environments. Changing the values is not likely to help much, and inappropriate values can have a dramatic negative effect on system performance.

If you do decide to change `ts_dptbl`, we recommend that you include at least 40 time-sharing global priorities. A range this large gives the scheduler enough leeway to distinguish processes based on their CPU use, which it must do to give good response to interactive processes. The default configuration has 60 time-sharing priorities. Figure 2-8 show a simple `ts_dptbl` and charts its affect and the scheduling of three processes with distinctly different execution behavior.

**Figure 2-8**
*A Simplified Scheduling Example.*
*The table shows the quantum length for each priority label and how the priority for the next scheduling period will be assigned. The graph shows priority assignment over time for three different kinds of processes: an I/O-intensive one, a compute-bound one, and a process that does some of both.*

*All processes start at Priority 9. If a process goes to sleep (e.g. blocks for I/O) before its quantum is exhausted, then it will have higher priority in the next time slice. If a process uses its entire quantum, it will have lower priority in the next time slice.*

the quantum or time slice: the maximum amount of time a process with this priority may use the CPU before the scheduler gives another process a chance. specified in clock ticks.

the new priority for a process that exhausts its quantum

global priorities. higher numbers run first.

the new priority for a process that goes to sleep rather than timing out

| glbpri | qntm | tqexp | slprt |
|--------|------|-------|-------|
| 0      | 100  | 0     | 1     |
| 1      | 90   | 0     | 2     |
| 2      | 80   | 1     | 3     |
| 3      | 70   | 1     | 4     |
| 4      | 60   | 2     | 5     |
| 5      | 50   | 2     | 6     |
| 6      | 40   | 3     | 7     |
| 7      | 30   | 3     | 8     |
| 8      | 20   | 4     | 9     |
| 9      | 10   | 4     | 9     |

**Process Priority Over Time**

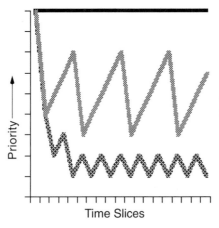

**Process 1**: an I/O bound job that repeatedly computes for 5 clock ticks and then waits for I/O.

**Process 2**: a process that computes for about 35 clock ticks between I/O requests.

**Process 3**: a CPU-intensive process that computes for 100 clock ticks and then does I/O.

The default global priority of a time-sharing process is the priority in the middle of ts_dptbl. This is the priority assigned to a process if it is changed to a time-sharing process with default parameters. This is also the priority initially assigned to the init process if INITCLASS is set to TS. The descendants of init, normally including all login shells and other user processes, inherit its class and current scheduler parameters.

## The Kernel-Mode Parameter Table ts_kmdpris

The scheduler uses the kernel-mode parameter table ts_kmdpris to manage sleeping time-sharing processes. A default version of ts_kmdpris is delivered with the system, and there is seldom a reason to change it. ts_kmdpris is specified in the ts file in the master.d directory. It is automatically built into the kernel as part of system configuration.

■ *Note*       The kernel assumes that it has at least 40 priorities in ts_kmdpris. It panics if it does not.

The kernel-mode parameter table is a one-dimensional array of global priorities. The kernel assigns these priorities to sleeping processes based on their reasons for sleeping. If a user process sleeps because it is waiting for an important resource, such as an inode, it sleeps at a priority near the high end of the ts_kmdpris priorities, so that it may get and free the resource quickly when the resource becomes available. If a user process sleeps for a less important reason, such as a wait for terminal input, it sleeps at a priority near the low end of the ts_kmdpris priorities.

The default kernel-mode parameter table is simply a one-dimensional array of the integers from 60 through 99, which means that time-sharing processes sleep at priorities between the default real-time priorities and the default time-sharing priorities.

In the default configuration, the priorities in ts_kmdpris happen to be exactly the same as the priorities used by system class processes, because the tunable parameter MAXCLSYSPRI is the same as the highest priority in ts_kmdpris. This overlap is designed to be consistent with the scheduler behavior of previous releases of the UNIX system, because these priorities produce good performance in most environments. But the overlap is not necessary. The System V Release 4 scheduler introduces a logical separation between the priorities of system processes and sleeping time-sharing processes; an administrator may configure a machine so that the two sets of processes have different ranges of global priorities.

## The Real-Time Parameter Table `rt_dptbl`

The scheduler uses `rt_dptbl`(4), the real-time scheduler (or dispatcher) parameter table, to manage real-time processes. A default version of `rt_dptbl` is delivered with the system, and an administrator may change it to suit local needs. `rt_dptbl` is specified in the `rt` file in the `master.d` directory. It is built into the kernel as part of system configuration if the `system` file contains the line

```
INCLUDE:RT
```

You may adjust the size and values of `rt_dptbl` depending on the applications on your system. Figure 2-9 shows a simple `rt_dptbl`.

**Figure 2-9**
*Part of a simple real-time dispatch table.*
Processes with priority 105 always run before any other processes. A process with priority 105 runs for 10 clock ticks or until it sleeps, whichever happens first. Because 105 is the highest priority, a process at this priority would be preempted after its quantum only if there were another process with priority 105. Processes at priority 104 run for 20 clock ticks, and so on. The lowest real-time priority specified in this table is 100; a process with priority 100 runs for 100

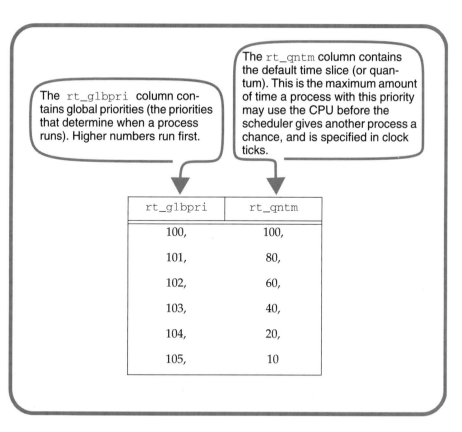

The `rt_glbpri` column contains global priorities (the priorities that determine when a process runs). Higher numbers run first.

The `rt_qntm` column contains the default time slice (or quantum). This is the maximum amount of time a process with this priority may use the CPU before the scheduler gives another process a chance, and is specified in clock ticks.

| rt_glbpri | rt_qntm |
|-----------|---------|
| 100,      | 100,    |
| 101,      | 80,     |
| 102,      | 60,     |
| 103,      | 40,     |
| 104,      | 20,     |
| 105,      | 10      |

The default real-time priority is the lowest priority configured in `rt_dptbl`. This is the priority assigned to a process if it is changed to a real-time process and no priority is specified. This is also the priority assigned to the `init` process and all its children if `INITCLASS` is set to `RT`.

Though `rt_dptbl` contains default time slices for real-time priorities, users with the appropriate privilege can set real-time priority and time slice independently. Users can specify any time slice they want for a real-time process, including an infinite time slice. The system assumes that real-time processes voluntarily give up the CPU so other work can get done.

## Changing the Scheduler Configuration

Changing scheduler configuration requires changing one or more of the tunable parameters or the configuration tables `rt_dptbl`, `ts_dptbl`, and `ts_kmdpris`. You can change any of these by changing the appropriate file in the `master.d` directory and rebuilding the kernel as described in Chapter 8, *Configuring UNIX*. Changes made in this way are permanent. This is the only way to change the size of the configuration tables. You can make temporary changes on running systems with the `dispadmin` command, described in the next section.

For systems that do not need real-time processes, it may make sense to remove the real-time class, thereby making it impossible to create real-time processes. By not having real-time processes, you avoid their non-pageable u-blocks and you avoid the possibility of a runaway process monopolizing the machine. To remove the real-time scheduler class:

**Step 1** Replace the `INCLUDE:RT` line from the `/etc/system` file with

    `EXCLUDE:RT`

**Step 2** Rebuild the kernel.

There should be no reason to remove the time-sharing scheduler class. An application can put its crucial processes into the real-time class, and thereby ensure that they always run before any time-sharing process. However, if you have a compelling reason to remove the time-sharing class, here's how to do it:

**Step 1**  Replace the INCLUDE:TS line from the /etc/system file with:

    EXCLUDE:TS

**Step 2**  In the kernel file in master.d, change INITCLASS to RT. This makes init and all its descendants real-time processes.

**Step 3**  Rebuild the kernel.

## Installing a Scheduler Class

By default, both the time-sharing and the real-time scheduler classes are installed. If you remove one of them and then decide you really did want it after all, you can reinstall the class with one of the following procedures:

To install the time-sharing class:

**Step 1**  Make sure that the TS module is in the /boot directory.

**Step 2**  Insert the INCLUDE:TS line in the /etc/system file. (The TS module is automatically configured unless it is explicitly excluded.)

**Step 3**  Build the kernel.

To install the real-time class:

**Step 1**  Make sure that the RT module is in the /boot directory.

**Step 2**  Insert the INCLUDE:RT line is in the /etc/system file. (The RT module is not configured unless it is explicitly included.)

**Step 3**  Build the kernel.

When you re-install a scheduler class, you should also check the value of the tunable parameter INITCLASS to make sure that your configuration is assigning the default scheduler class you want.

# ❏ Changing Scheduler Parameters with
## `dispadmin`

The `dispadmin`(1M) command allows you to change or retrieve scheduler information in a running system. Changes made using `dispadmin` do not survive a reboot. To make permanent configuration changes, you must change the scheduler parameter tables in the `master.d` directory as described in the section above on configuration. However, you can use `dispadmin` to get an effect equivalent to changing configuration tables by calling `dispadmin` from a startup script that changes the configuration automatically at boot time.

The `dispadmin` command has three forms:

▲ `dispadmin -l` lists the configured scheduler classes.

▲ `dispadmin -g [-r` *res*`] -c` *class* gets scheduler parameters for the specified class.

▲ `dispadmin -s` *config* `-c` *class* sets scheduler parameters for the specified class from *config*.

## Listing Scheduler Classes

To list the currently installed scheduler classes, type `dispadmin -l`. Figure 2-10 shows the output for the default configuration.

```
$ dispadmin -l
CONFIGURED CLASSES
==================

SYS     (System Class)
TS      (Time Sharing)
RT      (Real Time)
```

**Figure 2-10**
*Output from* `dispadmin -l`*. It shows the scheduler classes that are defined in the current system configuration.*

## Listing Scheduler Class Parameters

To list the current parameters for a specific scheduler class, type

```
dispadmin -g [-r res] -c class
```

where *class* is RT or TS. By default, dispadmin reports time slices in milliseconds. If you specify the -r *res* option, dispadmin reports time slices in units of *res* intervals per second. For example, a *res* of 1000000 reports time slices in microseconds (millionths of a second).

Scheduler parameters are class specific. The parameters for the default classes are described in the sections above on the scheduler parameter tables; ts_dptbl holds time-sharing parameters and rt_dptbl hold real-time parameters.

Figure 2-11 shows part of the output of dispadmin -g for the real-time and time-sharing classes.

```
$ dispadmin -c RT -g      #  list real-time parameters
# Real Time Dispatcher Configuration
RES=1000


#   TIME QUANTUM          PRIORITY
#   (rt_quantum)          LEVEL
            1000      #      0
            1000      #      1
            1000      #      2
             ...             ...
            1000      #      9
             800      #     10
             800      #     11
             800      #     12
             ...             ...
             800      #     19
             700      #     20
             ...             ...
             100      #     50
             100      #     51
             100      #     52
             ...             ...
             100      #     59



$ dispadmin -c TS -g      #  list time-sharing parameters
# Time Sharing Dispatcher Configuration
RES=1000


#ts_quantum ts_tqexp  ts_slprtts_maxwait  ts_lwaitPRIORITY LEVEL
      1000       0        10        5         10      #  0
      1000       0        11        5         11      #  1
      1000       1        12        5         12      #  2
       ...      ...       ...      ...        ...      ...
      1000       4        19        5         19      #  9
       800       5        20        5         20      # 10
       800       5        21        5         21      # 11
       800       6        22        5         22      # 12
       ...      ...       ...      ...        ...      ...
       800       9        29        5         29      # 19
       ...      ...       ...      ...        ...      ...
       100      40        55        5         55      # 50
       100      41        55        5         55      # 51
       100      42        56        5         56      # 52
       ...      ...       ...      ...        ...      ...
       100      48        59        5         59      # 58
       100      49        59        5         59      # 59
```

**Figure 2-11**
*Output from*
*dispadmin -g.*
*The real-time param-*
*eters are shown in*
*the top half of the fig-*
*ure. and detail the*
*relationship between*
*time slice length and*
*priority. The time-*
*sharing parameters*
*in the bottom half*
*include the time*
*slice length*
*(ts_quantum),*
*the new priority for a*
*process that*
*exhausts its quan-*
*tum (ts_tqexp),*
*and the new priority*
*for a process that*
*blocks before its time*
*is up (ts_slp).*

## Setting Scheduler Class Parameters

To set scheduler parameters, type

```
dispadmin -s config -c class
```

where *class* is RT or TS and *config* is a configuration file. The configuration file must be in the class-specific format produced by the -g option. The meanings of the parameters are described in the sections above on the scheduler parameter tables; ts_dptbl holds time-sharing parameters and rt_dptbl holds real-time parameters.

The following examples show how to set the parameters for the default classes as specified in the configuration files rt.config and ts.config. In each case, dispadmin is used to generate a file containing the current configuration, which is carefully edited to incorporate the desired changes. The newly modified file becomes the argument to a second dispadmin command that effects the changes. You must be the super-user root to set scheduler class parameters.

**Figure 2-12**
*Setting scheduler parameters with* **dispadmin -s**

```
$ dispadmin -c RT -g >rt.config   #get real-time parameters
$ ed rt.config
...
$ dispadmin -c RT -s rt.config   # set real-time parameters

$ dispadmin -c RT -g >ts.config   # get time-sharing parameters
$ ed ts.config
...
$ dispadmin -c TS -s ts.config   # set time-sharing parameters
```

The files that specify the new scheduler parameters must have the same number of priority levels as the current table that is being overwritten. To change the number of priority levels, you must change the ts file or the rt file in the master.d directory as described in the section above on configuration.

# ❏ Paging Behavior

The scheduling algorithm just described is heavily influenced by memory management policies and behavior. A process must be at least partially in memory in order to run. (Recall the $R_s$ state in Figure 2-5.) The memory manger decides which processes will reside at least partially in memory and administers the secondary memory on a swap device. It monitors the amount of primary memory available and may occasionally write inactive pages of a process's virtual address space to the secondary store to make room for newly-referenced pages of this process or for another process that is ready to run.

Historically, UNIX systems moved entire processes between primary and secondary store, a technique called *swapping*. This made sense on machines with limited address space and limited physical memory.

As address spaces increased and memory prices dropped, a demand paging technique where *pages* rather than entire processes are moved between primary and secondary store began to make sense. The first implementation of a demand paging policy was in BSD 4.0 UNIX; it is now found in most UNIX implementations, including System V Release 4.

Machines with a paged memory architecture and restartable instructions can support a kernel that implements a demand paging policy. Demand paging allows process page to be independent of physical memory size, limited only by the number of address bits in a virtual address.

The demand paging process is transparent to the user. A paging daemon, `pageout`, uses a least-recently used (LRU) algorithm to select pages for transfer to the swap space on secondary storage.

Processes tend to have *locality of reference*, executing instructions and referencing data that are close to the last instruction or data reference (instruction sequences and arrays of data, loops, subroutines, etc) rather than jumping randomly from place to place. A *working set* is the set of pages that a process has referenced in the last $n$ memory accesses, where $n$ is the *window* of the working set. The working set is a subset of the pages that currently reside in memory for a given process; memory-resident pages not in the working set are candidates for being paged out.

When a process references a page that is not in memory, a page fault occurs and the process is suspended until the selected page has been read into memory. When the process is scheduled to run again, it restarts at the instruction that was executing when the fault occurred.

**Figure 2-13**
*State diagram for LRU paging algorithm.*
*The longer a page stays in memory without being referenced, the more it ages. It becomes a candidate for swapping out when it reaches state $A_n$. A reference to the page resets its age (state $A_0$),*

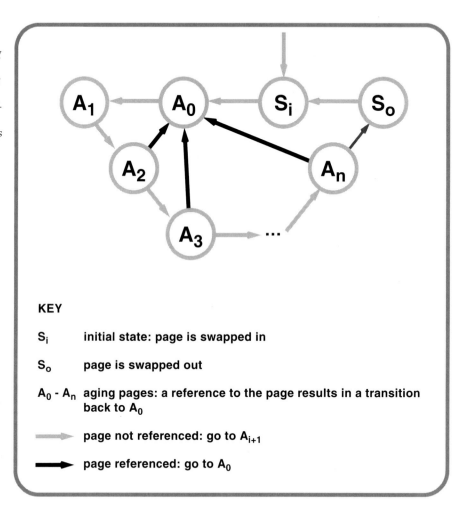

**KEY**

$S_i$         initial state: page is swapped in

$S_o$        page is swapped out

$A_0$ - $A_n$  aging pages: a reference to the page results in a transition back to $A_0$

⟶         page not referenced: go to $A_{i+1}$

⟶         page referenced: go to $A_0$

Several paging parameters are configurable:

▲   the amount of paged memory

▲   the low-water mark to start up the `pageout` daemon. It wakes up when the low-water mark is reached and removes all pages that are sufficiently aged.

- increase it to make the daemon more active

- decrease it to make the daemon less active

▲ low-water mark for user pages

▲ low water mark for kernel pages

Several options to `sar` are useful in detecting thrashing and reconfiguring the kernel or buying more memory:

▲ The `sar -g` option reports page-out and memory freeing activities:

- the number of times per second file that systems receive page-out requests

- the number of pages that are paged-out per second

- the number of pages per second that are placed on the freelist by the page-stealing daemon. If this value is greater than 5, it may be an indication that more memory is needed.

- the number of pages per second scanned by the page-stealing daemon. If this value is greater than 5, the page-out daemon is spending a lot of time checking for free memory. This implies that more memory may be needed.

- the percentage of `s5` inodes taken off the freelist which had reusable pages associated with them. These pages are flushed and cannot be reclaimed by processes. If this value is greater than 10 percent, then the freelist of inodes is considered to be page-bound and the number of `s5` inodes should be increased.

▲ The `sar -p` option reports paging-in activity:

- the number of page faults per second that are satisfied by reclaiming a page currently in memory

- the number of times per second file systems receive page-in requests

- the number of pages paged in per second

- the number of page faults from protection errors per second

- the number of address translation page faults per second

- the number of faults per second caused by software lock requests requiring physical I/O

▲ The `-r` option records the number of memory pages and swap file disk blocks that are currently unused.

▲ The CPU utilization is listed by `sar -u`. At any given moment the processor is either busy or idle. When busy, the processor is in either user or system mode. When idle, the processor is either waiting for input/output completion or is waiting for work. `sar -u` lists the percentage of time that the processor is in system mode (`%sys`), in user mode (`%user`), waiting for input/output completion (`%wio`), and idle (`%idle`).

In typical timesharing use, `%sys` and `%usr` are about the same value. In special applications, either of these may be larger than the other without anything being abnormal. A high `%wio` generally means a disk slowdown has occurred. A high `%idle`, with degraded response time, may mean memory constraints are present; time spent waiting for memory is attributed to `%idle`.

▲ The `-w` option reports swapping and switching activity:

  • the number of transfers into memory per second.

  • the number of 512-byte blocks transferred for swap-ins (including initial loading of some programs) per second.

  • the number of transfers from memory to the disk swap area per second. If greater than 1, you may need to increase memory or decrease the amount of buffer space.

  • the number of blocks transferred for swap-outs per second.

  • the number of process switches per second. This should be 30 to 50 on a busy 4- to 6-user system.

There is more information about `sar` and monitoring paging behavior in Chapter 6, *Monitoring System Activity.*

## ❏ Process Accounting

Process accounting allows you to keep track of the following data about each process run on your system:

▲ the user and group IDs of those using the process,

▲ the beginning and elapsed times of the process,

▲ the CPU time for the process (divided between users and the system),

▲   the amount of memory used, the commands run, and

▲   the controlling `tty` during the process.

Every time a process dies, the `exit` program collects these data and writes them to the file `/var/adm/pacct`.

The `pacct` file has a default maximum size of 500 blocks that is enforced by the accounting shell script `ckpacct` (normally run as a `cron` job). If `ckpacct` finds that `/var/adm/pacct` is over 500 blocks, it moves the file to `/var/adm/pacct?` where? is the next unused increment (expressed as a number).

## Accounting Programs

All the C language programs and shell scripts necessary to run the accounting system are in the `/usr/src/cmd/acct` directory. The `acctcom` program is stored in `/usr/bin`; all other binary programs are stored in `/usr/lib/acct`. These programs, which are owned by `bin` (except `accton`, which is owned by `root`), do various functions. For example, `/usr/lib/acct/startup` helps initiate the accounting process when the system enters multi-user mode. The `chargefee` program is used to charge a particular user for a special service, such as performing a file restore from tape. Other essential programs in the `/usr/lib/acct` directory include `monacct`, `prdaily`, and `runacct`. These and other programs are discussed in more detail in the following sections.

## Setting Up Non-Prime Time Discounts

UNIX system accounting provides facilities to give users a discount for non-prime time system use. For this to work, you must inform the accounting system of the dates of holidays and the hours that are considered non-prime time, such as weekends. To do this, you must edit the `/etc/acct/holidays` file that contains the prime/non-prime table for the accounting system. The format is composed of three types of entries:

▲   *comment lines*. Comment lines are marked by an asterisk in the first column of the line. Comment lines may appear anywhere in the file.

▲   *year designation lines*. This line should be the first data line (noncomment line) in the file and must appear only once. The line consists of three fields of four digits each (leading white space is ignored). For example, to specify the year as 1990, prime time start at 9:00 A.M., and non-prime time start at 4:30 P.M., the following entry would be appropriate:

```
1990    0900    1630
```

A special condition allowed for in the time field is that the time 2400 is automatically converted to 0000.

▲ *company holidays lines*. These entries follow the year designation line and have the following general format:

*month/day          holiday*

The *month/day* field indicates the date of the holiday. The *holiday* field is actually commentary and is not currently used by other programs. See Figure 2-5 for an example holiday list.

**Figure 2-14**
*Holiday List*
*Here are some*
*potential holidays*
*for 1993.*

```
#cat /etc/acct/holidays
1/1         New Year's Day
1/18        Martin Luther King, Jr. Day
2/15        President's Day
3/17        Saint Patrick's Day
4/6         Passover
4/9         Good Friday
5/31        Memorial Day
7/4         Independence Day
9/6         Labor Day
9/16        Rosh Hashanah
9/25        Yom Kippur
10/11       Columbus Day
11/11       Veteran's Day
11/25       Thanksgiving Day
11/26       Day after Thanksgiving
12/9        Hanukkah
12/24       Day before Christmas Day
12/31       Day before New Year's Day
#
```

During real time, you should monitor /var/adm/wtmp because it is the file from which the connect accounting is geared. If the wtmp file grows rapidly, execute acctcon -l *file* </var/adm/wtmp to see which terminal line is the noisiest. If the interrupting is occurring at a furious rate, general system performance will be affected.

## Daily Usage Report

The daily usage report gives a breakdown of system resource utilization by user. Figure 2-15 shows a sample of this type of report.

The data provided include the following:

UID:     The user ID

LOGIN NAME:

> The login name of the user. This information is useful because it identifies a user who has multiple login names.

CPU (MINS):

> This represents the amount of time the user's process used the central processing unit. This category is broken down into `PRIME` and `NPRIME` (non-prime) utilization. The accounting system's idea of this breakdown is located in the `/etc/acct/holidays` file.

KCORE-MINS:

> This represents a cumulative measure of the amount of memory a process uses while running. The amount shown reflects kilobyte segments of memory used per minute. This measurement is also broken down into `PRIME` and `NPRIME` amounts.

CONNECT and (MINS):

> This identifies the amount of "real time" used. What this column really identifies is the amount of time that a user was logged into the system. If the amount of time is high and the number shown in the column labeled `# OF PROCS` is low, you can safely conclude that the owner of the login for which the report is being generated is a "line hog." That is, this person logs in first thing in the morning and hardly touches the terminal the rest of the day. Watch out for this kind of user. This column is also subdivided into `PRIME` and `NPRIME` utilization.

DISK BLOCKS:

> When the disk accounting programs have been run, the output is merged into the total accounting record (`daytacct`) and shows up in this column. This disk accounting is accomplished by the program `acctdusg`. For accounting purposes, a block is 512 bytes.

\# OF PROCS:

> This column reflects the number of processes that were invoked by the user. This is a good column to watch for large numbers indicating that a user may have a shell procedure that has run out of control.

\# OF SESS:

> The number of times a user logged on to the system is shown in this column.

\# DISK SAMPLES:

> This indicates how many times the disk accounting was run to obtain the average number of `DISK BLOCKS` listed earlier.

FEE:     An often unused field in the total accounting record, the `FEE` field represents the total accumulation of widgets charged against the user by the `chargefee` shell procedure; see `acctsh`(1M). The `chargefee` procedure is used to levy charges against a user for special services performed such as file restores.

## Daily Command Summary

The daily command summary report shows the system resource utilization by command. With this report, you can identify the most heavily used commands and, based on how those commands use system resources, gain insight on how best to tune the system. The daily command and monthly reports are virtually the same except that the daily command summary reports only on the current accounting period while the monthly total command summary tells the story for the start of the fiscal period to the current date. In other words, the monthly report reflects the data accumulated since the last invocation of `monacct`.

These reports are sorted by TOTAL KCOREMIN, which is an arbitrary but often useful yardstick for calculating "drain" on a system.

Figure 2-16 shows a sample daily command summary.

```
Jun 29 09:53 1990   DAILY USAGE REPORT FOR sfxbs Page 1


UID LOGIN  CPU(MINS)    KCORE(MINS)   CONNECT(MINS)   DISK   # OF # OF # DISK FEE
    NAME PRIME NPRIME PRIME NPRIME  PRIME  NPRIME  BLOCKS PROCS SESS SAMPLES
   0 TOTAL  5     12     6    16     131      51       0  1114   13    0      0
   0  root  2      8     1    11       0       0       0   519    0    0      0
   3  sys   0      1     0     1       0       0       0    45    0    0      0
   4  adm   0      2     0     1       0       0       0   213    0    0      0
   5  uucp  0      0     0     0       0       0       0    53    0    0      0
 399  rly   3      1     5     2     111      37       0   269    1    0      0
 798  jan   0      0     0     1      20      14       0    15    6    0      0
```

**Figure 2-15**
*A Daily Usage Report*

```
Jun 29 09:52 1990   DAILY COMMAND SUMMARY Page 1


                        TOTAL COMMAND SUMMARY
COMMAND  NUMBER  TOTAL    TOTAL    TOTAL   MEAN   MEAN    HOG   CHARS  BLOCKS
NAME      CMDS  KCOREMIN CPU-MIN REAL-MIN SIZE-K CPU_MIN FACTOR TRNSFD  READ

TOTALS    1114   2.44    16.69   136.33   0.15   0.01   0.12 4541666  1926

sh         227   1.01     2.45    54.99   0.41   0.01   0.04  111025   173
fmli        10   0.50     2.06     9.98   0.24   0.21   0.21  182873   223
vi          12   0.35     0.62    44.23   0.55   0.05   0.01  151448    60
sed        143   0.09     0.82     1.48   0.10   0.01   0.55   14505    35
sadc        13   0.08     0.19     1.45   0.44   0.01   0.13  829088    19
more         3   0.04     0.07     2.17   0.59   0.02   0.03   30560     1
cut         14   0.03     0.09     0.28   0.37   0.01   0.33     154    13
uudemon.    76   0.03     0.66     2.30   0.05   0.01   0.29   43661    13
uuxqt       29   0.03     0.30     0.72   0.08   0.01   0.42   80765    35
mail         4   0.02     0.06     0.09   0.37   0.01   0.60    4540     9
ckstr       21   0.02     0.11     0.13   0.17   0.01   0.85       0     4
awk         13   0.02     0.12     0.21   0.15   0.01   0.54     444     2
ps           2   0.02     0.10     0.13   0.17   0.05   0.77    8060    21
find         9   0.02     3.35     5.73   0.00   0.37   0.58  355269   760
sar          1   0.01     0.19     0.24   0.08   0.19   0.80  564224     4
acctdisk     2   0.01     0.01     0.06   1.02   0.01   0.22       0     9
mv          24   0.01     0.14     0.17   0.10   0.01   0.81    3024    36
...         ...   ...      ...      ...    ...    ...    ...      ...    ...
```

**Figure 2-16**
*A Daily Command Summary Report.*

The data provided include the following:

### COMMAND NAME

> The name of the command. Unfortunately, all shell procedures are lumped together under the name sh because only object modules are reported by the process accounting system. It's a good idea to monitor the frequency of programs called a.out or core or any other name that does not seem quite right. Often people like to work on their favorite version of backgammon, but they do not want everyone to know about it. acctcom is also a good tool to use for determining who executed a suspiciously named command and also if super-user privileges were used.

### PRIME NUMBER CMDS

> The total number of invocations of this particular command during prime time.

### NON-PRIME NUMBER CMDS

> The total number of invocations of this particular command during non-prime time.

### TOTAL KCOREMIN

> The total cumulative measurement of the amount of kilobyte segments of memory used by a process per minute of run time.

### PRIME TOTAL CPU-MIN

> The total processing time this program has accumulated during prime time.

### NON-PRIME TOTAL CPU-MIN

> The total processing time this program has accumulated during non-prime time.

### PRIME TOTAL REAL-MIN

> Total real-time (wall-clock) minutes this program has accumulated.

NON-PRIME TOTAL REAL-MIN
> Total real-time (wall-clock) minutes this program has accumulated.

MEAN SIZE-K
> This is the mean of the `TOTAL KCOREMIN` over the number of invocations reflected by `NUMBER CMDS`.

MEAN CPU-MIN
> This is the mean derived between the `NUMBER CMDS` and `TOTAL CPU-MIN`.

HOG FACTOR
> The total CPU time divided by the elapsed time. This shows the ratio of system availability to system utilization. This gives a relative measure of the total available CPU time consumed by the process during its execution.

CHARS TRNSFD
> This column, which may go negative because of overflow, is a total count of the number of characters pushed around by the `read` and `write` system calls.

BLOCKS READ
> A total count of the physical block reads and writes that a process performed.

## Total Command Summary

The monthly command summary is similar to the daily command summary. The only difference is that the monthly command summary shows totals accumulated since the last invocation of `monacct`. Figure 2-17 shows a sample report.

**Figure 2-17**
*A Total Com-*
*mand Summary*
*Report.*

```
                          TOTAL COMMAND SUMMARY
COMMAND  NUMBER    TOTAL    TOTAL     TOTAL    MEAN    MEAN    HOG       CHARS     BLOCKS
NAME     CMDS   KCOREMIN CPU-MIN  REAL-MIN  SIZE-K CPU_MIN FACTOR     TRNSFD       READ

TOTALS  301314 300607.70 4301.59 703979.81  69.88    0.01   0.01 6967631360   10596385

troff      480  58171.37  616.15   1551.26  94.41    1.28   0.40  650669248     194926
rnews     5143  29845.12  312.20   1196.93  95.59    0.06   0.26 1722128384    2375741
uucico    2710  16625.01  212.95  52619.21  78.07    0.08   0.00  228750872     475343
nroff     1613  15463.20  206.54    986.06  74.87    0.13   0.21  377563304     277957
vi        3040  14641.63  157.77  14700.13  92.80    0.05   0.01  116621132     206025
expire      14  13424.81  104.90    265.67 127.98    7.49   0.39   76292096     145456
comp      3483  12140.64   60.22    423.54 201.62    0.02   0.14    9584838     372601
ad_d        71  10179.20   50.02   1158.31 203.52    0.70   0.04   11385054      19489
as        2312   9221.59   44.40    285.52 207.68    0.02   0.16   35988945     221113
gone       474   8723.46  219.93  12099.01  39.67    0.46   0.02   10657346      19397
i10        299   8372.60   44.45    454.21 188.34    0.15   0.10   60169932      78664
find       760   8310.97  196.91    728.39  42.21    0.26   0.27   58966910     710074
ld        2288   8232.84   61.19    425.57 134.55    0.03   0.14  228701168     279530
fgrep      832   7585.34   62.62    199.11 121.14    0.08   0.31   22119268      37196
sh       56314   7538.40  337.60 291655.70  22.33    0.01   0.00   93262128     612892
du         624   5049.58  126.32    217.59  39.97    0.20   0.58   16096269     215297
ls       12690   4765.60   75.71    541.53  62.95    0.01   0.14   65759473     207920
vnews       52   4235.71   28.11    959.74 150.70    0.54   0.03   28291679      28285
...          ...      ...      ...       ...     ...     ...    ...        ...        ...
```

# 3

# *The File System*

## ❏ Overview

A *file system* is a collection of directories and files where users organize and store data. A *file* stores data, the electronic equivalent of a paper document. A *directory* is a place to organize related files, the electronic equivalent of a file folder. Continuing the analogy, the file system is like a filing cabinet, storing many file folders that contain many documents.

UNIX organizes files and directories hierarchically in a tree-like structure that makes it easy for users to locate and maintain their files. It also provides facilities for creating, accessing, copying, moving, and processing files, directories, or sets of files and directories in a simple, consistent way. Space for files is automatically allocated and deallocated when a file is created or deleted, and as it grows and shrinks in size.

UNIX System V Release 4 introduces Virtual File System (VFS), an architecture that makes it possible for files systems of various types to coexist on the same system. VFS provides a clearly defined, modular interface between file systems and the rest of the UNIX kernel. The modular nature of the architecture allows programmers to design and install new file system types in a clean, straight-forward manner. The following file system types are provided as standard options:

▲ s5, the traditional file system type supported in earlier releases of UNIX System V.

▲ ufs, a file system type based on the BSD "fast file system".

▲ bfs, a file system type that provides support for file system independent booting.

▲ rfs, a distributed file system type that supports Remote File Sharing capabilities.

▲ nfs, a distributed file system type originally introduced in the SunOS operating system that supports Network File System capabilities.

▲ proc, a file system type useful for debuggers and similar applications that must access the address space of running processes.

▲ fifofs, a file system type that provides access to pipe files.

▲ specfs, a file system type that provides a common interface to all device files.

The first three file system types, s5, ufs, and bfs are discussed in this chapter. The two distributed file system types, rfs and nfs, are described in Chapter 5, *Communications*. The final three are outside the scope of this book.

This chapter begins with a brief look at three file system types and offers some suggestions for creating and configuring your file system. Administrative tasks that can identify and correct file system problems are discussed, such as

▲ monitoring the free disk space

▲ monitoring files and directories that grow

▲ identifying and removing inactive files

▲ identifying large space users

▲ balancing file system space

The chapter ends with some hints for improving file system performance:

▲   controlling directory size

▲   assigning disk quotas

Chapter 4, *Storage Devices*, talks about the relationship between files systems and the media they reside on, including partitioning the drive.

## ❏ File System Organization

The starting point of any UNIX file system is a directory that serves as the root of that file system. There is exactly one file system that has the name `root`. Traditionally, the root directory of the `root` file system is represented by a single slash (/). Figure 3-1 shows part of a typical root file system.

A directory such as `/usr` that is used to form the connection between the `root` file system and another mountable file system is sometimes called a "leaf" or "mount point." Such a directory is the root of the file system that descends from it. The name of that file system is the name of the directory. In Figure 3-1 the `/usr` file system has been mounted.

**Figure 3-1**
*Mountable file systems.*
*The top portion of the drawing shows part of the* root *file system. Other file systems can be mounted at the leaves of the tree. The* /usr *file system, enclosed in the grey box, is an example. One directory,* john, *is expanded to show the* . *and* .. *files that contain pointers for traversing the directory tree.*

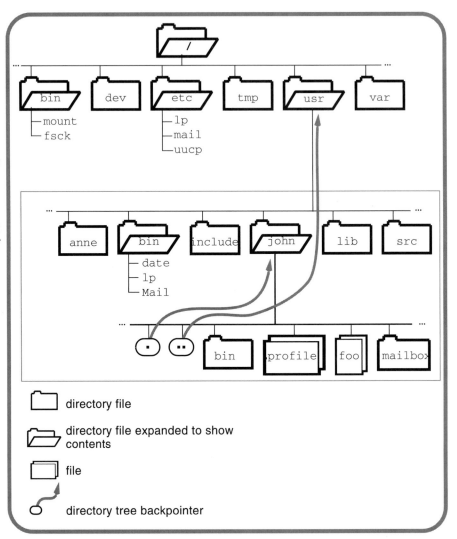

The collection of files and directories is the UNIX user's view of the file system. But file system performance is directly related to the operating system's view, that is, the underlying implementation.

UNIX System V Release 4.0 supports a variety of file system types (FSTypes) of varying characteristics, three of which are described here.

▲ the s5 file system, a hierarchical file system designed to minimize wasted disk space

▲ the `ufs` file system, a hierarchical file system designed to maximize I/O performance, and

▲ the `bfs` file system, a flat file system of contiguously allocated files used to boot the machine.

The next three sections briefly describe each FSType. Note the differences in block size, maximum file size, storage block access, etc.

## ❑ The s5 File System Type

The s5 file system is designed to use disk space efficiently. It divides the disk into small blocks (512, 1024, or 2048 bytes per block, set when the file system is created). Since disk space is allocated in blocks, a small block size minimizes the amount of space wasted in partially filled blocks, and minimizes the disk fragmentation (the extent to which files are non-contiguous). These are important considerations in file systems composed of many small files. However, large files will occupy many blocks and may require triple indirect addressing to access the data near the end of the file. Furthermore, since a block is the unit of data read and written for each disk access, and disk I/O operation will have high overhead (seek time and rotational delay).

The operating system views an s5 file system as a collection of addressable blocks of disk space that belong to one of four categories:

▲ *the boot block*. Block 0 is reserved for storing procedures used in booting the system. The boot block is unused in file systems that are not bootable

▲ *the superblock*. Block 1 holds the characteristics and status of the file system, including such things as

• file system name and size

• inode information, such as the total number allocated, the number free, and a partial list of available inodes

• storage block information, such as the number of free blocks and a partial list of available blocks

▲ *the i-list*, a variable number of blocks containing inodes

▲ *the storage block*s. The rest of the disk is storage blocks, some allocated to files, some used for indirect addressing for large files, and some unallocated and linked together in a free list.

The term *inode* stands for information node. A list of inodes is called an *i-list* and the position of an inode in an i-list is called an *i-number*.

An inode contains all the information about a file except its name, which is kept in a directory. Inodes are 64 bytes long with eight of them in a physical block. The length of an i-list is not fixed; it depends on the number of inodes specified when the file system is created.

An s5 inode contains:

▲ the type and mode of the file. The type can be regular, directory, block, character, symbolic link, or FIFO, also known as named pipe; the mode is the set of read-write-execute permissions

▲ the number of hard links to the file

▲ the owner-id and group-id of the file

▲ the number of bytes in the file

▲ an array of 13 disk block addresses

▲ the date and time the file was created, last accessed, and last modified

The heart of the inode is the array of disk block addresses. The first ten are direct addresses: they point directly to the first ten logical storage blocks of the contents of the file. If the file is larger than ten blocks, the 11th address points to an indirect block, which contains direct addresses instead of file contents; the 12th address points to a double indirect block, which contains addresses of indirect blocks. Finally, the 13th address in the array is the address of a triple indirect block, which contains addresses of double indirect blocks. Figure 3-2 illustrates this chaining of address blocks stemming from the inode.

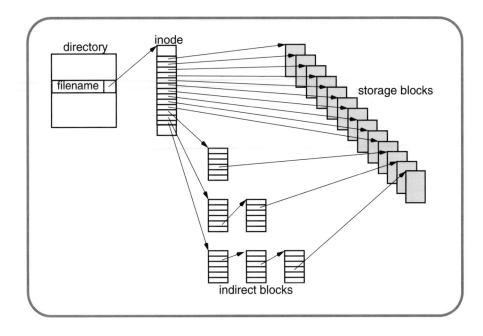

**Figure 3-2**
*Accessing storage blocks in an s5 file system.*
The file name is used to locate the inode, which in turn points to the storage blocks that contain the data. The first 10 blocks are addressed directly in the inode. Subsequent blocks are reached through single, double, or triple indirection, depending on how large the file is.

The table in Figure 3-3 shows the number of bytes addressable by the different levels of indirection in the inode address array for s5 file systems. These numbers are calculated using the logical block size of the file system and the number of bytes (4) used to hold an address.

| maximum number of addressable bytes | Block Size | | |
|---|---|---|---|
| | 512 bytes | 1024 bytes | 2048 bytes |
| direct blocks | 5120 bytes | 10240 bytes | 20480 bytes |
| single indirect blocks | 64 KB | 256 KB | 1 MB |
| double indirect blocks | 8 MB | 64 MB | 512 MB |
| triple indirect blocks | 1 GB | 16 GB | 256 GB |

**Figure 3-3**
*Maximum addressability for s5 file systems.*
The theoretical maximum file size is the size shown in the triple indirect addressing row. In practice, however, files size is limited by the size field in the inode.

The table shows the number of bytes addressable using the level of indirection in the column header plus all lower levels of addressing. For example, the table values for single indirect blocks also include bytes addressable by direct blocks; and the table values for triple indirect blocks include bytes addressable by direct blocks and single and double indirect blocks.

The theoretical maximum size of an s5 system file is the same as the size of a file addressable with triple indirection (shown in the last row of the table). In practice, however, file size is limited by the size field in the inode. This is a 32-bit field, so file sizes are limited to $2^{32}$ bytes = 4 gigabytes.

The rest of the space allocated to the file system is occupied by storage blocks. Blocks not currently in use are chained together in a free list, with each block in the list pointing to the next one. Blocks are allocated to files as needed to store the file contents and to act as indirect address blocks.

A directory file is a special file type that is readable by the user but writable only by the kernel. Each entry in the directory file consists of a 2-byte i-number and a 14-byte filename of the member file or subdirectory.

# ❑ The ufs File System Type

The ufs file system type is based on the BSD "fast file system" and is designed to address some of the performance limitations of the s5 file system design. It supports block sizes up to 8 KB: the bigger block size means that more bytes are read or written in each disk access, thus minimizing the overhead per byte. Since increasing the block size also increases the opportunity to waste space in partially used blocks, the ufs file system designers invented the notion of a *fragment*. Each block can be divided up into two, four, or eight fragments that can be assigned to files individually. Thus, the block is the I/O transfer unit while the fragment is the storage allocation unit.

As you may have suspected, the ufs FSType is considerably more complex in its design than the s5 FSType. In addition to the four categories of addressable blocks (the boot block, superblock, inodes, and storage blocks) found in s5, there are several additional disk-based data structures for keeping track of disk usage. There is also a radically different method of allocating and managing space, based on dividing the file system partition into subdivisions called *cylinder groups*. Each cylinder group has a copy of the superblock, offset from the start of the cylinder group such that the a superblock appears on each platter of a multiple-platter disk drive. If the first platter is lost, an alternate superblock can be retrieved.

Much of the information about the file system is stored in the superblock. A few of the more important things it contains are:

▲   the file system name

▲   the size and status of the file system

▲   the date and time of the last update

▲   the cylinder group size

▲   the number of data blocks in a cylinder group

▲   the summary data block

Each cylinder group also contains a *cylinder group map*. This is a block of data found in each cylinder group that records the block usage within the cylinder. This information is kept directly following the superblock copy for that cylinder group.

Cylinder group 0 is different than the others. In addition to a superblock and a cylinder group map, it has a *boot block* and a *summary information block*. The boot block is the first 8K in the partition. It is reserved for storing the procedures used in booting the system. If a file system will not be used for booting, the boot block is left blank. The summary block is used to record changes that take place as the file system is used, and lists the number of inodes, directories, fragments, and blocks within the file system.

An inode is 128 bytes long and contains all the information about a file except its name, which is kept in a directory. One inode is created for every 2K of storage available in the file system. This parameter can be changed when mkfs is used to create the file system, but it is fixed thereafter. A ufs inode contains:

▲   *the type and mode of the file. The type can be regular, directory, block, character, symbolic link, or FIFO, also known as named pipe; the mode is the set of read-write-execute permissions.*

▲   *the number of hard links to the file*

▲   *the user-id and group-id of the file*

▲   *the number of bytes in the file*

▲   *an array of 15 disk block addresses*

▲   *the date and time the file was created, last accessed, and last modified*

The heart of the inode is the array of 15 disk addresses. The first 12 are direct addresses; that is, they point directly to the first 12 logical storage blocks of the contents of the file. If the file is larger than 12 logical blocks, the 13th address points to an indirect block, which contains direct addresses instead of file contents; the 14th address points to a double indirect block, which contains addresses of indirect blocks. The 15th address is unused. Figure 3-4 illustrates this chaining of address blocks stemming from the inode.

**Figure 3-4**
*Accessing storage blocks in a ufs file system. The filename is used to locate the inode, which directly addresses the first twelve data blocks. Subsequent storage blocks are located through single or double indirection, depending on the size of the file.*

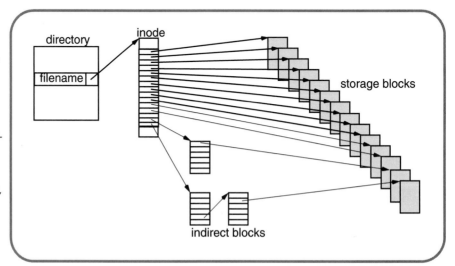

Figure 3-5 shows the number of bytes addressable by the different levels of indirection in the inode address array for ufs file systems. These numbers are calculated using the logical block size of the file system and the number of bytes used to hold an address.

**Figure 3-5**
*Maximum addressability for ufs file systems. Much bigger files can be addressed directly than in an s5 file system.*

| maximum number of addressable bytes | Block Size | |
|---|---|---|
| | 4096 bytes | 8192 bytes |
| direct blocks | 48 KB | 96 KB |
| single indirect blocks | 4 MB | 16 MB |
| double indirect blocks | 4 GB | 32 GB |

The theoretical maximum size of a ufs file system is the same as the size of a file addressable with double indirection. In practice, however, file size is limited by the size field in the inode. This is a signed 32-bit field, so file sizes are limited to $2^{31}$ bytes = 2 gigabytes. Because of the large size of ufs logical blocks, double indirect blocks rarely appear in ufs file systems. The result is that data retrieval in large files is much quicker than it would otherwise be.

The rest of the space allocated to the file system is occupied by storage blocks. Blocks are allocated to files as needed to store the file contents and to act as indirect address blocks. The block size is determined at the time a file system is created, and can be either 4096 or 8192 bytes; the fragment size may be set to 512, 1024, 2048, or 4096 bytes. The default ufs file system has 8 KB blocks and 1 KB fragments.

A directory file is a special file type that is readable by the user but writable only by the kernel. Each entry in the directory file consists of an inode number and the filename of the member file or subdirectory. ufs filenames may be up to 255 characters long.

Unused blocks and fragments are marked as free in the block map kept in the cylinder group summary information block. Blocks are allocated to files using an algorithm that chooses the one that will minimize the disk overhead.

# ❏ The bfs File System Type

The bfs FSType is a special-purpose file system. It contains all the stand-alone programs (e.g. unix) and all the text files necessary for the boot procedures. The bfs file system is a contiguous flat file system to allow quick and simple booting. The only directory bfs supports is the root directory. No directories or special files can be created in the bfs file system, just regular files.

A bfs file system consists of three parts:

▲ *the superblock*. The bfs superblock is quite different from its counter-part in s5 and ufs file systems. Because there is no file hierarchy storage blocks are allocated contiguously, much of the mechanism in the other superblocks is unnecessary. Instead, the bfs superblock contains:

- *the magic number,* a redundancy check and means of self-identification.

- *the size of the file system,* represented as starting and ending byte offsets.

- *the sanity words.* These are four words used to promote sanity during compaction. They are used by the `fsck` command to recover if there has been a system crash at any time during the process of compaction.

▲ *the inodes,* which contain all the information about a file except its name, which is kept in the `root` directory. An inode is 64 bytes long and includes the following information:

  - the i-number or zero if the inode is available

  - addresses of the first and last data blocks

  - the disk offset to the end-of-file (in bytes)

  - the file attributes

  - the type and mode of the file

  - the user ID of the owner of the file

  - the group ID to which the file belongs

  - the number of hard links to the file

  - the date and time the file was created, last accessed, and last modified

▲ *the storage blocks.* The size of the storage blocks is 512 bytes. The storage blocks are used to store the `root` directory and the regular files. The `root` directory blocks contain 16-byte entries. Each entry represents a file and consists of 2 bytes for the i-number and 14 bytes for the file name.

Figure 3-6 shows how the inode information about a file is used to locate the storage blocks that comprise the file.

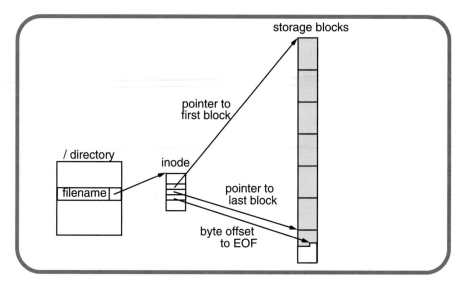

**Figure 3-6**
*Accessing storage blocks in a bfs file system. There are no indirect blocks and only one directory.*

The data or storage blocks for a file are allocated contiguously. The next available data block is always the block immediately following the last block of the last file in the directory. When a file is deleted, its data blocks are released The freed blocks will be reused when and if:

▲   the deleted file was the last file stored in the file system, or

▲   the system compacts the unused space into one contiguous block.

Compaction is a way of recovering data blocks by shifting files until the gaps left behind by deleted files are eliminated. This operation can be very expensive, but it is necessary because of the method used by bfs to store and delete files.

The system recognizes the need for compaction and automatically does it when:

▲   the system has reached the end of the file system and there are still free blocks available, or

▲   the system deletes a very large file and the file after it on disk is small and is the last file in the file system. (Small files are files of no more than 10 blocks; large files are files of 500 or more blocks.)

# ❑ Selecting a File System Type

The default file system type is the s5 file system type with a logical block size of 2K (2048 bytes). For most applications this should be best. Depending on the average size of the file, however, you may want to change either the logical block size or even the file system type of the file system. There are three logical block sizes of s5 file systems: 512 byte, 1K (1024 bytes), and 2K (the default). The ufs file system has two logical block sizes: 4K (4096 bytes) and 8K (8192 bytes). Each has its advantages and disadvantages in terms of performance.

The UNIX kernel uses the logical block size when reading and writing files. If the logical block size of the file system is 2K, whenever I/O is done between a file and memory, 2K chunks of the file are read into or out of memory.

Large logical block size improves disk I/O performance by reducing seek time and also decreases CPU I/O overhead. On the other hand, if the logical block size is too large then disk space is wasted. The extra space is lost because even if only a portion of a block is needed the entire block is allocated. For example, if files are stored in 1K (1024 bytes) logical blocks, then a 24-byte file wastes 1000 bytes. If the same 24-byte file is stored on a file system with a 2K (2048 bytes) logical block size, then 2024 bytes are wasted. However, if most files on the file system are very large this waste is reduced considerably.

For a file system with mostly small files, small logical block sizes (512 byte and 1K) have the advantage of less wasted space on disk. However, CPU overhead may be increased for files larger than the block size.

The maximum number of blocks that can be allocated to a file system is close to the total number of sectors on the disk device. This maximum may be reduced by space set aside for swapping or paging. Also, recall that under ufs a 2 gigabyte upper limit is imposed by the size field in the inode.

The maximum number of inodes that can be specified for s5 is 65,500. The ufs FSType does not have a rigid upper limit. Rather, roughly one inode is created automatically for each 2K of data space, although this default can be overridden at the time the file system is created.

The size of a block on a disk is 512 bytes, the same as a disk sector. However, internal file I/O works with logical blocks rather than with 512-byte physical blocks. The size of a logical block is set with the mkfs(1M) command, discussed later in the chapter. s5 uses logical block sizes of 512, 1024, and 2048 bytes; the default is 1024 byte blocks. ufs, on the other hand, uses logical block sizes of 4096 and 8192 bytes; the default is 8192 byte blocks.

Because of the large block size used by ufs, small files could waste a lot of space. To deal with this, ufs has a subdivision of a block called a fragment. When a ufs file system is created using mkfs, the fragment size may be set to 512, 1024, 2048, or 4096 bytes. When a block must be fragmented, the remaining fragments are made available to other files to use for storage. The information on which fragments are in use and which are available is kept in the cylinder group summary information block.

The sar -u command, described in Chapter 6, *Monitoring System Activity,* can help determine if large I/O transfers are slowing the system down.

## ❏ Creating a File System

In the UNIX system, file systems are kept on random-access disk devices. You must format and partition the disk before you create a file system on it. Formatting and partitioning are discussed in Chapter 4, *Storage Devices.* For this discussion, we will define the terms and assume that the disk is already formatted and partitioned appropriately.

Disks must be formatted into addressable sectors before they are usable on UNIX. A disk *sector* is a 512-byte portion of the storage medium that can be addressed by the disk controller. The number of sectors is a function of the size and number of surfaces of the disk device. Sectors are numbered from zero on up.

A *partition* consists of one or more sectors. Up to 16 partitions can be defined on a hard disk; fmthard(1M) command is used to associate the starting points of partitions with sector numbers. Partition tags 0-8 are reserved. Chapter 4, *Storage Devices,* has more information about disk partitions and their relationship to file systems.

Once a disk is formatted the next step is to define the file system. The `mkfs` command is used for this purpose. The general format of the `mkfs` command follows (shown on two lines for readability):

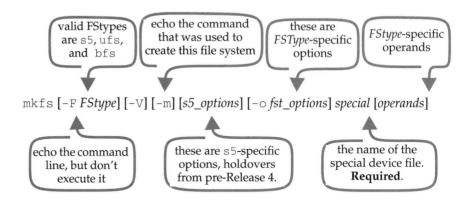

`mkfs` constructs a file system by writing on the *special* file, which must be specified. The file system is created based on the *FSType*, the *fst_options*, and *operands* specified on the command line.

The *FSType* must either be specified on the command line (with the -F option) or be determinable from /etc/vfstab by matching an entry in that file with one of the *operands* specified. (See the section "The *vfstab File*" in this chapter and vfstab(4) for more information.)

The -V option causes the command to echo the completed command line. The echoed line will include additional information derived from /etc/vfstab. This option can be used to verify and validate the command line. It does not cause the command to execute.

The -m option is used to return the command line which was used to create the file system. The file system must already exist; this option provides a means of determining the attributes used in constructing the file system. Note that file systems cannot be constructed for all *FSTypes*, only s5, ufs, and bfs.

*s5_options* are options supported by the s5-specific module of the *command* and are described in the next section.

The -o option is used to specify *FSType*-specific options if any. *fst_options* are options specified in a comma-separated list of keywords and keyword-attribute pairs for interpretation by the *FSType*-specific module of the command.

*operands* are *FSType*-specific and are described in the sections that follow.

### Choosing Logical Block Size

Logical block size is the size of the blocks that the UNIX kernel uses to read or write files. The logical block size is usually different from the physical block size, which is the size of the smallest block that the disk controller can read or write, usually 512 bytes.

The mkfs command allows the administrator to specify the logical block size of the file system. By default, the logical block size is 1024 bytes (1K) for s5 file systems and 8192 bytes (8K) for ufs file systems. The root and usr file systems are delivered as 2048-byte s5 file systems. Besides 1K and 2K file systems, the s5 file system also supports 512-byte file systems while the ufs file system supports 4096-byte (4K) as well as 8K systems.

To choose a reasonable logical block size for your system, you must consider both the performance desired and the available space. For most ufs systems, an 8K file system with a 1K fragment size gives the best performance, while for most s5 systems, a 1K file system provides the best performance: both offer a good balance between disk performance and use of space in primary memory and on disk. For special applications running under s5 (such as s5 file servers) that use large executable files or large data files, a 2K file system may be a better choice.

## ❑ Using mkfs to Create an s5 File System

When used to make an s5 file system, the mkfs command builds a file system with a root directory and a lost+found directory. It is usually invoked in one of the following ways:

    mkfs  [-F s5]  [-b *blocksize*]  *special blocks* [ :*inodes*]  [*gap blocks/cyl*]
    mkfs  [-F s5]  [-b *blocksize*]  *special proto* [*gap blocks/cyl*]

As discussed earlier, the file system type, s5, is specified on the command line if no entry has been set up for *special* in the vfstab(4) file by the administrator. See the *"The vfstab File"* section later in this chapter.

Notice that neither form of the command names the file system that is to be created (for this function see labelit(1M)); instead, both forms identify the file by the filename of the special device file on which it will reside. The *special* device file, traditionally located in the directory /dev, is associated with the identifying controller and unit numbers (major and minor, respectively) for the physical device. See Chapter 4, *Storage Devices*.

In the first form of the command the only other information that must be furnished on the mkfs command line is the number of 512-byte sectors the file system is to occupy. The second form lets you include that information in a prototype file that can also define a directory and file structure for the new file system.

Both forms of the command let you specify information about the inter-record gap and the blocks per cylinder. If this information is not given on the command line, default values are used. Figure 3-7 shows the recommended values for use with the mkfs command for devices using the s5 file system type. The recommended values are different from the defaults that will be used if no values are specified: gap 10, size 162.

The recommended gap size depends on the logical block size of the file system. By default, the file system has a logical block size of 1024 bytes. With the -b option, you can specify a logical block size of 512 bytes, 1024 bytes, or 2048 bytes. You may also specify the number of inodes. If the number of inodes is omitted, the command uses a default value of one inode for every four logical storage blocks, rounding down to a modulo 16 value if necessary to fill the final inode block.

| Device (Manufacturer) | Gap Size | | | Blocks per Cylinder |
| --- | --- | --- | --- | --- |
| | 512-byte blocks | 1K blocks | 2K blocks | |
| 10MB | 8 | 10 | 12 | 72 |
| 30MB | 8 | 10 | 12 | 90 |
| 72MB (CDC Wren II) | 8 | 10 | 12 | 162 |
| 72aMB (Micropolis) | 8 | 10 | 12 | 144 |
| 72bMB (Priam) | 8 | 10 | 12 | 162 |
| 72cMB (Fujitsu) | 8 | 10 | 12 | 198 |

**Figure 3-7**
*Inter-record Gap and Blocks/Cylinder Recommendations for s5*

If you use the first form of the command, the file system is created with a
root directory and a lost+found directory. If you use a prototype file, it
may include information that allows the command to build and initialize a
directory and file structure for the file system. The format of a prototype file is
described on the mkfs(1M) manual page of the *User's Reference Manual/System Administrator's Reference Manual*.

A sample command follows:

```
mkfs  -F  s5  -b  2048  /dev/rdsk/c0d0s2  12  44
```

This command creates an s5 file system with 2K blocks with an inter-record
gap of 12 and 44 blocks per cylinder.

## Summary: Creating and Converting s5 File Systems

Here is a summary of the steps to create a new file system or convert an existing one to a new logical block size:

1.  If the new file system is to be created on a disk partition that contains
    an old file system, back up the old file system.

2.  If the new file system is to be created from an old file system, run the labelit(1M) command, which reports the mounted file system name and the physical volume name of the old file system (see volcopy(1M).) These labels are destroyed when you make the new file system, so you must restore them.

3.  If the new file system is to be created from an old file system and the new file system will have a larger logical block size, then, because of fragmentation, the new file system will allocate more disk blocks for data storage than the old. Use the fsba(1M) command to find out the space requirements of the old file system with the new block size.

    Use the information you get from the fsba command to make sure that the disk partition to be used for the new file system is large enough. Use the prtvtoc(1M) command to find out the size of your current disk partitions. If the new file system requires a disk re-partition, see "*Formatting Hard Disks*" in Chapter 4.

4.  Use the mkfs(1M) command with the -b option to make the new file system with the appropriate logical block size.

5.  Run the labelit command to restore the file system and volume names.

6.  Populate the new file system. For example do a restore from a file system backup, or, if your system has two hard disks, do a cpio(1) from a mounted file system. (The volcopy(1M) and dd(1M) commands copy a file system image; they cannot convert logical block size.)

## ❏ Using mkfs to Create a ufs File System

When used to make a ufs file system, the mkfs command builds a file system with a root directory and a lost+found directory. The number of inodes is calculated as a function of the file system size.

The syntax for the mkfs command when it is used to create a ufs file system is the following:

```
mkfs -F ufs [-o specific_options] special size
```

The *specific_options* are a comma-separated list that allow you to control the parameters of the file system. The more important ones are as follows (for a complete list, see the ufs-specific mkfs(1M) manual page):

▲ nsect - The number of sectors per track on the disk. The default is 18.

▲ ntrack - The number of tracks per cylinder on the disk. The default is 9.

▲ bsize - The primary block size for files on the file system. It must be a power of two, currently selected from 4096 or 8192 (the default).

▲ fragsize - The smallest amount of disk space that will be allocated to a file. It must be a power of two, currently selected from the range 512 to 8192. The default is 1024.

▲ cgsize - The number of disk cylinders per cylinder group. This number must be in the range 1 to 32. The default is 16.

▲ free - The minimum percentage of free disk space allowed. Once the file system capacity reaches this threshold, you must be a privileged user to allocate disk blocks. The default is 10.

A sample command follows:

```
mkfs -F ufs -o bsize=4096,nsect=18,ntrack=9 \
     /dev/rdsk/c0d0s2 35340
```

The above command line is shown on two lines for readability. It creates a ufs file system with 4K blocks, 18 sectors per track, and 9 tracks per cylinder that will occupy 35,340 sectors in the disk partition called /dev/rdsk/c0c0s2.

## Summary: Creating and Converting ufs File Systems

Here is a summary of the steps required to create a new file system or convert an old one to a new logical block size:

1.  If the new file system is to be created on a disk partition that contains an old file system, back up the old file system.

2.  If the new file system is to be created from an old file system, run the labelit(1M) command, which reports the mounted file system

name and the physical volume name of the old file system (see volcopy(1M).) These labels are destroyed when you make the new file system, so you must restore them.

3. Use the mkfs(1M) command to make the new file system with the appropriate logical block size.

4. Run the labelit(1M) command to restore the file system and volume names.

5. Populate the new file system. For example do a restore from a file system backup, or, if your system has two hard disks, do a cpio(1M) from a mounted file system. (The volcopy(1M) and dd(1M) commands copy a file system image; they cannot convert logical block size.)

# ❑ Using mkfs to Create a bfs File System

When used to make a bfs file system, the mkfs command builds a file system with a root directory.

The syntax for the mkfs command when making a bfs file system is as follows:

    mkfs [-F bfs] *special blocks* [*inodes*]

If the number of inodes is not specified on the command line, the default number of inodes is calculated as a function of the file system size.

Although any disk can have multiple boot file systems defined on it, you will not normally want more than one boot file system on one disk.

The following procedure shows how to define a new boot file system and assumes that the disk you are using is already bootable. See the section *"Making New Bootable Disks"* in Chapter 4,*Storage Devices*, for instructions on making new bootable disks.

## Defining a New Boot File System on a Bootable Disk

1.  Use the `prtvtoc`(1M) command to identify the type and size of the current disk partitions on the disk. If your new `bfs` file system requires a disk repartition, see *"Making New Bootable Disks"* in Chapter 4 for information on partitioning a bootable disk.

2.  Use the `mkfs`(1M) command to make a `bfs` file system in the appropriate partition of the disk.

3.  Mount the new boot file system.

4.  Populate the new file system; that is, copy into the new `bfs` file system all the required bootable programs and data files used during the boot procedure. See *"The `stand` and `boot` Partitions"* in Chapter 4 for information about these files.

# ❏ The `vfstab` File

Since the generic commands work on multiple FSTypes (e.g., `mount` can mount both `s5` and `ufs` file systems), they require FSType-specific information which may be provided explicitly on the command line or implicitly through the file system table `/etc/vfstab`.

The file system table contains a list of default parameters for each file system. It is an ASCII file that should be maintained by the system administrator. Each record contains space separated information about a file system in the format:

*special fsckdev mountp fstype fsckpass automnt mntopts*

The meaning of each field is as follows:

> *special*      the block special device for local devices or the resource name for remote file systems (e.g. `rfs` and `nfs`). (For more information on remote file systems, see the *Network Applications Guide).*

> *fsckdev*     the character special device that corresponds to the *special*. The block special device is used if the character

special device is not available. Use a "–" where there is no applicable device.

*mountp*     the default mount directory (mount point)

*fstype*     the type of the file system on the special device

*fsckpass*     the pass number to be used by ff, fsck, and ncheck to decide whether to check the file system automatically. Use "–" to inhibit automatic checking of the file system.

*automnt*     yes or no for whether the file system should be automatically mounted by mountall when the system is booted.

*mntopts*     a list of comma-separated options that will be used in mounting the file system. Use "–" to indicate no options. See mount(1M) for a list of the available options.

Lines beginning with the # character are comments.

## ❏ Maintaining a File System

Once a file system has been created and made available, it must be maintained regularly so that its performance remains satisfactory. Four tasks should be part of routine maintenance to ensure that disk space does not become so scarce that system performance is degraded. They are:

▲   monitoring the percent of disk space used,

▲   monitoring files and directories that grow,

▲   identifying and removing inactive files, and

▲   identifying large space users.

## Monitoring the Percent of Disk Space Used

Monitoring disk space may be done at any time to see how close to capacity your system is running. Until a pattern has emerged, it is advisable to check every day. To do this, use the df(1M) command as follows:

```
df -t
```

The -t option causes the total allocated blocks and files to be displayed, as well as free blocks and files. When no file systems are named, information about all mounted file systems is displayed. If information on unmounted file systems is needed the file system name must be specified. For more information on the numerous options available to df, see the df(1M) manual page in the *User's Reference Manual/System Administrator's Reference Manual*.

## Monitoring Files and Directories that Grow

Almost any system that is used daily has several files and directories that grow through normal use. Some examples are shown in Figure 3-8.

| File | Use |
|------|-----|
| /var/adm/wtmp | history of system logins |
| /var/adm/sulog | history of su(1) commands |
| /var/cron/log | history of actions of /usr/sbin/cron |
| /var/help/HELPLOG | actions of /usr/bin/help |
| /var/spell/spellhist | words that spell(1) fails to match |

**Figure 3-8**
*Files that grow through normal use.*

The frequency with which you should check growing files depends on how active your system is and how critical the disk space problem is. A good way to limit the size of such files is the following:

```
tail -50 /var/adm/sulog > /var/tmp/sulog
mv /var/tmp/sulog /var/adm/sulog
```

This sequence puts the last 50 lines of /var/adm/sulog into a temporary file, and then it moves the temporary file to /var/adm/sulog, thus truncating the file to the 50 most recent entries.

## Identifying and Removing Inactive Files

Part of the job of cleaning up heavily loaded file systems involves locating and removing files that have not been used recently. The find(1) command locates files that have not been accessed recently. find searches a directory tree beginning at a point named on the command line. It looks for filenames that match a given set of expressions, and when a match is found, performs a specified action on the file.

The example find command below can be used to generate a list of pathnames for all files that have not been modified in 60 days.

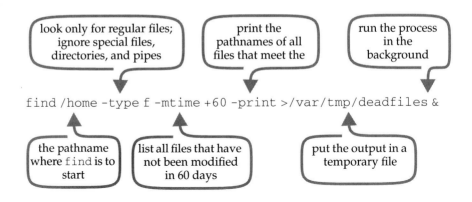

```
find /home -type f -mtime +60 -print >/var/tmp/deadfiles &
```

look only for regular files; ignore special files, directories, and pipes

print the pathnames of all files that meet the

run the process in the background

the pathname where find is to start

list all files that have not been modified in 60 days

put the output in a temporary file

## Identifying Large Space Users

Two commands provide useful information: du(1M) and find(1).

du produces a summary of the block counts for files or directories named in the command line. For example:

```
du /home
```

displays the block count for all directories in the /home file system. Optional arguments allow you to refine the output somewhat. For example, du -s may be run against each user's login to monitor individual users.

The find command can also be used to locate specific files that exceed a given size limit.

```
find /home -size +10 -print
```

This example produces a display of the pathnames of all files (and directories) in the /home file system that are larger than 10 (512-byte) blocks.

# ❑ Improving and Controlling File System Usage

Making files is easy under the UNIX operating system. Therefore, users tend to create numerous files using large amounts of space. The file systems containing the following directories should maintain, at the very least, the following start-of-day counts.

| | |
|---|---|
| /tmp | 2000 to 4000 512-byte blocks |
| /usr | 500 to 1000 512-byte blocks |
| /home | 3000 to 6000 512-byte blocks |
| /var | 4000 to 8000 512-byte blocks |

Other file systems should have 6 to 10 percent of their capacity available.

The default system configuration is set up so that the file blocks are allocated in an optimum manner.

## Balancing File System Space

You can also control file system space by balancing the load between file systems. To do this, user directories often need to be moved. Users should be notified of moves well enough in advance so that they can program around the expected change.

In order to move directories and manipulate the file system tree, you must use the find and cpio commands. The following command sequence shows how to do this. This example moves directory trees userx and usery from file system fs1 to fs2 where, presumably, there is more space available.

```
cd /fs1
find userx usery -print -depth | cpio -pdm /fs2
rm -rf /fs1/userx /fs1/usery
```

Once this sequence is entered, verify that the copy was made. Then change the userx and usery default login directories with the usermod shell command. You must also notify userx and usery, preferably via mail, that they have been moved and that their pathname dependencies may need to be changed.

Whenever moving users in this way, make sure that users with common interests are in the same file system. Furthermore, move groups of users with a single cpio command, as shown in the example above, otherwise linked files will be unlinked and duplicated.

## Controlling Directory Size

Very large directories are inefficient and can affect performance. Two directories in particular, /var/mail and /var/spool/uucp, tend to get very large and should be monitored periodically. If a directory becomes bigger than 10 logical blocks (forty, 512-byte blocks or 1280 entries for a 2K logical block size) or 2560 entries, whichever is smaller, then directory searches are likely causing performance problems. The find command, as shown below, can ferret out such problem directories.

```
find / -type d -size +40 -print
```

◆ *Note*        find thinks in terms of 512-byte blocks.

Another important thing to remember is that removing files from directories *does not* make those directories any smaller. When a file is removed from a directory, the inode (file header) number is nulled out, leaving an unused slot. Over time the number of empty slots may become quite large. For example, if you have a directory with 100 files in it and you remove the first 99 files, the directory still contains the 99 empty slots, at 16 bytes per slot, preceding the active slot. In effect, unless a directory is reorganized on the disk, it will retain the largest size it has ever achieved.

Use the `/usr/sbin/cmpress` shell command to compress the whole file system. During reorganization, the system can be up but the file system being compressed must be unmounted. Root reorganization should be done once a week (requires a system reboot) and user file systems should be reorganized once a month in order to maintain maximum system performance.

If you want to compress a single directory, you must perform a series of commands in order to perform this procedure. These commands are as follows:

```
mkdir /var/omail
mv /var/mail /var/omail
chmod 777 /var/omail
cd /var/omail
find . -print | cpio -plm ../mail
cd ..
rm -rf omail
```

You can also reduce directory size by locating inactive files, backing them up, and then deleting them. The `find` command can be used to locate inactive files. For example:

```
find / -mtime +90 -atime +90 -print > filename
```

where *filename* will contain the name of the files neither written to nor accessed within a specified time period. In this example, we used 90 days (+90). If these inactive files are causing problems, it is wise to first contact the user to see if these files can be deleted.

# ❑ Assigning Disk Quotas

The quota system is built around limits on the two principal resources of a file system: inodes and data blocks. For each of these resources, users may be assigned quotas. A quota in this case consists of two limits, known as the soft and hard limits. The hard limit represents an absolute limit on the resource, blocks or inodes, that the user may never exceed under any circumstances. Associated with the soft limit is a time limit set by the administrator. Users may exceed the soft limits assigned to them for a limited amount of time set by the administrator. This allows the user to temporarily exceed limits if necessary, as long as they are back under those limits before the time limit expires. An example of such a situation might be the generation of a large file that is then printed and deleted.

In summary, for each user, you can assign quotas (soft and hard limits) for both blocks and inodes. You can also define a time limit that applies to all users on a file system indicating how long they can exceed the soft limits. There are actually two time limits: one for blocks and one for inodes. You may define different time limits for different file systems. Also, users may have different quotas set on different file systems.

## Using Quotas

Before turning quotas on for a file system for the first time:

▲ If the quotas are for a file system listed in `/etc/vfstab`, enter an "`rq`" in the `mntopts` field for that file system. If there is an "`rw`" in that field in the table, it should be replaced by "`rq`".

▲ Mount the file system and `cd` to the mount point. Create a file called `quotas`. This file should be owned by `root`, and not writable by others.

▲ Execute `edquota -t` to change the time limits for exceeding the soft limits for blocks owned and inodes owned. These limits are initially set to the values defined for `DQ_FTIMELIMIT` and `DQ_BTIMELIMIT` in `/usr/include/sys/fs/ufs_quota.h`, normally one week. If you leave either time limit (the one for exceeding the block limit or the one for exceeding the inode limit) at 0, or if you set either limit to 0, the default values will apply. You can, of course, change them to something else.

▲ Execute `edquota`, with or without the `-p` option, to set user quotas. Once you have set the quotas for a user, you can use the `-p` option to set the same quotas for another user. Note that because you are not limited to UIDs that are already being used, you may set quotas for future users.

Before turning on quotas on a file system, always run `quotacheck` on the file system. This will sync up the quotas with the actual state of the file system, so that if the file system has been used since the last time the quotas were turned on, all of the quotas will be updated to reflect the current state. This also provides a sanity check on the `quotas` file.

Use `quotaon` to turn quotas on, and `quotaoff` to turn them off. If you use the `-a` option with either, the command will execute the desired action on each `ufs` file system with "`rq`" in the `mntopts` field of its `vfstab` entry. Otherwise, you must invoke the command on each individual file system.

To report on quotas an administrator can use `repquota` or `quot` to get information on all users on a file system, or use `quota` to get information on a single user. Normal users can use `quota` to get information on their own quotas; they cannot get information on anyone else's quotas.

## The Effects of Quotas on the User

The following are the major effects of the use of quotas on users:

▲ If a user exceeds his or her soft limit for blocks or inodes, the timer is started. If the user then reduces usage to a level under the soft limit, the timer is turned off and all is well. But if the user still has not reduced usage to an appropriate level when the timer expires, any further attempts by the user to acquire more file system resources will fail and the user will receive error messages saying that the file system is full. These messages will persist until the user has reduced usage to a level below the soft limit.

▲ If a user tries to exceed the hard limit at any time, the attempt will fail and the utility will indicate that it has run out of space.

▲ Because no warning is given when the user has exceeded the soft limit, users should be advised to run `quota` frequently. Users should be encouraged to include `quota` in their `.profile` so that it runs when they log in.

# ❑ Checking a File System for Consistency

When the UNIX operating system is brought up, a consistency check of the file systems should always be done. This check is often done automatically as part of the boot process. Included as part of that process is a sanity check of each file system on the hard disk using the -m option to fsck. The sanity check returns a code for each file system indicating whether the consistency checking and repair program, fsck(1M), should be run.

fsck should also be used to manually check file systems that are not mounted automatically when the system boots. If inconsistencies are discovered, corrective action must be taken before the file systems are mounted. The remainder of this section is designed to acquaint you with the command line options of the fsck utility, the type of checking it does in each of its phases, and the repairs it suggests.

It should be said at the outset that file system corruption, while serious, is not all that common. Most of the time a check of the file systems finds everything all right. The reason we put so much emphasis on file system checking is that if errors are allowed to go undetected, the loss can be substantial.

## The fsck Utility

The file system check (fsck) utility is an interactive file system check and repair program. fsck uses the information contained in the file system to perform consistency checks. If an inconsistency is detected, a message describing the inconsistency is displayed. At that point you may decide whether to have fsck ignore the inconsistency or attempt to fix it. Reasons you might choose to have fsck ignore an inconsistency are that you think the problem is so severe that you want to fix it yourself, or that you plan to go back to an earlier version of the file system. Whatever your decision, you should not ignore the inconsistencies fsck reports. File system inconsistencies do not repair themselves. If they are ignored, they get worse.

The fsck administrative command is used to run the fsck utility to check and repair inconsistencies in a file system. With the exception of the root file system, a file system should be unmounted while it is being checked. If this is not possible, care should be taken that the system is quiescent and that it is rebooted immediately afterwards if the file system checked is a critical one.

The `root` file system should be checked only when the computer is in run level S and no other activity is taking place in the machine. The system should be rebooted immediately afterwards.

The generic format of the `fsck` command is:

    fsck  [-F *FSType*] [-V] [-m] [*special* ...]

    fsck  [-F *FSType*] [-V] [*current_options*] [-o *specific_options*] [*special* ...]

The -F is used to specify the *FSType* on which the command must act. The *FSType* must be specified on the command line or must be determinable from /etc/vfstab by matching an entry in that file with the *special* specified.

The -V option causes the command to echo the completed command line. The echoed line will include additional information derived from /etc/vfstab. This option can be used to verify and validate the command line. It does not cause the command to execute.

The -m option is used to perform a sanity check only. This option is usually used before mounting file systems because it lets the administrator know whether the file system needs to be checked.

*current_options* are options supported by the s5-specific module of the *command*.

The -o option is used to specify *FSType*-specific options if any. *specific_options* are options specified in a comma-separated list of keywords and/or keyword-attribute pairs for interpretation by the *FSType*-specific module of the command.

If the file system is inconsistent, the user is prompted for concurrence before each correction is attempted. It should be noted that some corrective actions will result in some loss of data. The amount and severity of data loss may be determined from the diagnostic output. The default action for each correction is to wait for the user to respond `yes` or `no`. If the user does not have write permission, `fsck` defaults to a `no` action.

# ❏ Checking s5 File Systems

Here is the s5 specific format of the fsck command; the options and arguments are described in Figure 3-10. (The second command line is shown on two lines for readability.)

    fsck  [-F s5]  [*generic_options*]  [*special* ...]

    fsck  [-F s5] [*generic_options*] [-y][-n][-p][-s*X*][-S*X*][-t*file*] \
        [-1][-q][-D][-f] [*special* ...]

# *Example*

The command line below shows fsck being entered to check the usr file system. No options are specified. The system response means that no inconsistencies were detected. The command operates in phases, some of which are run only if required or in response to a command line option. As each phase is completed, a message is displayed. At the end of the program a summary message is displayed showing the number of files (inodes) used, blocks used, and free blocks.

**Figure 3-9**
*An fsck example.*

```
# fsck -F s5 /dev/rdsk/c1d0s2

/dev/rdsk/c1d0s2
File System: usr Volume: usr

** Phase 1 - Check Blocks and Sizes
** Phase 2 - Check Pathnames
** Phase 3 - Check Connectivity
** Phase 4 - Check Reference Counts
** Phase 5 - Check Free List
289 files 6522 blocks 3220 free
#
```

| Option | Use |
|--------|-----|
| -y | Specifies a "yes" response for all questions. This is the normal choice when the command is being run as part of a shell procedure. It generally causes fsck to correct all errors. |
| -n | Specifies a "no" response for all questions. fsck will not write the file system. |
| -p | This option causes fsck to correct any innocuous inconsistencies. Unreferenced blocks, misaligned directories, incorrect link counts and bad free lists are some examples of inconsistencies which are automatically corrected. |
| -s$X$ | Specifies an unconditional reconstruction of the free list. The $X$ argument specifies the number of blocks per cylinder and the number of blocks to skip (inter-record gap). The default values are those specified when the file system was created. See the *"Using* mkfs *to Create an* s5 *File System"* section of this chapter for more information. |
| -s$X$ | Specifies a conditional reconstruction of the free list, to be done only if corruption is detected. The format of the $X$ argument is the same as described above for the -s option. |
| -t*file* | Specifies a scratch file for use in case the file system check requires additional memory. If this option is not specified, the process asks for a filename when more memory is needed. |
| -l | This option causes damaged files to be identified by their logical names in addition to the inode numbers. |
| -q | Specifies a "quiet" file system check. Output messages from the process are suppressed. |
| -D | Checks directories for bad blocks. This option is used to check file systems for damage after a system crash. |
| -f | Specifies that a fast file system check be done. Only Phase 1 (check blocks and sizes) and Phase 5 (check free list) are executed for a fast check. Phase 6 (reconstruct free list) is run only if necessary. |
| *special* | Names the special device file associated with a file system. If no device name is specified, fsck checks all file systems named in /etc/vfstab with a numeric fsckpass field. |

**Figure 3-10**
*fsck options.*

## s5  File System Components Checked by `fsck`

The phases of `fsck` and the messages that may appear in each phase are described in Appendix A. These are the s5 components that will be checked for consistency:

▲  *the superblock.* Every change to the file system blocks or inodes modifies the superblock. If the CPU is halted and the last command involving output to the file system is not a `sync` command, the superblock will almost certainly be corrupted. The superblock can be checked for inconsistencies involving:

   • *the file system size and inode list size.* The number of blocks in a file system must be greater than the number of blocks used by the superblock plus the number of blocks used by the inode list. The number of inodes must be less than the maximum number allowed for the file system type. While there is no way to check these sizes precisely, `fsck` can check that they are within reasonable bounds. All other checks of the file system depend on the reasonableness of these values.

   • *the free-block list.* The free-block list starts in the superblock and continues through the free-list blocks of the file system. Each free-list block can be checked for

      ■  list count out of range

      ■  block numbers out of range

      ■  blocks already allocated within the file system

   A check is made to see that all the blocks in the file system were found.

   The first free-block list is in the superblock. The `fsck` program checks the list count for a value less than 0 or greater than 50. It also checks each block number to make sure it is within the range bounded by the first and last data block in the file system. Each block number is compared to a list of previously allocated blocks. If the free-list block pointer is not 0, the next free-list block is read and the process is repeated.

   When all the blocks have been accounted for, a check is made to see if the number of blocks in the free-block list plus the number of blocks claimed by the inodes equals the total number of blocks in the file system. If anything is wrong with the free-block list, `fsck` can rebuild it leaving out blocks already allocated.

- *the free-block count.* The superblock contains a count of the total number of free blocks within the file system. The `fsck` program compares this count to the number of blocks it finds free within the file system. If the counts do not agree, `fsck` can replace the count in the superblock by the actual free-block count.

- *the free inode count.* The superblock contains a count of the number of free inodes within the file system. The `fsck` program compares this count to the number of inodes it found free within the file system. If the counts do not agree, `fsck` can replace the count in the superblock by the actual free inode count.

▲ *the inodes.* The list of inodes is checked sequentially starting with inode 1 (there is no inode 0). Each inode is checked for inconsistencies involving

- *format and type.* Each inode contains a mode word. This mode word describes the type and state of the inode. Inodes may be one of six types:

  - regular
  - directory
  - block special
  - character special
  - FIFO (named-pipe)
  - symbolic link

  Inodes may be in one of three states: unallocated, allocated, and partially allocated. This last state means that the inode is incorrectly formatted. An inode can get into this state if, for example, bad data are written into the inode list because of a hardware failure. The only corrective action `fsck` can take is to clear the inode.

- *Link Count.* Each inode contains a count of the number of directory entries linked to it. The `fsck` program verifies the link count of each inode by examining the entire directory structure, starting from the root directory, and calculating an actual link count for each inode.

  Discrepancies between the link count stored in the inode and the actual link count as determined by `fsck` may be of three types:

  - *the stored count is not 0, the actual count is 0.* This can occur if no directory entry appears for the inode. In this case `fsck` can link the disconnected file to the `lost+found` directory.

■ *the stored count is not 0, the actual count is not 0, but the counts are unequal.* This can occur if a directory entry has been removed but the inode has not been updated. In this case fsck can replace the stored link count by the actual link count.

■ *the stored count is 0, the actual count is not 0.* In this case fsck can change the link count of inode to the actual count.

• *duplicate blocks.* Each inode contains a list of all the blocks claimed by the inode. The fsck program compares each block number claimed by an inode to a list of allocated blocks. If a block number claimed by an inode is on the list of allocated blocks, it is put on a list of duplicate blocks. If it is not on the list of allocated blocks, it is put on it. If this process produces a list of duplicate blocks, fsck makes a second pass of the inode list to find the other inode that claims each duplicate block. (A large number of duplicate blocks in an inode may be caused by an indirect block not being written to the file system.) Although it is not possible to determine with certainty which inode is in error, in most cases the inode with the most recent modification time is correct. The fsck program prompts the user to clear both inodes.

• *bad block numbers.* The fsck program checks each block number claimed by an inode to see that its value is higher than that of the first data block and lower than that of the last block in the file system. If the block number is outside this range, it is considered a bad block number.

Bad block numbers in an inode may be caused by an indirect block not being written to the file system. The fsck program prompts the user to clear the inode.

■ *Note*     A bad block number in a file system is not the same as a bad (that is, unreadable) block on a hard disk.

• *inode size.* Each inode contains a 32-bit (4-byte) size field. This field shows the number of characters in the file associated with the inode. A directory inode within the file system has the directory bit set in the inode mode word.

If the directory size is not a multiple of 16, fsck warns of directory misalignment and prompts for corrective action.

For a regular file, a rough check of the consistency of the size field of an inode can be performed by using the number of characters shown in the size field to calculate how many blocks should be associated with the inode, and comparing that to the actual number of blocks claimed by the inode.

▲ *indirect block*s. Indirect blocks are owned by an inode. Therefore, inconsistencies in an indirect block directly affect the inode that owns it. Inconsistencies that can be checked are:

- blocks already claimed by another inode

- block numbers outside the range of the file system

The consistency checks for direct blocks described in the bullet items *"duplicate blocks"* and *"bad block numbers"* above are also performed for indirect blocks.

▲ *directory data blocks*. Directories are distinguished from regular files by an entry in the mode field of the inode. Data blocks associated with a directory contain the directory entries. Directory data blocks are checked for inconsistencies involving:

- *directory inode numbers pointing to unallocated inodes*. If a directory entry inode number points to an unallocated inode, `fsck` can remove that directory entry. This condition occurs if the data blocks containing the directory entries are modified and written out while the inode is not yet written out.

- *a bad inode number*. If a directory entry inode number is pointing beyond the end of the inode list, `fsck` can remove that directory entry. This condition occurs if bad data are written into a directory data block.

- *incorrect directory inode numbers for " . " and " . . " directories*. The directory inode number entry for " . " should be the first entry in the directory data block. Its value should be equal to the inode number for the directory data block.

  The directory inode number entry for " . . " should be the second entry in the directory data block. Its value should be equal to the inode number for the parent of the directory entry (or the inode number of the directory data block if the directory is the root directory). If the directory inode numbers for " . " and " . . " are incorrect, `fsck` can replace them with the correct values.

- *directories disconnected from the file system*. The `fsck` program checks the general connectivity of the file system. If a directory is found that is not linked to the file system, `fsck` links the directory to the `lost+found` directory of the file system. (This condition can occur when inodes are written to the file system but the corresponding directory data blocks are not.) When a file is

linked to the `lost+found` directory, the owner of the file must
be notified.

▲ *regular data blocks*. Data blocks associated with a regular file hold the
file's contents. `fsck` does not attempt to check the validity of the contents of a regular file's data blocks.

# ❏ Checking `ufs` File Systems

This section describes the use of `fsck` with `ufs` file systems. It assumes that
you are running `fsck` interactively and that all possible errors may be
encountered. When an inconsistency is discovered in this mode, `fsck`
reports the inconsistency so that you can choose a corrective action. (You can
also run `fsck` automatically using the -y, -n, or -o ˉp options; see Figure
3-10 for an explanation of these and other `fsck` options.)

## `ufs` File System Components Checked by `fsck`

The phases of `fsck` and the messages that may appear in each phase are
described in Appendix B. This section describes the kinds of consistency
checks applied to each component of a `ufs` file system.

▲ *the superblock*. The most commonly corrupted item in a file system is
the summary information associated with the superblock, because it
is modified with every change to the blocks or inodes of the file system and is usually corrupted after an unclean halt. The superblock is
checked for inconsistencies involving:

- *file system size*. The file system size must be larger than the number of blocks used by the superblock and the number of blocks
  used by the list of inodes. While there is no way to check these
  sizes precisely, `fsck` can check that they are within reasonable
  bounds. All other file system checks require that these sizes be
  correct. If `fsck` detects corruption in the static parameters of the
  default superblock, `fsck` requests the operator to specify the
  location of an alternate superblock (e.g. block 32).

- *free block list*. `fsck` checks that all the blocks marked as free in
  the cylinder group block maps are not claimed by any files. When
  all the blocks have been initially accounted for, `fsck` checks that
  the number of free blocks plus the number of blocks claimed by

the inodes equals the total number of blocks in the file system. If anything is wrong with the block allocation maps, fsck will rebuild them, based on the list it has computed of allocated blocks.

- *free block count.* The summary information associated with the superblock contains a count of the total number of free blocks within the file system. fsck compares this count to the number of free blocks it finds within the file system. If the two counts do not agree, then fsck replaces the incorrect count in the summary information by the actual free block count.

- *free inode count.* The summary information contains a count of the total number of free inodes within the file system. fsck compares this count to the number of free inodes it finds within the file system. If the two counts do not agree, then fsck replaces the incorrect count in the summary information by the actual free inode count.

▲ *the inodes.* The list of inodes in the file system is checked sequentially starting with inode 2 (inode 0 marks unused inodes; inode 1 is saved for future generations) and progressing through the last inode in the file system. Each inode is checked for inconsistencies involving:

- *format and type.* Each inode contains a mode word. This mode word describes the type and state of the inode. Inodes may be one of six types: regular, directory, symbolic link, special block, special character, or named-pipe. Inodes may be in one of three allocation states: unallocated, allocated, and neither unallocated nor allocated. This last state means that the inode is incorrectly formatted. An inode can get into this state if bad data are written into the inode list. The only possible corrective action fsck can take is to clear the inode.

- *link count.* Each inode counts the total number of directory entries linked to the inode. fsck verifies the link count of each inode by starting at the root of the file system, and descending through the directory structure. The actual link count for each inode is calculated during the descent.

  If the stored link count is non-zero and the actual link count is zero, then no directory entry appears for the inode. If this happens, fsck will place the disconnected file in the lost+found directory. If the stored and actual link counts are non-zero and unequal, a directory entry may have been added or removed without the inode being updated. If this happens, fsck replaces the incorrect stored link count by the actual link count.

Each inode contains a list, or pointers to lists (indirect blocks), of all the blocks claimed by the inode. Since indirect blocks are owned by an inode, inconsistencies in an indirect block directly affect the inode that owns it.

- *duplicate blocks.* fsck compares each block number claimed by an inode against a list of already allocated blocks. If another inode already claims a block number, then the block number is added to a list of duplicate blocks. Otherwise, the list of allocated blocks is updated to include the block number.

  If there are any duplicate blocks, fsck performs a partial second pass over the inode list to find the inode of the duplicated block. The second pass is needed, since without examining the files associated with these inodes for correct content, not enough information is available to determine which inode is corrupted and should be cleared. If this condition does arise, then the inode with the earliest modify time is usually incorrect, and should be cleared. If this happens, fsck prompts the operator to clear both inodes. The operator must decide which one should be kept and which one should be cleared.

- *bad block numbers.* fsck checks the range of each block number claimed by an inode. If the block number is lower than the first data block in the file system, or greater than the last data block, then the block number is a bad block number. Many bad blocks in an inode are usually caused by an indirect block that was not written to the file system, a condition which can only occur if there has been a hardware failure. If an inode contains bad block numbers, fsck prompts the operator to clear it.

- *inode size.* Each inode contains a count of the number of data blocks that it contains. The number of actual data blocks is the sum of the allocated data blocks and the indirect blocks. fsck computes the actual number of data blocks and compares that block count against the actual number of blocks the inode claims. If an inode contains an incorrect count fsck prompts the operator to fix it.

  Each inode contains a 32-bit size field. The size is the number of data bytes in the file associated with the inode. The consistency of the byte size field is roughly checked by computing from the size field the maximum number of blocks that should be associated with the inode, and comparing that expected block count against the actual number of blocks the inode claims.

- ▲ *data associated with an inode.* An inode can directly or indirectly reference three kinds of data blocks. All referenced blocks must be the same kind. The three types of data blocks are: plain data blocks, symbolic link data blocks, and directory data blocks. Plain data blocks contain the information stored in a file; symbolic link data blocks contain the path name stored in a link. Directory data blocks contain directory entries. `fsck` can only check the validity of directory data blocks.

▲ *directory data blocks.* Directory data blocks are checked for inconsistencies involving:

- *directory inode numbers pointing to unallocated inodes.* If the inode number in a directory data block references an unallocated inode, then `fsck` will remove that directory entry.

- *bad inode number.* If a directory entry inode number references outside the inode list, then `fsck` will remove that directory entry. This condition occurs if bad data are written into a directory data block.

- *incorrect directory inode numbers for " . " and " . . ".* The directory inode number entry for " . " must be the first entry in the directory data block. The inode number for " . " must reference itself; e.g., it must equal the inode number for the directory data block. The directory inode number entry for " . . " must be the second entry in the directory data block. Its value must equal the inode number for the parent of the directory entry (or the inode number of the directory data block if the directory is the root directory). If the directory inode numbers are incorrect, `fsck` will replace them with the correct values. If there are multiple hard links to a directory, the first one encountered is considered the real parent to which " . . " should point; `fsck` recommends deletion for the subsequently discovered names.

- *directories that are not attached to the file system.* `fsck` checks the general connectivity of the file system. If directories are not linked into the file system, then `fsck` links the directory back into the file system in the `lost+found` directory.

# ❑ Checking `bfs` File Systems

All I/O for `bfs` file systems is synchronous. Thus, `bfs` files systems will not get corrupted even if proper shutdown procedures are not observed.

Corruption of a `bfs` file system is likely to occur only if the system crashes during the process of compaction. `fsck` checks the sanity words stored in the `bfs` superblock to see if compaction was in progress when the system crashed. If it was, `fsck` completes the compaction of the file system.

# 4

# *Storage Devices*

## ❑ Overview

As a system administrator, you are responsible for controlling the resources of your system and for granting access to them. Among those resources are the devices used for storing data, such as disks and tapes. There is a special file for each device in the /dev directory and a database that contains information about all devices on your system.

Each file has a special composition and, depending on the type of device it represents, resides either in the /dev directory or in a subdirectory under /dev. How your system interacts with a device is defined by three attributes of the file in the /dev directory associated with that device: the name, the composition (that is, the major and minor device numbers), and the location of the file. Special files connect devices to device drivers.

The most common storage devices on UNIX systems are:

▲ *hard disk devices*. The UNIX operating system keeps all system software and user files on hard disks. Hard disks are available in a variety of sizes, providing a flexible range of storage capacity that

allows you to add more devices as your user population and computing needs grow.

▲ *floppy diskette devices*. Floppy diskette drives are generally used to
load software packages or user files onto the hard disk, to back up
user files, and sometimes to back up file systems.

▲ *tape devices*. Tape drives are used primarily for high-speed file system
backups and file system or individual file restoration services. Your
computer may be equipped with cartridge, 9-track, or other type of
tape drives. Because of their high storage capacity, tapes provide an
efficient way of storing data.

▲ *SCSI devices*. Small Computer System Interface (SCSI) devices are a
group of devices that adhere to the American National Standards
Institute (ANSI) standard for connecting intelligently-interfaced
peripherals to computers. The SCSI bus is a daisy-chained arrangement originating at a SCSI adapter card that interconnects a number
of SCSI controllers. Each controller interfaces the device to the bus
and has a different SCSI address that is set on a switch located on the
controller. This address determines the priority that the device is
given, with the highest address having the highest priority.

SCSI storage devices include tape, hard disk, floppy diskette, and
write-once-read-many (WORM) devices. SCSI tape devices are
incompatible with tape devices that use similar media (such as cartridge tapes).

Because SCSI devices are daisy-chained together from a single
adapter card, they do not require major hardware or software
changes and are therefore easily adaptable to your computer. SCSI
devices will work on most computers with UNIX System V Release
2.0.5, Release 3.0, and later software versions.

## Device Identification Via Special Files

Before you can use any device with a computer running the UNIX operating
system, the device must first be made known to the system. Devices delivered
with your computer are automatically identified when the system is booted
for the first time.

Directory listings for special files show two decimal numbers (called the *major*
and *minor device numbers*) in the place where directory listings for regular files
show the character counts. Figure 4-1 shows part of the output produced by

running the `ls -l` command on a user's directory and on the directories under the /dev directory.

```
# ls -l
-rw-r----- 1 abc other   1050 Apr 23 08:14 dm.ol
#
# ls -l /dev/dsk /dev/rdsk
/dev/dsk:
brw------- 2 root sys    17,0 Apr 15 10:59 c1d0s0
brw------- 2 root sys    17,1 Apr 12 13:51 c1d0s1
...
/dev/rdsk:
crw------- 2 root sys    17,0 Apr 15 10:58 c1d0s0
crw------- 2 root sys    17,1 Apr 12 13:51 c1d0s1
...
#
```

**Figure 4-1**
*Directory listings for a user's directory and /dev.*
Note the major and minor numbers instead of a file size in the /dev directories. The leading 'b' or 'c' in the permissions field of the special files indicates whether it is a block or character device.

In Figure 4-1, file dm.ol is a regular file; all other files shown are device files. Four of the fields in this listing identify a file as a device: the first field, the fifth and sixth fields, and the last field.

▲  In the first field of this listing, the first character shows the type of file. Entries for regular files have a dash (–) in this position; entries for device files have the letters b (for block devices) or c (for character devices) in this position.

▲  For a regular file, the fifth and sixth fields show the character count (as one field); for a device file, these fields show the major and minor device numbers for the appropriate device.The major number specifies to the kernel which device driver is used for that device. The drvinstall command assigns major numbers to drivers that do not conflict with existing drivers. Major numbers for drivers are in the /etc/master.d/README file under the heading External Major Numbers. Major numbers serve as an index to the appropriate block or character switch table.

The minor number specifies which device or subdevice is connected to the device driver. Minor numbers are passed to the device driver when a specific device driver function is called. The procedure for determining minor numbers for special files is device dependent.

Block files can have the same major and minor numbers as character files. However, such file pairs either have different filenames or are in different directories (for example, `/dev/dsk/c0d0s0` and `/dev/rdsk/c0d0s0`).

▲   The last field shows (by its location in the `/dev` directory) how the system interacts with the device. For example, devices in the `/dev/dsk` directory are treated as block devices and devices in the `/dev/rdsk` directory are treated as character (or raw devices).

The following sections describe device types and partitions. For more information on the organization of device names and the file system, refer to Chapter 3, *The File System*. For more information on the attributes of files and directories, refer to the `ls`(1) command in the *User's Reference Manual/System Administrator's Manual*.

## Block and Character Devices

All devices are either block type or character type; the classification of a device as one of these two types depends on how the device is accessed. When data are accessed in fixed-length blocks (that is, when the device does not permit access until a block of data has been accumulated), such a device is classified as a block device. Examples of block devices are disk drives and tape drives.

When data are accessed in chunks consisting of a specific number of characters (usually one), such a device is classified as a character device. File maintenance utilities may also use character devices. In the UNIX system, standard C language subroutines transfer data to these types of devices one character at a time. Examples of character devices are terminals and printers.

Most devices provide both character and block access; however, one type of access to a device is usually preferred. For example, a tape device has both types of access, but the preferred access type is block; character access to tape devices is possible but uses considerably more tape to store the same data, so block access is preferred. On the other hand, terminals prefer a character access type. Block access is possible, but the characters you type would not be echoed to the screen until you pressed a carriage return. The two special files for each device are explained next.

## Summary

Devices are identified by special files in specific directories. The conventions used in positioning a device file depends on the type of computer and whether the device is internally or externally controlled. Standard file positions are used to identify the floppy diskette, hard disk, and cartridge tape devices. A distinction is made between character (raw) and block devices. Raw devices usually do not hold files or file systems and their names are positioned in the raw device directory (usually a `tty` assignment in the `/dev` directory that is linked to a file in the `/dev/rdsk` directory). Terminals, line printers, and tape drives are examples of raw devices. Block devices usually hold files and file systems and their names are positioned in the block device directory (usually `/dev/dsk` for disk devices). Floppy diskette and hard disk drives are examples of devices that are best accessed a block at a time.

The rest of this chapter addresses a series of topics that relate to storage devices with a focus on hard disk drives. The topics include:

▲ device properties: how to define and characterize a device to the system.

▲ suggestions for device management

▲ formatting, partitioning, and repartitioning disks

▲ bad block handling

▲ a look at the `/stand` and `/boot` partitions

▲ creating bootable disks

▲ managing device attributes, groups, and reservations

# ❏ Properties of Devices

UNIX devices have several properties that are established and maintained by the system administrator, among them:

▲ *the device alias*, a unique name by which a device is known to the administrator. It is defined in the device database in `/etc/device.tab` (see *"Managing Device Attributes"* later in this chapter for more information). The device alias is mapped to the pathname.

▲ *device attributes*, stored in the device database and described in *"Managing Device Attributes"*. Each entry in the database consists of a set of attributes and their value for that device. The device entries should be created by the device installation script, if written for UNIX System V Release 4 or a later release. However, you will need to create entries for any device whose installation script does not do so.

▲ *device drivers* that manages signals between a device and the operating system. If you want to design, install, and debug your own device drivers, look at the suggested reading list in the *Preface*. It lists several books, written for advanced C programmers, that can help you.

▲ *device partitions* that set aside specific areas of the device for booting, swapping, and file systems. Device partitions should fall on cylinder boundaries to obtain the best possible file system performance, since the read/write heads will not have to move to find a partition; all partitions will be under the read/write heads at the same time. The number of blocks assigned to the boot and swap partitions on a root device are chosen so that the next partition will start on a cylinder boundary.

Up to sixteen partitions can be defined on a SCSI hard disk. Partitions 0 through 5 are reserved for system use and partition 6 defines the full user disk. Partition 7 is reserved for the boot blocks and the VTOC. You can assign partitions 8 through 15 for your users. Partitioning strategies and repartitioning procedures are described in subsequent sections of this chapter.

▲ *device groups* allow you to perform an action, or a set of actions, on several devices at the same time. For example, if you want to back up several devices on a regular basis, you can create a group for those devices. Then, whenever performing the backup operation, you can use the group name in place of a device name and every device in that group will be backed up. See *"Managing Device Groups"* later in this chapter.

▲ *device reservations* allow a user to reserve a device for exclusive use with the devreserv command. Reserving a device places it on a device reservation list and any new attempt to reserve that device will fail until the existing reservation is canceled. See *"Managing Device Reservations"* later in this chapter.

# ❏ Suggestions for Managing Storage Devices

Storage device management depends a lot on the size of your user population and how your resources are utilized. If there is a large user community with a lot of resources, managing your storage devices may take a lot of your time. The following are some suggestions for administering storage devices:

▲ When formatting floppy diskettes, format the entire box at once and label the box clearly so that you know that they are already formatted.

▲ When repartitioning a hard disk, make sure that you do a complete system backup before starting. This may be unnecessary if the hard disk contains a straight file system.

▲ If resources become depleted in one but not both of the /tmp and /var/tmp directories, ask users to distribute temporary files more evenly to both of these directories. (To do this, the TMPDIR environment variable may be defined in the user's profile as TMPDIR=/tmp or TMPDIR=/var/tmp.)

▲ When assigning a device for mounting the user file systems on a dual disk computer, such as the /home, home2, home3, etc., assign them to the second drive so that backups and restores are easier to do. However, allowing / and /usr to share the same disk can create performance problems.

▲ For a more secure computer, mount the /usr file system with read only permission.

▲ After copying valuable files from a floppy diskette to another medium, use the write-protect tab on the floppy diskette to prevent inadvertent erasure of the data.

▲ When copying large files, the value of ulimit may need to be changed to a number as large or larger than the character count of the largest file (ulimit=*number* where *number* is larger than the character count of the file as determined with ls -l *filename*).

# ❑ Formatting Disks

Before you can use a disk to store information, it must be formatted to impose an addressing scheme onto the media. Formatting maps both sides of the disk into tracks and sectors that can be addressed by the disk controller. A portion of the disk is reserved for data having to do with the specific disk. The VTOC resides in that area and shows how the partitions on the disk are allocated. On a hard disk, another reserved area maps portions of the disk that may not be usable. Formatting a previously used disk, in addition to redefining the tracks, erases any data that may be there.

◆ *Note*        Unusable portions of the hard disk are called bad blocks. Bad block handling is discussed later in the next section.

A disk sector is a 512-byte portion of the storage medium that can be addressed by the disk controller. The number of sectors is a function of the size and number of surfaces of the disk device. Sectors are numbered from zero on up. Hard disks are shipped from the factory already formatted.

Diskettes are made to be usable in more than one machine. Manufacturers produce diskettes unformatted, leaving it to customers to format them for the particular machine on which they are to be used. The command to use to format a diskette is fmtflop(1M). A related command, format(1M) is used to format a SCSI hard disk.

◆ *Note*        The fmthard command does not format hard disks. This command is used to *partition* hard disk devices (other than the root device) and to install a VTOC.

# ❑ Bad Block Handling

A disk is a magnetic medium on which digital data (measured in bits and bytes) are stored in logical sections called "blocks." A block usually contains 512, 1024, or 2048 bytes of data and is handled by the UNIX system as a single unit. Because the bit density is very high (millions of bits of data are packed into a small space), the magnetic properties of a disk must be precisely uniform. Variations in uniformity mean that some bit patterns may be stored more easily in one block than in another. This variation in uniformity is normally insignificant. However, when these variations become so great that data can no longer be stored reliably in a particular block, that block is labeled "bad." There are three categories of bad blocks, each of which is described under *"Bad Block Recovery"* later in this chapter.

If the pattern of data stored in a block coincidentally matches the nonuniformity of the disk, a bad block may escape recognition. However, the nonuniform block will eventually be discovered if the disk remains active. Bad blocks are discovered when a data read or write fails after several successive attempts. Read failures alone do not guarantee the existence of a bad block because they may also be caused by problems in the format of the disk, a failure in the disk controller, or hardware flaws. Write failures generally signal problems with the disk's format or failures in the disk or disk controller hardware.

The bad block handling feature does not distinguish genuine bad blocks from other types of problems; it reports all types of read and write failures, most of which are not caused by bad blocks. (Reports can be viewed by issuing the command `hdelogger -f`.) The distinction is unimportant, however, because all read and write failures indicate problems that must be repaired.

To fix read and write problems, you must reformat the disk or arrange to repair the hardware. In either case, you should call your service representative; especially if several failures occur about the same time.

## How the UNIX System Handles Bad Blocks

You cannot really "fix" a bad block; you can only find a way to work around it. One way you can work around a bad block is by using a *media-specific data area*. A media-specific data area is a small portion of a disk that is isolated from the default data area; that is, it is not used by normal UNIX system commands and system calls. This isolated portion of the disk contains a description of the properties of the disk and other media-specific data.

The media-specific data area includes a set of blocks called the *surrogate image region*. The purpose of this region is to hold the data that should have been stored in a bad block. The media-specific data area also includes a mapping table to map a bad block on the disk to one of the surrogate image blocks. The disk driver software in the operating system has a map showing the original location of the data in the bad block and the new location of that data in the surrogate image block. Data are read from or written to the surrogate image block via the addresses in this mapping table. Address mapping is transparent to software programs accessing the data.

The UNIX system has a software feature called bad block handling. This feature extends the useful life of an integral hard disk by

▲ detecting and recording blocks that are no longer usable.

▲ reminding you that you need to "fix" some bad blocks that have been identified.

▲ restoring the usability of the disk in spite of the bad blocks that exist.

Most disk drives are manufactured with a few defective blocks. Bad blocks detected in the manufacturer's quality control checks are identified on a label on the drive when it is delivered. The bad block handling feature provides special software for recording the known bad blocks and for mapping any additional ones that are encountered. If a surrogate block becomes bad, the software remaps the original bad block to a new surrogate block.

◆ *Note*       This feature can be used only with hard disk devices. There is no comparable feature for diskettes or tapes.

New bad blocks will seldom occur if you do not move or vibrate the disk drive while the disk is spinning. When a new bad block does occur, the data stored in the bad block are lost and the disk may be unusable in its current state. The bad block handling feature helps restore the usability of a disk. How much data you lose depends on the adequacy of the backup procedures you have established.

## Blocks that Cannot Be Mapped

There are a few special blocks in the isolated portion of the disk that cannot be mapped: the disk block containing the physical description of the disk and the disk block or blocks containing the mapping table. All other blocks, including the surrogate image blocks, can be mapped.

## When Are Bad Blocks Detected?

Bad blocks are detected when read or write operations fail for several successive attempts. When these failures occur, data being read or written at the time are lost, but the system can restore the use of the disk by mapping the bad blocks to usable surrogate blocks.

There are several questions that are frequently asked about bad block handling.

▲ *Why doesn't the system try to discover that a given block is bad while the system still has the data in memory?*

Besides the undesirable increase in system size and complexity, severe performance degradation would result. Also, a block can become defective after the copy in memory no longer exists.

▲ *Why doesn't the system periodically test the disk for bad blocks?*

Because there is no reasonable and reliable way of reading a block and always detecting whether its bad or not. Even if a thorough bit pattern test could be devised using ordinary read and write operations, it would take so long that you would never run it. The disk manufacturer has tested the disk using extensive bit pattern tests and special hardware. All manufacturing defects have been identified.

▲ *Why are disks with manufacturing defects used?*

By selling disks that contain a modest number of defects, manufacturers can greatly increase their yield and thereby reduce the cost of each disk. Many manufacturers take advantage of this cost reduction to provide a more powerful system at a low price.

# ❑ Bad Block Recovery

The bad block handling feature provides mechanisms for detecting bad blocks and mapping them to surrogate blocks. The remainder of this section describes three ways that recovery from bad blocks can be handled.

## Automatic Recovery from a Bad Block

One of the tasks that the UNIX system performs regularly is a check of the hard disks for bad blocks. (This check is always performed when the system is in multi-user state, that is, in system state 2.)

The UNIX system keeps track of the location of each file on a disk by recording several data about it in a "virtual node" (vnode) table. Two of the data items in this table identify the location of the file (the physical block number on the disk that specifies the sector, head, and cylinder numbers) and its size (the number of data blocks occupied by the file).

The following scenario explains the automatic process of handling bad blocks. Physical block 3 is a surrogate block on the disk for physical block 42. Block 42 is a block in the middle of a text file that is five data-blocks long. Block 3 has become a bad block since the file was last read. Now the file needs to be read again. When block 42 is reached, the driver for the integral disk sees that block 42 is mapped to block 3 and attempts to read block 3. But block 3 is now bad and cannot be read. When the integral disk driver determines that block 3 is unreadable, the following messages are sent to the system console:

```
WARNING: unreadable CRC hard disk error: maj/min = 17/0

        block # = 3

WARNING:
hard disk: cannot access sector 3, head 0, cylinder 0, on drive 0

Disk Error Daemon: successfully logged error for block 3 on disk
maj=17 min=0
```

◆ *Note*    CRC stands for Cyclic Redundancy Check, an error checking method. The numbers assigned to maj and min are the major and minor device numbers of the disk on which the error occurred. (See the "*Device Identification Via Special Files*" section at the beginning of this chapter for a complete description of major and minor device numbers.)

The attempt to read this text file has failed. When you notice the message on the console, run the shutdown command to change the system to single-user state (system state 1). While shutdown is running, the following message is sent to the system console:

```
Disk Error Daemon: Disk maj=17 min=0: 1 errors logged
```

In this scenario, a bad block has been identified, reported, and logged by automated mechanisms in the system. Most bad blocks are handled in this way. The following sections describe how these automated mechanisms work.

## Identifying Disks

Disks are identified by their major and minor device numbers (on both single-disk and multi-disk computers). Messages printed by the bad block handling mechanisms use the major and minor numbers rather than any other names. The utilities of the bad block handling feature can be given these numbers as arguments when more specialized operations must be used.

## Detecting Bad Blocks

The disk driver detects a bad block when the disk fails to access that block after several attempts. To be sure that the problem is not being caused by the position of a read or write head, the driver repositions the read and write heads between access attempts. When the driver is still unable to access this block, it can safely be assumed that the block is defective.

## Reporting and Logging Bad Blocks

When a block is determined to be inaccessible, the disk driver reports the defective block to the bad block logging mechanism which, in turn, notifies the system administrator by sending a message to the system console. For example, in the scenario described above, the following message was sent to the console:

```
WARNING: unreadable CRC hard disk error: maj/min = 17/0

        block # = 3
```

This output is used as input to the hard disk error logger commands. In this case, for example, device 17/0 and block #3 would be arguments to the hdelogger commands.

The disk driver also reports the error by displaying the following message on the system console:

```
WARNING: hard disk: cannot access sector 3, head 0, cylinder 0,
on drive 0
```

The logging mechanism then attempts to record the error in the disk error log located in the isolated portion of the disk. If the error is logged successfully, the following message is sent to the system console:

```
Disk Error Daemon: successfully logged error for block 3 on disk
maj=17 min=0
```

The logging mechanism is run by the driver for the hard disk error log (hdelog) and by a hard disk error daemon process called hdelogger that is, in turn, run by the /sbin/init process. The error log driver provides both mechanisms for reports and access to the reserved disk areas needed by the bad block handling feature. (This driver can queue a maximum of 18 reports.) Because one track on a 10-megabyte or 30-megabyte disk has 18 sectors, a bad track can have up to 18 reports, one for each bad sector. The disk error daemon gets reports from this queue and adds each report to the disk error log.

The disk error daemon has another reporting role. When the system state changes (for example, when you turn on your computer, shut it off, or shut down to system state 1), a daemon process checks the error log. If the daemon finds outstanding bad block reports in a log, it sends a message to the system console. For example, in the scenario described earlier, the following message was sent:

```
Disk Error Daemon: Disk maj= 17 min= 0: 1 errors logged
```

The `hdelogger` daemon runs in system states 2, 3, and 4.

◆ *Note*     The bad block handling daemon does not run in system states 1, 5, or 6. System state 1 (also referred to as "s" or "S") is single-user state. System states 5 and 6 are used for returning to firmware and for rebooting the operating system, respectively.

## Interactive Recovery from a Bad Block

Not all bad block errors can be handled automatically; recovery from some types of errors requires your assistance. Which recovery procedure is required depends on the system state of the computer when the error occurred.

## Errors in System State 1 (Single-User State)

If errors happen while your system is in system state 1, the error reports stay queued until a system state is used in which the bad block handling daemon will also run. However, if you shut your system off or reboot it without going to another system state, the error reports in the queue are lost. When errors occur while in system state 1, only the messages from the logging mechanism and disk driver are sent to the system console.

If you get errors while in system state 1 and you are not ready to fix them (the mechanism for fixing them takes error reports from the queue as well as from the disk error logs), you can switch to another system state to force them to be logged. You will get a `successfully logged` message for each error that occurred. When all reports are logged, you can switch back to system state 1

When you do, a reminder message from the disk error daemon will be sent to the console.

## System Panics and Firmware-Detected Errors

If there is a disk error that results in the loss of a critical operating-system path, such as the path to the swap space, the operating system panics. A system panic occurs after the reports from the logging mechanism and disk driver are sent to the console, but before the report is logged.

◆ *Note*        If an error is detected by the firmware, the error is reported to the console, but it is not logged. In these cases, **you must write down this console report.** When the system comes back up, use the /usr/sbin/hdeadd command and manually add this handwritten report to the disk error queue.

The following is an example of a bad block error message from the firmware.

```
id 0 CRC error at disk address 00010211
```

Because the arguments to the hdeadd and hdefix commands must be in decimal format, the hexadecimal disk address (00010211) must be converted to the decimal values of the cylinder, track, and sector. Figure 4-2 shows how the hexadecimal number is converted to decimal format, and how this decimal number translates to the address on the disk.

**Figure 4-2**
*Sample disk address conversion*

|  |  | Physical Cylinder Number High | | Physical Cylinder Number Low | | Physical Head Number | | Physical Sector Number | |
|---|---|---|---|---|---|---|---|---|---|
| Hex Address | | 0 | 0 | 0 | 1 | 0 | 2 | 1 | 1 |
| Binary | | 0000 | 0000 | 0000 | 0001 | 0000 | 0010 | 0001 | 0001 |
| Decimal | | Cylinder 1 | | | | Track 2 | | Sector 17 | |

In this example, the hexadecimal number 00010211 is translated to cylinder 1, track 2, and sector 17. These decimal numbers are then used as arguments to the -B option of the hdeadd and hdefix commands (that is, -B 1 2 17).

The following screen shows example messages that appear when a bad block causes a system panic. Assume that physical block number 463 is in your swap space. Although, unknown to you, this block has recently become bad, the operating system writes data into it. (These data cannot be read with the disk's current pattern of magnetic biases.) When the operating system tries to read this block, the disk driver determines that the block is unreadable, reports the condition, and fails the read. The swapper process runs next, discovers the read failure, and causes the panic. All process activity is precluded at this point, including the disk error daemon, and the following messages are sent to the console.

```
WARNING: unreadable CRC hard disk error: maj/min = 17/0

         block # = 463


WARNING:
hard disk: cannot access sector 13, head 0, cylinder 5, on drive 0
```

◆ *Note*      Because of the system panic, the system cannot record this error. Therefore you must write down or print out the numbers 17/0 and 463.

Unless you are already in system state 5, you must bring the system down to system state 1 with the shutdown command (/sbin/shutdown -y -g0 - i1) to minimize the chances of getting another swap-generated panic. Once you are in system state 1, enter the following command:

```
hdeadd -ia -D 17 0 -b 463
```

This command reports the bad block to the operating system's logging mechanism. If this swap error occurred on Saturday, January 13, 1990, at 02:01:00 hours, the full report would be as follows:

```
# hdeadd -a -iD 17 0 -b 463
hdeadd: logging the following error report:
        disk maj= 17 min= 0
        blkaddr= 463, timestamp= Sat Jan 13 02:01:00 1990
        readtype= 1, severity= 2, badrtcnt= 0, bitwidth= 0
WARNING: unreadable CRC hard disk error: maj/min = 17/0


        block # = 463



Disk Error Daemon: successfully logged error for block 463 on
disk maj=17 min=0
#
```

You can also use the `hdelogger -f` command to double check the error status and obtain the following report (assuming this is the only error in the log).

```
# hdelogger -f

Disk Error Log: Full Report for maj= 17 min= 0
        log created:  Mon Jan  1 12:13:14 1990
        last changed: Sat Jan 13 02:01:04 1990
        entry count: 1
phys blkno   cnt   first occurrence      last occurrence
0:     463    1    Jul 13 02:01:00 1990   Jul 13 02:01:00 1990
TOTAL: 1 errors logged
#
```

If the firmware detected the error, it may not be possible to boot the system from your hard disk. However, if you have a floppy diskette device on your system and a bootable floppy containing the bad block utilities, you can boot from this diskette and try to repair the bad blocks as described in *"Manual Recovery from a Bad Block"* below. If you do not have a floppy diskette device on your system or if you do not have a bootable floppy containing the bad block utilities, contact your service representative.

# The Special Case of a Bad Error Log Block

Though unlikely, the new bad block could be the block in which the disk error log resides. Obviously, if the system cannot access the log because this log resides in a bad block, errors cannot be recorded. An auxiliary mechanism of the `hdefix` command, however, allows you to add bad blocks to the defect map, as discussed next.

# Manual Recovery from a Bad Block

To fix a bad block manually:

**Step 1**   Completely shut down the machine to system state 1

```
shutdown -y -g0 -i1
```

**Step 2**   Unmount all file systems except `root`

```
umountall -k
```

**Step 3**   Force any queued reports from the disk error queue to the error log.

```
/sbin/hdefix -a
```

If an error is reported while you are in system state 1, you need not switch system states to get it processed.

The `hdefix -a` command updates the defect map appropriately (remember that bad surrogate blocks are replaced, not mapped), removes any reports for the block (there may be more than one) from the disk error log, and identifies the use of the block. If the bad block is in a file system, the file system is marked bad.

If any block (or surrogate of such a block) in the normally accessible portion of the disk has been processed, the `hdefix` command forces an immediate reboot that checks the integrity of the root file system while coming back up. You must manually check the integrity of any other file system you want to mount.

You can also specify which disk and block(s) are to be fixed by using additional arguments to the `hdefix` command. In the swap panic example above, you could have specified the bad block to be fixed by entering the following command from system state 1:

```
hdefix -a -D 17 0 -b 463
```

When you specify a block number, hdefix ignores the contents of the error log and the error queue. If there is a report in the log for this block, the report remains in the log after you have finished. As a result, when reviewing the log, you may incorrectly interpret it to mean this block is still bad. However, when you issue the command hdefix -a, the fix list is taken from the log and queue and the log is cleaned up automatically.

## ❑ Dealing with Data Loss

Although the useful life of disk hardware is greatly extended with the bad block handling feature, once a bad block is logged, the data in the block are lost. You must be prepared to restore files or file systems from archives. When restoring data from archives, users may encounter unavoidable inconveniences in the form of lost files and lost work on existing files.

Under rare circumstances, a bad block may occur in the Volume Table of Contents (VTOC) block. In such a case, you may have to reformat the disk and restore the contents of the entire disk from an archive. Sometimes you may also need to restore the special code (the program) for booting the system (it is not in a file system).

## ❑ Partitioning a Hard Disk

A partition consists of one or more sectors. Up to 16 partitions can be defined on a hard disk, up to 8 on a floppy diskette. On a hard disk, the fmthard(1M) command is used to associate the starting points of partitions with sector numbers. prtvtoc may be used to see the partitions assigned. fmthard gives the number of sectors allocated to a partition and a hex code tag that tells how the partition is to be used. Partition tags 0-8 are reserved.

The partitions are allocated to accommodate the root(/), /usr, /stand, /var, /home, local file systems, swapping space, and a small partition for the boot program. In multiple-disk systems, /usr is typically put on one disk while / and /home share the other. Figure 4-3 is an example of the partitions for a 72-megabyte disk drive that has been configured to be the root device of a system. Figure 4-4 shows five file systems defined on this drive: /, /usr, /stand, /var, and /home. Space has also been set aside for the boot file and for swap space.

The default partitions are fundamentally a compromise. After your system has been in operation for a few months, you may feel that a different arrangement would better serve the needs of your users.

| Partition | Use | Starting Sector | Size in sectors | Inodes |
|-----------|-----|-----------------|-----------------|--------|
| c1d0s0 | root | 14256 | 17010 | 2112 |
| c1d0s1 | swap | 100 | 14156 | - |
| c1d0s2 | usr | 36774 | 96066 | 12000 |
| c1d0s3 | stand | 31266 | 5508 | 55 |
| c1d0s4 | unassigned | | | |
| c1d0s5 | unassigned | | | |
| c1d0s6 | entire disk | 0 | 149526 | - |
| c1d0s7 | boot | 0 | 100 | - |
| c1d0s8 | var | 132840 | 10044 | 1248 |
| c1d0s9 | home | 142884 | 6642 | 800 |
| c1d0sa | unassigned | | | |
| c1d0sb | unassigned | | | |
| c1d0sc | unassigned | | | |
| c1d0sd | unassigned | | | |
| c1d0se | unassigned | | | |
| c1d0sf | unassigned | | | |

**Figure 4-3**
*Default disk partitions for a 72MB drive. There are 162 blocks per cylinder and a rotational gap of 10 blocks.*

**Figure 4-4**
*Physical lay-
out of disk par-
titions.*
*The boot partition
begins in the inner
most cylinder.
Space is allocated
out from the cen-
ter.*

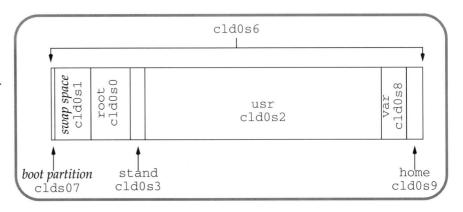

## Planning to Change Hard Disk Partitions

The basic question to ask yourself when deciding to partition your hard disks
is whether you should have a larger number of smaller file systems or stay
with the default partitions. However, other questions also influence this decision. Some of these other questions are:

▲ What group IDs are defined? Are the right number of groups
defined? Are users appropriately assigned to these groups?

▲ What type of processing is done by these groups? Does their work
require temporary data storage? Is there a big difference between the
type of processing done by one group and that done by other groups?

▲ Has software that affects the current plan for space requirements
been added to the system? Will such software be added in the future?

The `sadp` command provides performance information about your existing
file system arrangement and is described in Chapter 7, *Performance Tools*.

Hard disk repartitioning can be done in conjunction with a full system
restore. The `fmthard` command can be used to redefine partitions on disks
other than the root disk.

If you find that your users need a large region of temporary space, you may
want to create a separate partition for `/var/tmp`. If you do this, position the
partition at the beginning of a disk different from your root and `/usr` partitions, if possible, to help balance your disk loads.

### Changing Partitions to Increase Swap Space

If you frequently get console messages warning of insufficient memory, it may mean that either the amount of main memory or the swap area configuration is insufficient to support user demands. Before adding more main memory, you can first try to expand the swap area. There are three things you should do before expanding the swap area:

1. Run prtvtoc(1) to identify the sizes of your present partitions. (Use sysadm storage_devices to obtain this information via a menu.)

2. Decide what the new partition sizes should be. (The disk is already fully allocated. Increasing the size of the swap partition means that you must reduce the size of another partition.)

3. Perform a complete system backup. (The process of changing partitions may erase the entire disk.) See backup(1M) for more details.

You are now ready to reload the operating system. See your computer installation manual for a description of how to perform this operation.

## ❏ The boot and stand Partitions

The *boot file system*, /stand, contains bootable programs. The *boot partition*, /boot, is a separate disk partition (not a file system) that holds the programs used to load the files found in the boot file system. On most computers, the boot process is basically a three step process:

▲ you turn your machine on, and the firmware loads the mboot program from the boot partition into a special area of memory

▲ mboot in turn loads another program from the boot partition, called boot

▲ boot then loads the bootable operating system /stand/unix

The bootable operating system unix is found in the stand partition, which has a file system defined on it that contains all the bootable programs and data files used during the boot procedure. It can be identified using the prtvtoc(1M) command as the partition with the tag of 6 (indicating

V_STAND). The file system defined on this partition is mounted by default as /stand.

Some of the files in /stand are described in Figure 4-5.

**Figure 4-5**
*The /stand file system.*

| File Name | Description |
|---|---|
| unix | This is the bootable operating system. When the boot program is loaded, it searches for and loads this program into memory, and then passes control to it. Once the bootable operating system is running, various system daemons are started, and the system enters one of the init states (see the description of /sbin/inittab in this chapter). Note that the filename unix is linked to /stand/-unix for compatibility with earlier releases; you can enter unix or /stand/unix at any prompt requiring the name of the bootable operating system. |
| system | This is the system configuration file; it contains a description of the hardware and software modules that must be included in the bootable operating system (/stand/unix) for correct configuration of the system. If the time stamp of the system file is newer than the time stamp of the /stand/unix file, a reconfiguration of the bootable operating system is necessary before the boot program can pass control to it. Note that the filename system is linked to /stand/system for compatibility with earlier releases; you can enter system or /stand/system at any prompt requiring the name of the system configuration file. |
| mUNIX | This is a version of the UNIX operating system that is run only during the configuration of a new bootable operating system (unix). |
| mini_system | This is the system configuration file for the mUNIX program. |

See Chapter 8, *Configuring UNIX*, for more information on the operating system files in /stand.

## Operations on the boot Partition

The only operation performed on the boot partition is the loading of the boot programs; no file system is defined on this partition.

The boot programs are loaded using the newboot(1M) command. The boot programs are found in the root file system under the /usr/lib directory. The command is used as follows:

```
newboot /usr/lib/boot /usr/lib/mboot /dev/rdsk/c1d1s7
```

The special file used in the example above may vary depending on the number of disks you have connected to your computer. See newboot(1M) for a complete description of this command.

This command is normally not used unless you are manually repartitioning your hard disks or creating a new bootable disk (see *"Making New Bootable Disks"* later in this chapter). In the delivered system, a boot partition is defined on the first integral hard disk. This partition already contains the boot and mboot programs.

## Operations on the stand Partition

In the delivered system, the stand partition contains a file system of type bfs; this boot file system is mounted as /stand by default.

The boot file system is a flat file system, with only one directory. You can copy and move regular files to and from a boot file system, but cannot make directories or create other special files in the bfs file system. You can, however, use file system commands such as mount(1M), umount(1M), and fsck(1M).

It is recommended that you use this file system for boot- and configuration-related files only.

You can use mkfs to create bfs-type file systems on other disk partitions or on other disks (to make them bootable). See the section called *"Making New Bootable Disks"* in this chapter, *"Using mkfs to Create a bfs File System"* in Chapter 3, and the mkfs(1) manual page for more information. Having multiple boot file systems on one or more disks is particularly useful in an operating system development environment.

 **▼ Caution**    You must define bfs-type file systems only on hard disk partitions with a tag of 6. Do not make bfs-type file systems on any other devices. Similarly, do not make a file system of any other type than bfs in a partition with a tag of 6. Doing so may render your machine unbootable. See the references cited in the above paragraph, and the fmthard(1M) and prtv-toc(1M) manual pages in the *User's Reference Manual/System Administrator's Reference Manual* for more information.

Any disk can contain stand and boot partitions. Thus it is possible to boot the system from any disk that has both, as long as the root file system is also accessible (though not necessarily on the same disk).

A disk can also have multiple stand partitions with a boot file system defined on each one. Each partition can contain a version of the bootable programs. The next part firmware command (described below) can be used to switch partitions from which you can request a manual boot from firmware mode. You can manually request a boot from any stand partition on any disk from the firmware prompt.

▼ *Caution*        Note that while you can request a boot from any stand partition on any disk from firmware, configuration of a new operating system will work only on the stand partition found in /etc/vfstab. For example, if you specify a system file at the firmware prompt that is in a stand file system other than the one found in /etc/vfstab, the configuration process will fail, even if you made the correct /stand partition the current partition using the next part command.

Although any disk can be made bootable, only one disk will actually be booted when the system is powered up: the default boot disk defined in Non-Volatile RAM (NVRAM). You can change the default boot disk using the procedure in this chapter titled *"Changing Default Boot Parameters."*

If you define multiple stand partitions on the default boot disk, the one used during the boot procedures will be the one with the smallest partition number. For example, suppose you have a default boot disk that has three stand partitions, all with bfs-type file systems defined on them that contain one or more bootable programs (such as unix or dgmon), and the device names for the three partitions are /dev/dsk/c1d0s3 for slice 3, /dev/dsk/c1d0s5 for slice 5, and /dev/dsk/c1d0s8 for slice 8. On reboot and powerup, the system will boot from slice 3 (/dev/dsk/c1d0s3); the other stand partitions will be ignored.

When you are in firmware mode, however, you can access all stand partitions on a disk. When you enter firmware mode, the following prompt is displayed:

```
Enter name of program to execute [ ]:
```

If the brackets are empty, as shown above, just press ( *return* ) . The following prompt is displayed, after a list of possible load devices:

```
Enter Load Device Option Number [1 (HD70)]:
```

After pressing ( *return* ) at this prompt (regardless of whether you change the load device or accept the default shown in brackets), the following prompt is displayed:

```
Enter name of boot file (or 'q' to quit):
```

Pressing ( *return* ) at the above prompt lists the contents of the first boot partition, /dev/dsk/c1d0s3. This partition is the working partition.

If you enter next part at the prompt, slice 5 (/dev/dsk/c1d0s5) becomes the working partition. You can then either choose a program from this partition or enter next part again. If you enter next part, slice 8 (/dev/dsk/c1d0s8) becomes the working partition.

Once you reach the last stand partition defined on the disk, you can enter next part to make the first boot file system the working partition again (in our example, slice 3 (/dev/dsk/c1d0s3)).

See the next section, *"Changing Default Boot Parameters"*, for more detail on firmware prompts and commands.

The file /etc/vfstab contains the pathname of the stand partition to be mounted during single- and multi-user states and is used during configuration of a new operating system on powerup or reboot. This should always be the one defined on the lowest numbered partition on your default boot disk (usually partition 3). The device name has the form /dev/dsk/c?d?s3.

## Boot Scenarios

There are several reasons that a system boot takes place:

▲ Power is newly applied to the machine. In this case, the boot program looks for the `unix` and `system` files in the first boot partition on the default boot disk. If `unix` has the same or a later timestamp than `system`, then the boot program loads and executes `unix`; if `system` is newer, the boot program will execute mUNIX, and then build-sys(1M) to configure a new `unix`. When the new `unix` is built, the system boots the new `unix` and the system comes up in the state defined by the `initdefault` entry in `/sbin/inittab`. (See inittab(4).)

▲ A reboot of the machine is explicitly requested while the UNIX system is running (e.g., `init 6` or `shutdown -i6`). In this case, all system activity is stopped (all processes are killed, etc.). The system checks to see if a new `unix` needs to be configured (as above), and if so, configures one. Then, the system unmounts all file systems and boots `unix`. The system comes up in the state defined by the `initdefault` entry in `/sbin/inittab`.

▲ A reboot is requested from firmware. From the firmware prompt, the user can specify the name of any executable (such as `unix`) or text file (such as `system`) in `/stand`. If an executable is specified, the boot program loads it and branches to it. If a text file is specified, the boot program starts mUNIX, and then executes buildsys(1M) to configure a new `unix`, using the text file specified as the `system` file for the new `unix`. When the new `unix` is built, the system loads and executes it, and comes up in the state defined by the `initdefault` entry in `/sbin/inittab`.

▲ A crash occurs and the machine automatically reboots. In this case, the procedure is the same as for the first case, above.

See Chapter 8, *Configuring UNIX*, for a description of the configuration process.

# ❑ Changing Default Boot Parameters

■ *Note*     Before you change to a new default boot device, you must make
            sure that the disk is a valid bootable disk. See the procedure in this
            guide for making a device bootable before executing the `flt-
            boot`(1M) command.

In the delivered AT&T 3B2 Computer, the default boot program name is
NULL and the default bootable device is the first hard disk connected to the
first disk controller. What this means is that when you are in firmware mode
and attempt to boot the system, you will be prompted for a manual boot program name. After you enter the name of the program you want, the system
will, by default, attempt to locate and load the program whose name you supplied from the default boot device.

You may change the default manual boot program to any bootable program
name in the `/stand` directory using the `fltboot` command (see `flt-
boot`(1M)). Once you do this, the program name you select will be displayed
in firmware mode as the default boot program. Similarly, you can change the
default boot device that is booted on powerup or reboot.

The `fltboot` command is interactive, so no command line parameters are
required. Two prompts are displayed, one for changing the default boot program and one for changing the default boot device. Pressing ( *return* ) without entering a value at either prompt leaves the current value unchanged.

The following paragraphs explain how these defaults are displayed in firmware mode.

When you bring the system down to firmware mode (see *"Changing to Firmware Mode,"* in this chapter) the following prompt is displayed:

```
Enter name of program to execute [   ]:
```

Note that the brackets in the prompt are empty. This means that the default
manual boot program name in Non-Volatile RAM (NVRAM) is null. If you
change the default boot program using `fltboot`, the name you supply to
`fltboot` will appear in the brackets shown above.

You have three options at this prompt:

- use `next part` to switch working partitions
- enter a program name and press ( _return_ )
- press ( _return_ ) without entering a program name

The `next part` command changes the current working partition, if more than one is defined, on the default boot disk.

All these options cause the firmware to list the possible load devices connected to your machine and display the following prompt:

```
Enter Load Device Option Number [1 (HD70)]:
```

The brackets in this prompt show the default boot device for your machine, in this case a 70-Mbyte hard disk. You can enter a ( _return_ ) at this prompt, or choose another device and press ( _return_ ) . If you change the default boot device using `fltboot`, the device you supply to `fltboot` will appear in the brackets shown above.

What happens next depends on what appeared in the brackets in the previous prompt, and whether you entered the `next part` command or not.

If you had entered `next part`, a message appears telling you the current working partition, and the following prompt is displayed:

```
Enter name of boot file (or 'q' to quit):
```

If you did not enter `next part`, and either entered a program name or accepted the default contained in brackets, the system will boot from the current working partition using the name in brackets.

If you did not enter `next part`, and the brackets were empty, as shown above, the following prompt is displayed:

```
Enter name of boot file (or 'q' to quit):
```

If you press  at this prompt (regardless of how you got to it), the contents of the current working partition is displayed, and the above prompt is repeated:

```
Enter name of boot file (or 'q' to quit):
```

At this point, you have the option of choosing one of the displayed programs, or entering next part to change the working partition to the next defined stand partition. If the currently displayed partition is the only one defined on the disk, then the system will tell you so, and you must then choose one of the displayed programs, or abort the boot procedure (enter q). Otherwise, entering next part again makes the first partition the working partition.

# ❑ Making New Bootable Disks

Each time you turn on your computer, reboot, or manually request a boot from firmware mode, the programs and data files used to boot the computer are read from the hard disk or the floppy disk and loaded into memory for execution. For normal operations, you need to know little more. You know where the programs reside (in /stand) and you know how to reconfigure some of these programs (like the bootable operating system) should the configuration of your computer change.

This section shows you how to make additional bootable hard disks, should the need arise. For example, you may want to make another bootable hard disk for development purposes.

After making a new bootable disk, you can bring your machine down to the firmware level (shutdown -i5) and request a boot from the new bootable disk.

### Making a New Bootable Hard Disk

▼ *Caution*    This procedure should be used by experienced system administrators only. Users unfamiliar with disk partitioning, multi-disk operations, and the operation of the system in both firmware mode and during the boot process should not attempt this procedure.

Suppose you are the only system administrator around and even your mother wouldn't claim that you are experienced. But you *have* to make a new bootable disk. Read this section several times before you start. Then, put your existing bootable disk in a very safe place and follow the directions exactly.

During the process of installing the system software on your computer, the disk attached to the first hard disk controller is made a bootable disk and becomes the default hard disk for the boot process. This disk has a pathname of the form `/dev/rdsk/c1d0s6`, for the character special file (raw device), and `/dev/dsk/c1d0s6`, for the block special file (block device).

Whenever you power up or reboot your computer, the disk described above is the disk from which the boot programs, associated data files, and the bootable operating system are taken. The computer loads the boot program found in the `boot` partition of the default hard disk. The boot program will then load the bootable operating system found in the boot file system in the first `stand` partition on the default hard disk. (In most delivered systems, the default hard disk is the first integral hard disk connected to the first disk controller.)

When the system is in firmware mode, you can request a reboot from any bootable hard disk connected to your system, regardless of which device contains the root file system.

If your computer has more than one hard disk, you can make any disk a bootable disk.

A bootable disk must have at least two partitions defined on it:

▲   a   `boot` *partition*. This partition holds the `boot` program that loads and executes the bootable operating system.

▲   *a* `stand` *partition* that has a file system of type `bfs` defined on it. This boot file system contains all the bootable programs for your computer, as well as all data files needed by these programs. The boot file system is like other file systems in that it can be mounted and unmounted under any directory. By default it is mounted as `/stand`.

You can make any disk connected to your computer bootable, and either boot that disk from firmware, or make it the default boot disk. However, you should be aware that maintaining two or more bootable devices, depending on your intentions, may involve constantly mirroring changes made in one boot file system to other boot file systems. If you make changes to your machine's configuration, such as adding a new hardware or software module, changing tunables, etc., you may want to copy the bootable operating system to all boot file systems, so that each contains a valid bootable operating system for your machine's current configuration.

For example, suppose you have a two-disk system, with boot file systems and boot partitions on both disks (Disk A and Disk B). Assume that the boot file system on Disk A is mounted as /stand and the boot file system on Disk B is mounted as /stand2. Disk A is the disk booted when the system come up and on a shutdown -i6.

Let's say that you install a new software driver, thereby the /stand/system file on Disk A, and reboot the machine. When the machine reboots, the firmware will detect a difference in the /stand/system file on Disk A, and will cause the configuration of a new bootable operating system (/stand/unix) on Disk A. After the configuration completes, the machine boots from Disk A.

Now you have two different bootable operating systems on the two disks; the one on Disk A knows about the new software driver you installed, while the one on Disk B does not.

A similar situation arises whenever you make other kinds of changes to the configuration of your system, such as the addition or removal of expansion boards, device drivers, and the like. It is a good idea to copy the bootable operating system to other boot file systems whenever you make changes to the configuration of your system.

In cases like this, request a boot from each defined boot file system on each disk. To do this, request a boot of the /stand/system file from firmware and then choose the appropriate disk.

Note that the boot program examines the Volume Table of Contents (VTOC) on each disk to find the boot file system. The boot file system used depends on which disk you request at the firmware prompt (on powerup and reboot, the default boot disk specified in Non-Volatile RAM is assumed). If you define multiple boot file systems on a disk (i.e., multiple stand partitions), you can use the next part firmware command to boot from a specific boot file system (see *"Operations on the stand Partition,"* in this chapter, for a description of the next part command).

Also note that the file systems mounted when the system comes up in multi-user state are specified in /etc/vfstab.

The following procedure shows how to make a hard disk bootable.

**Step 1**  If the hard disk you want to make bootable has data on it, perform a full backup of the hard disk. You will want to reload this data after you make the disk bootable.

**Step 2**  Use the prtvtoc(1M) command to list the partitions currently on the disk. In order to make the disk bootable, boot and stand partitions must exist on the disk and must have the following minimum sizes: boot, 100 512-byte sectors; stand, 5500 512-byte sectors. The command looks like the following:

```
prtvtoc /dev/rdsk/c?d?s0
```

where the question marks in the device name are replaced by the appropriate controller and drive number, respectively. See prtvtoc(1M)  to identify the partitions on the disk from the output.

**Step 3**  If Step 2 reveals that the boot and stand partitions do not exist, or do not meet the minimum sizes specified in Step 2, you must repartition the hard disk.

At a minimum, the disk must be formatted to contain boot and stand partitions, as well as a partition (partition 6) that contains the whole disk. Other partitions can be defined on remaining space on the disk as needed, including creating additional stand partitions.

You can partition a disk using either a restore procedure in the hardware guide for your computer, the fmthard(1M) command, or the sysadm devices menu.

**Step 4**  Make a boot file system on the stand partition using mkfs(1M). The command looks like the following:

```
mkfs -F bfs /dev/rdsk/c?d?s? 5500 [#inodes]
```

where the question marks in the device name are replaced by the appropriate controller, drive, and partition numbers, respectively. The #inodes parameter is optional; it specifies the maximum number of files permitted in the boot file system. If omitted, the system will choose a number of files based on the number of blocks specified. Under most circumstances, this parameter may be omitted. See mkfs(1M) and Chapter 3, *The File System*, for complete information on making a boot file system.

**Step 5** Mount the new /stand file system as /mnt:

```
mount -F bfs /dev/dsk/c?d?s? /mnt
```

Replace the question marks with appropriate controller, drive, and partition numbers, as above.

**Step 6** Copy the contents of /stand on the old bootable disk to /mnt. Use any copy method you like, but the following is recommended:

```
cd /stand
find. -type f -print | cpio -pumv /mnt
```

Note that you may have to raise the allowable file size limit using the ulimit shell command (see sh(1)) if /stand/unix is larger than the current maximum file size limit.

**Step 7** Use umount(1M) to unmount the boot file system from /mnt, as follows:

```
umount /mnt
```

**Step 8** Copy the boot programs from the old bootable disk to the new boot partition on the new bootable disk using the newboot(1M) command, as follows:

```
newboot /usr/lib/boot /usr/lib/mboot \
    /dev/rdsk/c?d?s7
```

Replace the question marks with appropriate controller and drive numbers. The partition number specified must be 7.

**Step 9** Make any other file systems desired on remaining disk partitions. If you performed a backup in Step 1, restore data from the backup to a file system on the new bootable disk.

**Step 10** Edit /etc/vfstab and /etc/boot_tab to match the new file system layout on your machine. These files determine the file systems that are mounted at boot time and where they are mounted. Use prtvtoc(1M) to list the partitions and file systems on all the disks, and compare this output to the above files. Then make changes so that the file systems you expect to be mounted at boot time are specified in these files.

You have now defined another bootable disk for your system. Right now, the only way to boot from this new disk is to explicitly request a boot from the disk from firmware. If you want this disk to become the default disk used at powerup and reboot, you must follow the instructions in the "Changing *Default Boot Parameters*" section earlier in this chapter.

# ❏ Managing Device Attributes

The system stores information about devices in a database that can be accessed by applications that depend on device specific information. This section explains how to examine the information in this database, how to create new entries, and how to change or remove existing entries.

## The Device Database

The device database resides in `/etc/device.tab`. It has one entry per device, consisting of a set of attributes that describe the device. This database is used by applications, such as the backup and restore services, which depend on device-specific information.

If you need to add, change or delete an entry, you can do so by using the `put-dev` command, as described in the procedures to follow.

◆ *Note*     You can have a device installed that does not have an entry in this database. However, applications that access the device database for information will not be able to use such a device.

## Creating a Device Entry

Each entry in the device database is composed of a list of attributes for a particular device. Every device must have the `alias` attribute assigned (this attribute defines the alias name for a device). No other attributes are required. The set of assigned attributes can, and probably will, vary from device to device. Figure 4-6 shows recommended values for the attributes of different types of devices.

| alias | description | medium | type |
|-------|-------------|--------|------|
| 9trackN | 9-track tape drive N | tape reel | 9-track |
| ctapeN | cartridge tape drive N | cartridge | ctape |
| dpartN | disk partition N | | dpart |
| diskN | integral disk drive N | | disk |
| disketteN | floppy diskette drive N | diskette | diskette |
| qtapeN | QIC tape drive N | cartridge | qtape |

**Figure 4-6**
*Recommended device attribute values.*

The following list defines the standard device attributes that can be defined for a device in the device database. However, there are no restrictions on what can be defined as an attribute. If you have an attribute you want to define, simply name it when invoking the putdev command.

| Attribute | Description |
|-----------|-------------|
| alias | The unique name by which a device is known. No two devices in the database may share the same alias name. The name is limited in length to 14 characters and should contain only alphanumeric characters and also the following special characters if they are escaped with a backslash: underscore (_), dollar sign ($), hyphen (-), and period (.). |
| bdevice | The pathname to the block special device node associated with the device, if any. The associated major/minor combination should be unique within the database and should match that associated with the cdevice field, if any. (It is your responsibility to ensure that these major/minor numbers are unique in the database.) |
| capacity | The capacity of the device or of the typical volume, if removable. |
| cdevice | The pathname to the character special device node associated with the device, if any. The associated major/minor combination should be unique within the database and should match that associated with the bdevice field, if any. (It is your responsibility to ensure that these major/minor numbers are unique in the database.) |
| cyl | Used by the command specified in the mkfscmd attribute. |

**Figure 4-7**
*Standard device attributes.*
*These are the standard attributes that can be defined for a device. In addition, you can define any other attributes you care about by naming the new attribute in a putdev command.*

| | Attribute | Description |
|---|---|---|
| *Figure 4-7 Continued* | desc | A description of any instance of a volume associated with this device (such as floppy diskette). |
| | dpartlist | The list of disk partitions associated with this device. Used only if type=disk. The list should contain device aliases, each of which must have type=dpart. |
| | dparttype | The type of disk partition represented by this device. Used only if type=dpart. It should be either fs (for file system) or dp (for data partition). |
| | erasecmd | The command string that, when executed, erases the device. |
| | fmtcmd | The command string that, when executed, formats the device. |
| | fsname | The file system name on the file system administered on this partition, as supplied to the /usr/sbin/labelit command. This attribute is specified only if type=dpart and dparttype=fs. |
| | gap | Used by the command specified in the mkfscmd attribute. |
| | mkfscmd | The command string that, when executed, places a file system on a previously formatted device. |
| | mountpt | The default mount point to use for the device. Used only if the device is mountable. For disk partitions where type=dpart and dparttype=fs, this attribute should specify the location where the partition is normally mounted. |
| | nblocks | The number of blocks in the file system administered on this partition. Used only if type=dpart and dparttype=fs. |
| | ninodes | The number of inodes in the file system administered on this partition. Used only if type=dpart and dparttype=fs. |
| | norewind | The name of the character special device node that allows access to the serial device without rewinding when the device is closed. |
| | pathname | Defines the pathname to an inode describing the device (used for non-block or character device pathnames, such as directories). |
| | type | A token that represents inherent qualities of the device. Standard types include: 9-track, ctape, disk, directory, diskette, dpart, and qtape. See Figure 4-5 for a list of recommended attributes for these device types. |
| | volname | The volume name on the file system administered on this partition, as supplied to the /usr/sbin/labelit command. Used only if type=dpart and dparttype=fs. |

| Attribute | Description |
|-----------|-------------|
| volume | A text string used to describe any instance of a volume associated with this device. This attribute should not be defined for devices which are not removable. See Figure 4-5 for sample volume descriptions. |

*Figure 4-7*
*Continued*

Use the putdev command to create an entry for a device in the device database. Execute

```
putdev -a alias [ attribute=value ...]
```

where *alias* is the alias name of the device to be added to the database and *attribute=value* is a list of attribute values to be associated with the device.

If the list of attributes described with the putdev command does not provide enough information for a device definition, you can use new attributes to satisfy the need. Such an attribute would be created simply by adding a definition for it to the attribute list of a device entry. (See the procedure entitled *"Modifying a Device Entry."*)

The following shows the command line required to add a device with the alias of diskette3 to the database:

```
putdev -a diskette3 desc="Floppy Diskette Drive 3" \
    type=diskette
```

## Listing Devices

Use the getdev command to generate a list of devices. Executed without any options, this command creates a list of all devices in the device database, as shown below:

```
# getdev
ctape1
disk1
disk2
diskette1
spool
#
```

You can customize lists by naming the devices to be included, by defining the criteria that a device must match before being included, or by supplying both device names and a list of criteria. Using getdev like this allows you to obtain answers to questions such as the following.

▲   For what devices is a format command defined?

▲   What devices besides spool are set up in the device database?

Name devices on the getdev command line by executing

    getdev [-e] *device* [ *device* ... ]

where *device* is the name of the device or devices that you want included in the list. All devices named will be included, unless you use the -e option, which specifies that the devices named should be excluded from the list.

To name criteria on the getdev command line, execute

    getdev [-a] *criteria* [*criteria* ... ]

where *criteria* is specified with expressions. The four possible expression types are:

| | |
|---|---|
| *attribute=value* | Selects all devices for which *attribute* is defined and is equal to *value*. |
| *attribute!=value* | Selects all devices for which *attribute* is defined and does not equal *value*. |

*attribute* : *          Selects all devices for which *attribute* is defined.

*attribute* ! : *        Selects all devices for which *attribute* is not
                         defined.

You can define a list of criteria simply by supplying more than one expression, each separated by white space. Devices must satisfy at least one criteria in the list unless the -a option is used. In that case, only those devices matching all criteria will be included.

# *Example*

In each of the following examples, a user question is posed, followed by a getdev command line that you would enter to obtain the answer to that question. The resulting output would be a list of devices.

▲   What devices besides spool are set up in the device database?

       getdev -e spool

▲   What devices have the fmtcmd attribute defined?

       getdev fmtcmd:*

▲   What devices do not have the fmtcmd attribute defined?

       getdev fmtcmd!:*

▲   What devices have the attribute type defined as disk or have the attribute part defined?

       getdev type=disk part:*

▲   What devices have the attribute type defined as disk and have the attribute part defined?

       getdev -a type=disk part:*

    (Note that this example differs from the previous one by requiring that a device adhere to both criteria, not just one.)

▲   What devices in the named list (`disk1`, `disk3`, and `disk5`) have the
     attribute `type` defined as `disk` or have the attribute `part` defined?

```
getdev type=disk part:* disk1 disk3 disk5.
```

## Listing Device Attributes

The `devattr` command displays the attribute values for a device. The display can be presented in two formats:

▲   The default format shows a list of attribute values, without a descrip-
     tive label for each attribute.

▲   The verbose format, requested with the `-v` option, displays the
     attribute as *attribute=value*.

To list device attributes, type

```
devattr [-v] device [ attribute ...]
```

where *device* is the pathname or alias of the device whose attributes should be
displayed and *attribute* is the specific attribute whose value should be displayed. If you do not name a specific attribute, all attributes associated with
the device are shown in alphabetical order. For example, executing

```
devattr -v diskette1
```

produces the display shown as follows.

```
alias='diskette1'
bdevice='/dev/diskette'
cdevice='/dev/rdiskette1'
copy='true'
desc='Floppy Drive'
erasecmd='true'
fmtcmd='/etc/fmtflop -v /dev/rdiskette'
mkfscmd='/etc/mkfs -F S51K /dev/diskette 1422:512'
mountpt='/install'
type='diskette'
volume='diskette'
```

To see only the value for the `mountpt` attribute, type

```
devattr diskette1 mountpt
```

This produces

```
/install
```

## Modifying a Device Entry

The `putdev` command can be used to modify existing attribute values for a device or to add new attributes to a device entry. To do so, execute

```
putdev -m device attribute=value [ attribute=value … ]
```

where *device* is the pathname or alias of the device entry being modified, *attribute* is the name of the attribute being modified, and *value* is the value that should be assigned to the attribute.

If the specified attribute currently exists for this device in the device database, `putdev -m` modifies the value. If the attribute does not exist, it is added and given the value *value*. The alias attribute cannot be changed with `putdev -m`. This prevents an accidental modification or deletion of a device's alias from the database.

To delete an attribute definition from a device entry, use the `-d` option of the `putdev` command as follows.

```
putdev -d device attribute
```

where *device* is the name of the device entry from which an attribute definition will be deleted and *attribute* is the name of the attribute. For example, executing

```
putdev -d diskette1 volume
```

removes the attribute `volume` from the device entry for `diskette1`.

To delete the value of an attribute but keep the attribute in the device entry, use the same format as above, but assign the attribute the value of null. For example, to remove the value of the `volume` attribute while retaining `volume` in the device entry, execute

```
putdev -m diskette1 volume=""
```

### Removing a Device Entry

The `putdev` command can be used to delete a device entry from the device database. To do so, execute

```
putdev -d device
```

where *device* is the pathname or alias of the device being deleted from the device database.

# ❑ Managing Device Groups

You can create device groups to allow you to perform an action, or a set of actions, on any number of devices by giving only the device group name. As an example, think about a multiple device computer center. If there were several different rooms, each with a number of devices, groups could be created consisting of the devices located in each room. Device operations could then easily be done on a room-by-room basis by use of the group name instead of a device name.

The device group database resides in /etc/dgroup.tab. It has one entry per device group, consisting of a membership list. You can read this database, but you should not edit it directly. For this, you must use the putdgrp command, as described in the procedures that follow.

## Creating a Device Group

Use the putdgrp command to create a device group. Execute

```
putdgrp group_name alias [ alias ... ]
```

where *group_name* is the name of the group you are creating and *alias* is the device alias of the member, or members, of the group. The following example creates a group called disk with two members (disk1 and disk2):

```
putdgrp disk disk1 disk2
```

## Listing Device Groups

Use the getdgrp command to generate a list of groups that are defined in the device group database. Executed without options, this command creates a list of all device groups. For example, executing getdgrp might generate a list such as this:

```
# getdgrp
ctape
disk
diskette
#
```

You can customize lists by naming the device groups to be included, by defining the criteria that the member of a group must match before being included, or by doing both. Using `getdgrp` like this allows you to obtain answers to questions such as:

▲   What device groups do I have access to besides `disk`?

▲   What groups have devices with the attributes `fmtcmd` defined?

Name device groups on the `getdgrp` command line by executing

> `getdgrp` [`-e`] *group_name* [ *group_name* … ]

where *group_name* is the name of the device group or groups that you want included in the list. All named groups will be included, unless you use the `-e` option, which specifies that the groups named should be excluded from the list.

To name criteria on the `getdgrp` command line, execute

> `getdgrp` [`-a`] *criteria* [ *criteria* … ]

where *criteria* is specified with expressions. The four possible expression types are:

| | |
|---|---|
| *attribute*=*value* | Selects all device groups with at least one member whose attribute *attribute* is defined and is equal to *value*. |
| *attribute*!=*value* | Selects all device groups with at least one member whose attribute *attribute* is defined and does not equal *value*. |
| *attribute*:* | Selects all device groups with at least one member whose attribute *attribute* is defined. |
| *attribute*!:* | Selects all device groups with at least one member whose attribute *attribute* is not defined. |

You can define a list of criteria simply by supplying more than one expression, each separated by white space. To be included in the list, at least one member of a device group must satisfy at least one criteria, unless the `-a` option is used. Then, only those device groups with a member matching all criteria will be included.

In each of the following examples, a user question is posed, followed by a `getdgrp` command line that you would enter to obtain the answer to that question. The resulting output would be a list of device groups.

▲ What device groups do I have access to besides `ctape`?

```
getdgrp -e ctape
```

▲ What device groups have members with the `fmtcmd` attribute defined?

```
getdgrp fmtcmd:*
```

▲ What device groups have members that do not have the `fmtcmd` attribute defined?

```
getdgrp fmtcmd!:*
```

▲ What device groups have members with the attribute `type` defined as `disk` or have the attribute `part` defined?

```
getdgrp type=disk part:*
```

▲ What device groups have members with the attribute `type` defined as `disk` and have the attribute `part` defined?

```
getdgrp -a type=disk part:*
```

(Note that this example differs from the previous one by requiring that a group have a member adhering to both criteria, not just one.)

▲ What device groups in the named list (`group1`, `group3`, `group5`) have members with the attribute `type` defined as `disk` or have the attribute `part` defined?

```
getdgrp type=disk part:* group1 group3 group5
```

## Listing the Members of a Device Group

To display a list showing the names of devices that belong to a group, execute

```
listdgrp group_name
```

where *group_name* is the name of the group whose member list should be displayed. For example,

```
listdgrp disk
```

might produce a list such as the following:

```
# listdgrp disk
disk1
disk2
#
```

## Modifying a Device Group

The putdgrp command can be used to change group definitions by adding or removing a device from the group definition. To do so, execute

```
putdgrp [-d] group_name alias [ alias ... ]
```

where *group_name* is the name of the group definition to be modified, and *alias* is the device alias of the device to be added to the group definition or, if the -d option is used, the name of the device to be deleted from the group definition. For example,

```
putdgrp disk disk3
```

would add the device disk3 to the group disk and

```
putdgrp -d disk disk3
```

would remove the device `disk3` from group `disk`.

### Removing a Device Group

To remove a device group definition from the database, execute

```
putdgrp-d group_name
```

where *group_name* is the name of the device group definition to be removed.

# ❏ Managing Device Reservations

Device reservation is provided to help manage device use. Reserving a device places it on the device reservation list. This list contains the name of any device that has been reserved and the process ID that requested the reservation.

When a process requests a reservation, the device reservation list is checked. If the device does not already appear in the list, then it is available, and is added so that any future request to reserve that device will be denied. When a reservation is canceled, the device name is removed from the device reservation list and thus is available for a new reservation.

It is important to note that use of the device reservation system is not mandatory and that, when it is used, device reservation does not place any constraints on access to the device. It is assumed that when a reservation fails, the person or process attempting the reservation will not use the device. However, there is no mechanism to prevent it. Also, processes that do not request a device reservation can use a device that is reserved, since such a process would not have checked the reservation status to find out if it was reserved or not.

As administrator, you can reserve a device for exclusive use, release the reservation once you are finished with it, and check the status of a device.

◆ *Note*     Device reservation activities can be done from within application programs. Unpredictable behavior may result, however, when applications collide on device usage. An example occurs when one application uses device reservation and another does not. Here, both may attempt to access the same device, and thus collide.

## Reserving a Device

To reserve a device for exclusive use, enter

```
devreserv key device
```

where *key* is a positive integer that will be associated with this reservation and must be used later to free this particular reservation. The key should be unique. A suggested convention is to use the process ID of the calling process as the key (for example, devreserv *key device*). *device* is either the alias or pathname of a device that should be reserved or a list of devices. If *device* is a list, then the first device in the list that is available will be reserved.

## Freeing a Reserved Device

To free a device reservation, enter

```
devfree key [ device ... ]
```

where *key* is the key to which the device has been reserved and *device* is the alias or pathname of the device(s) that should be freed from reservation. devfree can be executed with only the key argument, in which case all devices reserved to that process ID will be released.

## Checking Device Reservation Status

You can check device reservation status in either of two ways. You can list all devices that are currently reserved or you can list all devices that are currently reserved to a particular key.

To list all devices that are currently reserved, execute

```
devreserv
```

To list all devices that are currently reserved to a particular key, execute

```
devreserv key
```

# 5

# *Communications*

## ❑ Overview

This chapter addresses four different communication facilities of System V
Release 4.0:

▲ STREAMS, which provides interprocess communication services.

▲ Basic Network Utilities (BNU), which allows computer

▲ two file system types that provide file sharing across networks:
Remote File Sharing (RFS) and Network File System (NFS).

File sharing refers to the process of making resources on your local system
available to remote systems via a network, and conversely, to accessing
resources on remote systems from your local system.

## ❑ STREAMS

STREAMS is a general, flexible facility and a set of tools for developing
UNIX communications services. It supports the implementation of services
ranging from individual device drivers to complete networking protocol
suites. STREAMS defines a standard interface for character input and out-

put within the kernel and between the kernel and the rest of the UNIX system. The simple and open-ended mechanism consists of a collection of system calls, kernel resources, and kernel routines.

The standard interface and mechanism enable modular, portable development and easy integration of high performance network services and their components. STREAMS does not impose any specific network architecture and is upwardly compatible with the character I/O user level functions such as `open`, `close`, `read`, `write`, and `ioctl`.

A *Stream* is a full-duplex processing and data transfer path between a STREAMS driver in kernel space and a process in user space (see Figure 5-1(a)). The *Stream head* is the end closest to the user process. A STREAMS *pipe* is a bidirectional data transfer path in the kernel (see Figure 5-1(b)). It implements a connection between one or more user processes.

A STREAMS *driver* may be a device driver, servicing an external I/O device, or a software driver, commonly called a pseudo-device driver. The driver handles data transfer between the kernel and the service and does little or no processing of data, other than conversions between STREAMS data structures and the device's data structures.

A STREAMS *module* represents processing functions to be performed on data flowing on the Stream. It is a defined set of kernel-level routines and data structures used to process data, status, and control information. Data processing may involve changing the way the data is represented, adding or deleting header and trailer information, and collecting the data into and from packets. Each module is self-contained and functionally isolated from any other Stream component except its two neighboring ones. The module communicates with its neighbors by passing messages.

A *message* is a set of data structures used to pass data, status, and control information between user processes, modules, and drivers. Messages that are passed from the Stream head toward the driver or from the process to the device are said to travel *downstream* or *write-side* while messages in the other direction, from the device to the process or from the driver to the Stream head, travel *upstream* or *read-side*.

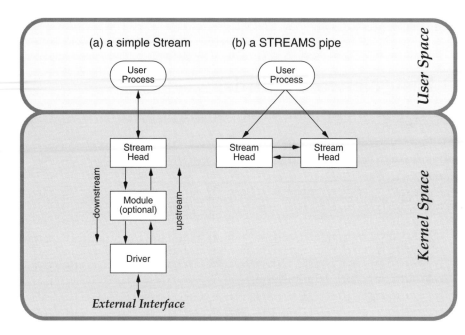

**Figure 5-1**
*Streams and pipes.*
*A stream pro-vides a full-duplex path between a user process and a STREAMS driver. The same mechanism can be used to imple-ment a pipe.*

## ❏ The Benefits of STREAMS

STREAMS provides a flexible, portable, and reusable set of tools for develop-ing UNIX system communication services. It allows a system programmer to easily create modules that offer standard data communication services and the ability to manipulate those modules on a Stream. Modules can be dynam-ically selected and interconnected from the user level. And it provides a sim-ple, standard user interface to the I/O subsystem. Thus,

▲ user level programs can be independent of underlying protocols and physical communication media.

▲ network architectures and higher level protocols can be independent of the underlying protocols, drives, and physical communication media.

▲ higher level services can be created by selecting and connecting lower level services and protocols.

Several system parameters referenced by STREAMS are configurable and are given in Chapter 8, *Configuring UNIX*.

# ❑ Basic Network Utilities

The Basic Network Utilities (BNU) package lets computers using UNIX communicate with each other and with remote terminals. The package includes:

▲ utilities for copying files between computers: `uucp`, `uuto`, `uuencode`, `uudecode`, `uupick`, and `uutry`.

▲ utilities for remote login and remote command execution: `cu`, `ct`, and `uux`.

▲ utilities for administering BNU: `uucleanup`, `uucheck`, and `uugetty`.

▲ utilities for checking status: `uulog`, `uuname`, `uuglist`, and `uustat`.

▲ network daemons: `uusched`, `uucico`, and `uuxqt`.

▲ database files in `/etc/uucp` that define and describe the remote computers that BNU will communicate with.

▲ log files that keep track of statistics about BNU operations.

Figure 5-2 shows a high level view of how BNU accomplishes the communication. The steps are:

**Step 1**   A user on the local machine issues a command requesting file transfer or remote execution communication with a remote computer (shown as phase A in the figure). Several BNU data base support files are read to determine if the remote computer is accessible and to establish a priority ordering for the request. Phase A ends when the request is queued, triggering the next phase.

**Step 2**   The `uucico` daemon wakes up when there is work in the `uucp` queue. It reads several of the data base support files to determine when and how the remote computer can be reached, how to handle data flow between the two computers, and whether the remote computer can handle the additional load of this request.

**Step 3**   The `uucico` daemon on the remote computer wakes up when the call from the local `uucico` comes in (phase C). The remote `uucico` reads its own data base support files to determine whether the calling computer is allowed access, and what action to take if it's not (phase C'). If access is allowed, the level of access is determined.

**Step 4**  Requests initiated on the local computer may contain commands to be executed on the remote computer (phase D). When these commands arrive at the remote computer, they are stored in a spool area. The uuxqt daemon on the remote computer will awaken and run them during this phase.

**Figure 5-2**
*Making a connection through BNU.*

The user issues a command (A). Several databases are consulted to process and queue the request. The *uucico* daemon takes the request from the queue (B), determines a means of contacting the remote machine, and places the call. The remote *uucico* daemon responds (C), placing the incoming data into the queue. The *uuxqt* daemon will execute any commands that are contained in the request (D).

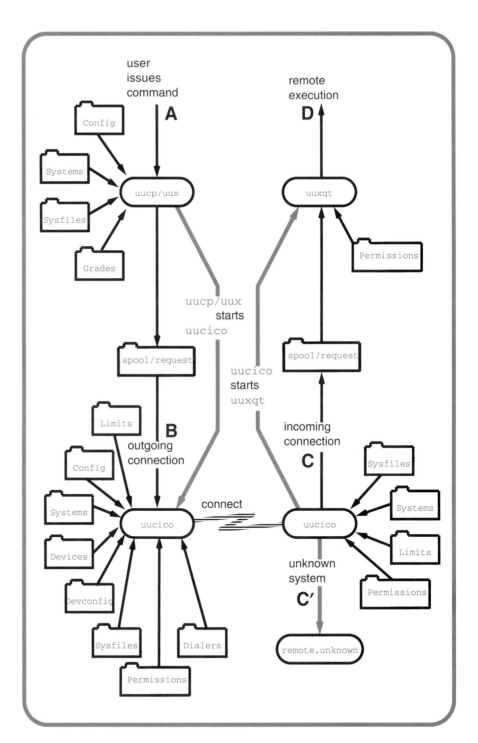

# ❏ BNU Database Support Files

The BNU support files are in the /etc/uucp directory. You can edit these files using the sysadm menus or manually, with your favorite test editor. The files are shown in Figure 5-2:

▲  Config contains parameters and values that can be changed to customize your BNU system.

▲  Devconfig contains network parameters.

▲  Devices contains information about the location and line speed of
   automatic call units (ACUs), direct links, and network devices.

▲  Dialcodes contains dial-code abbreviations that may be used in the
   telephone number field of Systems file entries.

▲  Dialers contains character strings required to communicate with
   network devices, ACUs, and direct links.

▲  Grades defines job grades and the associated permissions that users
   may specify to queue jobs to a remote computer.

▲  Limits defines the maximum number of simultaneous uucicos,
   uuxqts and uuscheds permitted on your machine.

▲  Permissions defines the level of access that is granted to computers
   when they attempt to transfer files or execute remote commands on
   your computer.

▲  Poll lists remote computers that are to be polled by your machine
   and the times to poll them.

▲  Sysfiles lets you assign different and multiple Systems,
   Devices, and Dialers files to uucico and cu.

▲  Systems contains information about remote systems, such as the
   remote system name, the connecting device, times to contact it, a telephone number or network address, and the uucp login ID and password.

We will discuss Config and Limits in more detail: they contain parameters that affect BNU performance.

## The `Config` File

The `/etc/uucp/Config` file allows the administrator to override certain parameters within BNU manually. Each entry in the `Config` file has the following format:

    *parameter* = *value*

where *parameter* is one of the configurable parameters and *value* is the value assigned to that parameter. See the `Config` file provided with your system for a complete list of configurable parameter names.

The following `Config` file entry sets the default protocol ordering to "Gge" and changes the "G" protocol defaults to 7 windows and 512-byte packets.

```
Protocol=G(7,512)ge
```

## The `Limits` File

The `/etc/uucp/Limits` file is used to control the maximum number of simultaneous BNU daemons (`uucico`, `uuxqt`, and `uusched`) that are running at a given time. The format of an entry in the `Limits` file is:

```
service=x      max=y
```

where $x$ can be `uucico`, `uuxqt`, or `uusched` and $y$ is the maximum number of running instances of $x$ that is allowed. The fields are order insensitive and lower case.

The following lines show the recommended limits. The `Limits` file is modified by editing it with your favorite text editor.

```
service=uucico    max=5
service=uuxqt     max=5
service=uusched     max=2
```

# ❏ BNU Log Files

BNU keeps eight log files, recording

▲ all commands that access the BNU utilities

▲ each action that changes the state of the BNU subsystem and queue

▲ all errors that occur as BNU executes

▲ information about file transfers

▲ accounting information so that users can be charged for BNU network use

▲ attempted security violations

▲ operation statistics that reflect BNU system performance

▲ attempts by unknown systems to connect to the machine (shown as C' in Figure 5-2).

We discuss three of these log files in more detail: they can help you monitor BNU service, detect and correct problems, and twiddle system parameters as needed.

## The Command Log

The command log, `/var/spool/uucp/.Admin/command`, contains the commands issued by the user, the administrator, and the operator. It can help the system administrator troubleshoot BNU problems. Figure 5-3 shows the format of an entry in the command log.

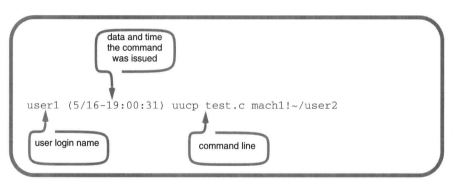

```
user1 (5/16-19:00:31) uucp test.c mach1!~/user2
```

data and time the command was issued

user login name

command line

**Figure 5-3**
*Format of an entry in the command log. All BNU commands are logged. This log entry was produced by a user command. Others may come from the BNU administrator or the console opera-*

## The Error Log

The error log, /var/spool/uucp/.Admin/errors, contains the error messages that are produced as BNU operates. In most cases, the errors are caused by file system problems. The format of a typical entry is shown in Figure 5-4.

**Figure 5-4**
*Format of an error log entry. The error log provides a record of all the errors encountered during BNU operation. Most errors are file system errors.*

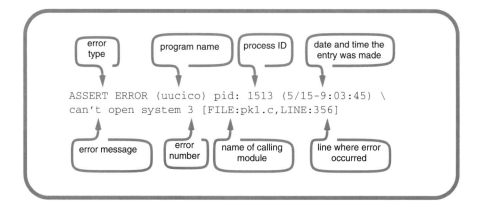

## The Performance Log

The BNU performance log, /var/spool/uucp/.Admin/perflog, contains statistics about the operation of uucico. The system administrator can turn performance logging on and off by creating and removing the log file: statistics are collected only if the log file exists when uucico starts.

Two types of records are written to the log file. Each is identified by a mnemonic type at the beginning of the record:

▲   conn records contain statistics about the successful establishment of connections

▲   xfer records contain statistics about file transfers

Figure 5-5 and Figure 5-6 show the formats of these two records. Each record is a string of ASCII fields separated by spaces and terminated with a line feed.

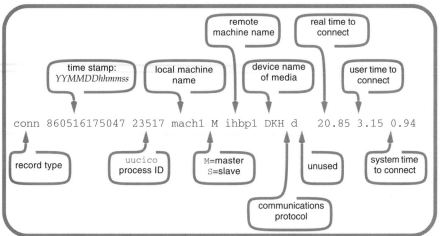

**Figure 5-5**
*Format of* `conn`
*entries in*
`perflog`.
*This* `conn` *entry shows that a successful connection was made to* `ihbp1`.

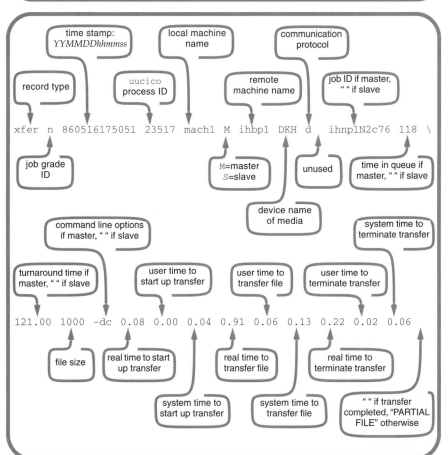

**Figure 5-6**
*Format of* `xfer`
*entries in*
`perflog`.
*This* `xfer` *entry shows that a 1000-byte files was transferred from* `mach1` *to* `ihpb1`.

## ❏ Detecting BNU Problems

Several monitoring tools are included in the BNU package to help you detect and correct basic networking problems. They include:

▲   uustat(1). Use the -q option to examine counts and reasons for failure to contact other machines.

▲   cu(1). Use the -d and -l options to place a call on a particular line (-l line) with debugging turned on (-d).

▲   uutry(1). Use this command to make a trial connection to a machine. It will start the uucico daemon in debugging mode. Debugging output can be found in /tmp/*machine*, where *machine* is the name of the remote computer you are trying to contact.

▲   uuname(1). Use this command to list the machines you can contact from your machine.

▲   uulog(1). Use this command to display the contents of the log directories for particular hosts.

▲   uucheck(1). Use the -v option to check for the presence of files and directories needed by uucp. It also checks the Permissions file and provides information on the permissions you have established.

## ❏ System V File Sharing

File sharing employs a *client/server* model. A computer that wishes to share file systems with other computers on a network acts as a *server*. Files are physically owned and managed by the server machine. A computer that wishes to access file systems that do not reside on its physical disk acts as a *client* of the server machine. Acting on behalf of its applications, the client makes requests to a server to access data in a file or to perform file manipulations. A single machine may be both a client and a server, if it wishes both to share its local file systems and to access remote file systems.

A server may offer any directory tree for access over the network. Once shared, an authorized client may mount the remote file system on any of its local directories. The mount procedure behaves in a manner similar to mounting local file systems. *Transparency* is the key to the usefulness of file sharing.

Once mounted, remote file systems look like local file systems from a user or application perspective. Applications, in most cases, run unchanged.

Since remote file systems may be mounted anywhere in the local tree, existing programs can run on several different computers while still having the same files and directory structure available to them. Creating the file environment is now mainly an administrative task, not one requiring program changes.

Servers do not need to make all their files accessible to network clients. In the following illustration, the server is sharing /pub. One client mounts /pub-lic/dac/bin on its local directory /usr/tools. The remote directory tree now appears to be a directory tree under /usr/tools, and files in that tree may be accessed as though they were local. Note that the client cannot access /pub/man. Another client, elm, has mounted only /pub/man on its local directory /usr/man/man and cannot access files under /pub/dac, even though the server has made them a shared resource.

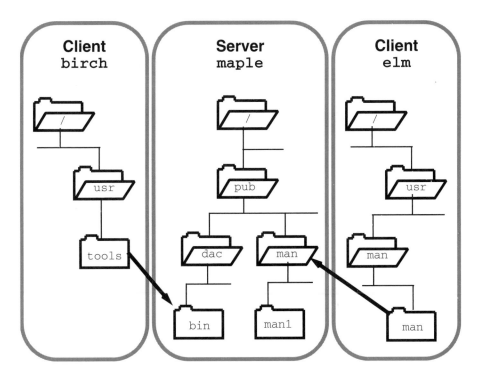

**Figure 5-7**
*File sharing.*
*Server* maple
*has made its*
/pub *directory*
*tree a shared*
*resource. Client*
birch *mounts*
/pub/dac/bin
*and can execute*
*the programs it*
*contains as if*
*they were local.*
*Client* elm *has*
*mounted*
/pub/man
*which will be*
*searched along*
*with the local*
man *directories*
*when a user*
*issues a* man *com-*
*mand.*

In a file sharing environment, a large number of users can access a program as though it were on their local machines, when actually the program resides an a single file server. This is a great benefit to small workstations, where disk space is at a premium. A user can have access to a much larger program repertoire than could fit on a private disk.

By having a resource reside physically on a single server, then distributed throughout the network, you can greatly simplify administration. First, you reduce the number of copies of various programs that need to be maintained on the network. Second, you reduce the problems involved in performing backups for a number of machines dispersed over a wide geographical area. By keeping files in a single location, this task becomes comparable to backing up a single machine.

Centralizing files on a few file servers not only simplifies administration, it helps maintain consistency of shared data files. When changes are made to a shared file, they become available to all users immediately.

As an alternative to centralizing files on a few file servers, files may be shared in a peer manner. When a single computer runs out of capacity, more computers can be added to a configuration. Files can be moved to the new computers, while a consistent view of the file system from the user's perspective is maintained.

## ❑ RFS vs. NFS

In UNIX System V Release 4.0, RFS and NFS have been integrated as file system types under the Virtual File System mechanism. This means that the benefits of both RFS and NFS can be realized on the same computer. RFS and NFS will operate on the same machine and over the same network. Since the same directory trees may be mounted simultaneously over RFS and NFS, applications that require one or the other can co-exist. However, RFS and NFS protocols are different, and do not inter-operate.

■ *Note*     Because RFS and NFS are implemented as file system types under the Virtual File System (VFS) mechanism, applications see a normal file system interface. The same open, read, write, and close operations as used for local files work for remote files. The distributed file system uses the VFS interface to take care of translations between the UNIX file system interface and internal protocols. For more information about Virtual File System, see Chapter 3, *File Systems.*

In Release 4.0, the syntax of administrative commands for RFS and NFS has been standardized to provide a uniform interface to distributed file systems. File system-dependent options allow differences to be accommodated, while integrating common features. Older forms of commands are still available to provide compatibility with previous systems.

Both RFS and NFS provide a comparable file sharing capability but have some differences, resulting from their different goals.

The goal of NFS is to provide file sharing in a heterogeneous environment potentially containing many different operating systems. The NFS internal protocol has been designed to be implementable on non-UNIX operating systems in order to provide an open file sharing capability. NFS clients and servers have been implemented on many operating systems ranging from MS-DOS to VMS. A secondary goal of NFS is to provide good recovery characteristics when file servers fail; this has resulted in a design where the NFS servers do not keep any state about clients accessing them. Thus, servers are not sensitive to client crashes, which results in a robust environment.

The major goal of RFS is to provide file sharing in a UNIX System V environment as transparently as possible. A file system shared using RFS closely supports UNIX file system semantics. This makes it relatively easy to migrate programs written to use the local file system.

The following sections highlight some of the similarities and differences between RFS and NFS.

▲   *shared objects.* An RFS server can share any local directory, and all local files and directories under the shared directory are made accessible to remote users. RFS clients can access all file types transparently, including ordinary files, directories, named pipes, and special devices. Because computers running RFS can access remote devices, expensive peripherals, such as tape drives, can be used for backups by smaller computers that could not justify the cost of a dedicated drive; media incompatibilities (such as diskette formats) can be overcome by using devices supporting required formats on remote computers; and the reliability of the environment can be increased by making remote devices such as printers available if the locally attached device breaks down.

An NFS server can share a file system or any part of file system, including a single file. All files and directories below the root of the shared resource are made available to clients. A machine cannot share a file hierarchy that overlaps with one that is already shared. For example, it is illegal to share both `/public` and `/public/tkit`.

▲ *transparency and consistency.* The same system calls and command syntax used to access local files are used to access RFS and NFS resources. Remote data is cached on both RFS and NFS clients. Cache consistency is guaranteed on RFS clients, but not on NFS clients.

▲ *location independence.* RFS provides a name server with which to register resource names; the administrator of the client does not need to know where a resource resides. If resources (such as on-line manual pages or line printers) are moved, the client does not need to know about the move or modify its actions to access the resources at their new locations.

The administrator of an NFS client machine must specify the name of the server machine when mounting an NFS file system. If a resource moves, all clients must be aware of the new location when mounting the resource.

▲ *heterogeneity.* RFS can operate over a network of computers running UNIX System V Release 3.0 and later System V releases, regardless of the underlying computer architecture.

NFS can operate on a variety of operating systems implemented on a variety of computer architectures.

▲ *network protocol independence.* RFS can run over any network protocol that conforms to the System V Transport Provider Interface and provides virtual circuit service. In Release 4.0, if multiple network protocols exist on the machine, RFS may run over all of them simultaneously.

NFS is built on top of the Remote Procedure Call (RPC) facility, which requires the User Datagram Protocol (UDP) transport. UDP is a protocol in the TCP/IP protocol family.

▲ *full semantics.* RFS supports full UNIX system semantics, including file and record locking, open with append mode, access to remote devices and pipes, and so on.

NFS takes advantage of a network locking facility called the Lock Manager. The Lock Manager supports the UNIX System V style of advisory and mandatory file and record locking.

▲ *application compatibility.* Since full file system semantics are supported, RFS allows all applications to run without recompilation.

Because NFS provides transparent access, within limits, NFS allows existing applications that do not attempt to use unsupported features to run without recompilation.

▲ *security*. RFS allows file access based on machine passwords and user and group IDs. It also provides an administrator with the ability to specify read-only access to resources; to share directories selectively; to restrict which machines can access resources; to unshare a resource to prevent further client mounts; and to force a client to unmount a resource.

NFS assumes global UID/GID space, and provides an administrator with the ability to restrict which machines can access resources; to specify read-only access to shared directories; and to unshare a directory, causing client access to that directory to fail. NFS also provides an option called Secure NFS, which supports encrypted machine and user identification along with ID mapping.

■ *state*. RFS servers maintain the state of local resources. The server knows which clients hold references to each of its files at any given time.

NFS servers do not maintain the state of local resources. The server does not know which client has its files open at any given time.

▲ *recovery*. With RFS, if a client crashes, the server removes the client's locks and performs other clean-up actions. If the server crashes, the client acts as if that portion of the file tree has been removed (reads fail, and so on).

With NFS, if the client crashes, the server is oblivious to it. If the server crashes, clients can either block until the server comes up or return an error after a timeout.

The rest of the chapter discusses RFS and NFS separately and covers parallel topics for each:

▲ an overview of the features

▲ a brief look at the system administration requirements

▲ detecting and recovering from problems.

# ❑ Remote File Sharing

The primary function of RFS is to allow computers running UNIX System V to selectively share resources (directories containing files, subdirectories, devices, and/or named pipes) across a network. It offers:

▲ *compatibility.* Once you mount a remote resource on your system it will look to your users as though it is part of the local system. You will be able to use most standard UNIX system features on the resource. Standard commands and system calls, as well as features like File and Record Locking, work the same on remote resources as the do locally. Applications should be able to work on remote resources without modification.

▲ *flexibility.* Since you can mount a remote resource on any directory on your system you have a lot of freedom to set up your computer's view of the world. You do not have to open up all your files to every machine on the network available to your computer's users.

▲ *performance.* The client caching feature of RFS provides substantial performance improvements over non-caching systems by reducing the number of times data must be read across the network. Client refers to the computer that is using a remote resource, while caching refers to the client's ability to store data in local buffer pools.

The first time a client process reads a block of data from a remote resource, it is placed in local buffer pools. Subsequent client processes reading a server file can avoid network access by finding the data already present in local buffers. This generally causes a large reduction in network messages, resulting in improved performance.

In order for client caching to work simply and reliably, the following features were built into it:

• *cache consistency.* Checking mechanisms are used to ensure that the cache buffers accurately reflect the contents of the remote file the user is accessing.

• *transparency.* The only difference users should see in caching and non-caching systems is improved response time. RFS-bases applications do not have to be changed to take advantage of client caching.

- *administration.* By default, client caching is on. It is possible to turn it off for an entire system or for a particular resource. There are tools for monitoring performance and parameters you can tune to customize RFS to your needs.

# ❏ Sharing Resources on RFS

An RFS network consists of *domains, servers, clients,* and *shared resources.* Each computer on an RFS network is assigned to a domain; there can be many domains on the network. Servers offer resources to clients. A shared resource is directory tree that can be accessed by clients on remote computers.

To create a shared resource on an RFS network, a resource identifier (the name that other computers will use to access the directory) is assigned to a pathname and registered as a sharable resource by the share command. Computers with proper access permissions can then mount the shared resource with the `mount -F rfs` command.

Figure 5-8 shows how two computers can share resources. In this example, the administrator of a computer named `maple` wants to share all files and directories under `/pub` with clients on an RFS network. The name of the resource is `PUBLIC`.

Another computer in `maple`'s domain, `birch`, wants to access part of `PUBLIC`, the `dac/bin` subtree. The `birch` administrator uses `dfshares` to make it accessible to users on `birch`, then creates a directory called `/usr/tools` and mounts `PUBLIC/dac/bin` on `/usr/tools`. Users on `birch` can now `cd` to the remote directory, list its contents, and run a remote program locally. If the shared resource directory contains the `/dev` directory, users could direct output to a remote device as though the device were on the local machine.

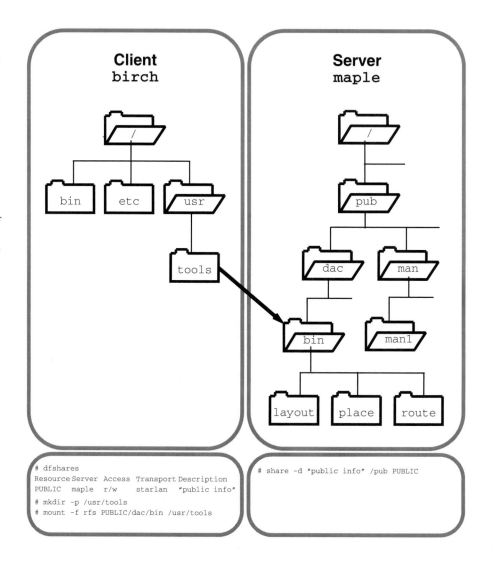

```
# dfshares
Resource Server  Access  Transport Description
PUBLIC   maple  r/w      starlan   "public info"
# mkdir -p /usr/tools
# mount -f rfs PUBLIC/dac/bin /usr/tools
```

```
# share -d "public info" /pub PUBLIC
```

# ❏ RFS Troubleshooting Techniques

As a domain name server, computers in your domain and other domains rely
on your machine for information about domain resources and domain member machines. RFS is designed to recover quickly when communication is cut
between machines and the name server. The following sections describe RFS
events that can occur and the recovery mechanisms designed to handle them.

## Primary Goes Down

All essential domain records are maintained on the primary domain server. The primary regularly distributes the most critical of these records to secondary domain name servers. (These records do not include files and directories under `/etc/rfs/auth.info`.)

If the primary goes down, domain name server responsibilities are passed to the first secondary name server listed in the `rfmaster` file. The secondary is only intended to take over temporarily, since has limited name service capabilities. The definitive domain records remain on the primary. Changing the name server should not affect any currently mounted resources.

While a secondary is acting domain name server, these functions cannot be done:

▲ *maintaining domain member lists*. Computers can be added or deleted from the domain membership list only by the primary name server.

▲ *changing RFS passwords*. Only the primary name server can change RFS authentication passwords.

The secondary will maintain lists of shared resources for the domain and continue basic name server functions. In most cases, the computers in the domain won't be aware that the primary is down. When the primary comes back up, the secondary should pass name server responsibilities back to the primary.

 ◆ *Note*    When a server machine crashes, the domain name server (primary or secondary) still has resources listed as being shared. The domain name server can unshare resources to clean up.

## Primary and Secondary Go Down

If all primary and secondary name servers go down at once, all information on shared resources will be lost. Active mounts and links, however, will not be disturbed. The problem is that when the primary comes back up, each computer will still think its resources are shared by the primary will have no record of those shares resources.

As soon as the primary is running, each computer can make sure its shared resources are in sync with those listed on the primary by restarting RFS. Stop the running RFS system, restart it, and reshare all your resources. This can be done automatically by going from `init` 3 to `init` 2 to `init` 3.

# ❑ Network File System

The Network File System (NFS) enables machines of different architectures running different operating systems to share resources across a network. NFS makes it possible for a machine to share local files and directories, and permits remote users to access those files and directories as though they were local to the user's machine.

NFS provides file sharing in a heterogeneous environment, potentially containing many different operating systems; it has been implemented on operating systems ranging from MS-DOS® to VMS. Two of its attributes are:

▲ *it defines an abstract model of a file system.* On each operating system, the NFS model is mapped into the local file system semantics. As a result, normal file system operations like `read` and `write` operate in the same way they would on a local file system.

▲ *it allows multiple machines to use the same files.* The same data can be accessible to everyone on the network. Storage costs can be kept down by having machines share applications, and database consistency and reliability is enhanced by having all users read the same set of files.

## NFS Resources

The objects that can be shared through NFS include any whole or partial directory tree or file hierarchy—including a single file. A machine cannot share a file hierarchy that overlaps one that is already shared. Special device files, as well as ordinary files, can be shared over NFS; however, peripheral devices such as modems and printers cannot be shared.

In most UNIX system environments, a shareable file hierarchy corresponds to a file system or to a portion of a file system; however, NFS works across operating systems, and the concept of a file system may be meaningless in other, non-UNIX system environments. Therefore, the term *resource* is used through-out this guide to refer to a file or file hierarchy that can be shared and mounted over NFS.

When you mount a local file system on a local mount point, you mount the entire file system, starting at its root. When you mount a remote resource through NFS, you are not restricted to mounting the entire file system. You can mount any directory or file in the file system tree, and gain access only to that directory or file and anything beneath it. For example, in Figure 5-9, the server, `maple`, is sharing its entire `/pub` file system. If client `elm` wants access only to the files and subdirectories in `/pub/man` on Machine A, it can mount `/pub/man`, rather than `/pub`; then, only `/pub/man` on `maple` appears in `elm`'s directory tree (`/pub/dac` is not accessible, for instance).

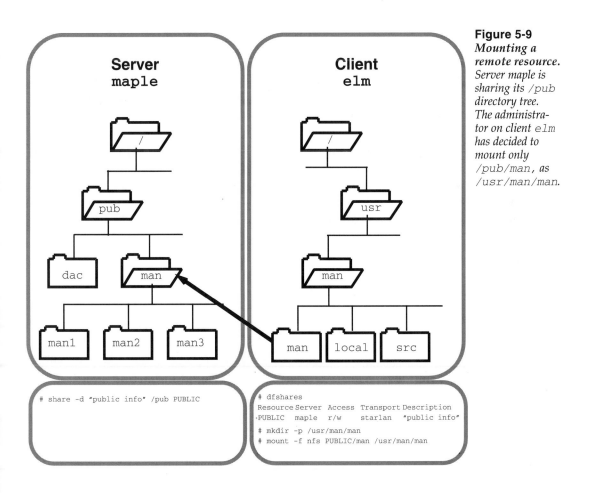

**Figure 5-9**
*Mounting a remote resource. Server maple is sharing its /pub directory tree. The administrator on client elm has decided to mount only /pub/man, as /usr/man/man.*

It would be illegal for maple to individually share /pub/dac and /pub/man if both resources reside on the same disk partition. In this case, you would have to share the parent, /pub, and leave it to each client to decide whether to mount /pub/dac or /pub/man or /pub (to provide access to both subtrees).

If you want to mount a single file, you must mount the file on a directory. Once it is mounted, you cannot remove it (using rm) or move it to another directory (using mv); you can only unmount it.

### NFS Servers and Clients

A machine that makes a local resource available for mounting by remote machines is called a *server*. A machine that mounts a resource shared by a remote machine is a *client* of that machine. Any machine with a disk can be server, a client, or both at the same time.

A server can support a *diskless* client, a machine that has no local disk. A diskless client relies completely on the server for all its file storage. A diskless client can act only as a client—never as a server.

Clients access files on the server by mounting the server's shared resources. When a client mounts a remote resource, it does not make a copy of the resource; rather, the mounting process uses a series of remote procedure calls that enable the client to access the resource transparently on the server's disk. The mount looks like a local mount, and users enter commands just as if the resources were local.

# ❑ NFS Administration

Your responsibilities as an NFS administrator depend on your site's requirements and the role of your machine on the network. You may be responsible for all the machines on your local network, in which case you may be responsible for installing the software on every machine, determining which machines, if any, should be dedicated servers, which should act as both servers and clients, and which should be clients only.

If your site has a network administrator, and you are the administrator of a client-only machine, you may be responsible only for mounting and unmounting remote resources on that machine.

Maintaining a machine once it has been set up involves the following tasks:

▲ Starting and stopping NFS operation.

▲ Sharing and unsharing resources as necessary during a server's work session.

▲ Mounting and unmounting resources as necessary during a work session.

▲ Modifying administrative files to update the lists of resources your machine shares and/or mounts automatically.

▲ Checking the status of the network.

▲ Diagnosing and fixing NFS-related problems as they arise.

▲ Setting up optional security features provided by Secure NFS.

▲ Setting up maps to use the optional automatic mounting facility called the Automounter.

# ❑ Monitoring NFS Performance

The `dfshares`, `share`, and `dfmounts` commands let you monitor shared resource availability on both local and remote systems. You can browse the list of resources being offered by remote servers with `dfshares`, identify the resources the local host is offering with `share`, and find out who is using what with `dfmounts`.

## Browsing Available Resources with the `dfshares` Command

The command `dfshares` allows you to "browse" remote servers to find out the names of remote resources available to your client machine. The syntax of the command is:

```
dfshares [-F nfs][-h][server ...]
```

where -F nfs indicates that resources shared over NFS should be displayed; -h indicates that a header should not be printed in the display; and *server* is a list of servers, separated by white space, whose shared resources should be displayed.

If NFS is the only file sharing package you have installed, you can omit the -F option.

Unless it is suppressed with the -h option, the output from the dfshares command is preceded by the header

```
    resource server access transport
```

where *resource* is of the form *server* : *pathname* and *server* is the name of the server sharing the resource. At this time, NFS does not populate the *access* and *transport* fields; a hyphen appears in place of access and transport information.

## Displaying Shared Local Resources with the share Command

You can obtain a list of all the NFS resources currently shared on your machine by entering

```
    share
```

If you have more than one distributed file system package installed, the share command without arguments displays *all* the resources shared on your system, including the resources shared through NFS.

You do not have to be the superuser to use the share command in this capacity.

## Monitoring Shared Local Resources with the dfmounts Command

The command dfmounts lets you display a list of shared resources by server that tells you which resources are currently mounted over NFS, and by which clients. The syntax of the command is

```
dfmounts [ -F nfs ] [ -h ] [ server ... ]
```

where -F nfs indicates that resources mounted over NFS should be displayed; -h indicates that a header should not be printed in the display; and *server* is a list of servers, separated by white space, whose shared resources should be displayed.

If NFS is the only file sharing package you have installed, you can omit the -F option.

Unless it is suppressed with the -h option, the output from the dfmounts command is preceded by the header

```
resource server pathname clients
```

where *resource* is of the form *server:pathname*; *server* is the name of the server from which the resource was mounted; *pathname* is the pathname of the shared resource as it appears in the second part of *resource*; and *clients* is a commaseparated list of clients that have mounted the resource.

The *server* can be any system on the network. If a *server* is not specified, dfmounts displays the resources of the local system that have been mounted by remote clients.


## ❑ NFS Troubleshooting Techniques


This section describes problems that may occur on machines using NFS services. Included are

▲  A summary of NFS sequence of events

▲  Strategies for tracking NFS problems

▲  NFS-related error messages.

Before trying to clear NFS problems, you need some understanding of the issues involved. This section contains enough technical details to give experienced network administrators a thorough picture of what is happening with their machines. If you do not yet have this level of expertise, note that it is not important to fully understand all the daemons, system calls, and files. However, you should be able to at least recognize their names and functions. In addition, you should be familiar with the following commands: mount(1M), share(1M), mountd(1M), nfsd(1M), and biod(1M).

## An Overview of the Mount Process

This section describes the remote mount process. It is not critical that you understand in depth how the daemons mentioned here work; however, you need to know that they exist, because you may need to restart them should they stop for any reason.

Here is the sequence of events when you first enter run level 3.

1.  The appropriate file in /sbin/rc3.d starts the mountd daemon and several nfsd daemons (the default is four). The nfsd daemons are used in server operation.

2.  The same file in /sbin/rc3.d executes the shareall program, which reads the server's /etc/dfs/dfstab file, then tells the kernel which resources the server can share and what access restrictions, if any, are on these files.

3.  The appropriate file in /sbin/rc3.d starts several (the default is four) biod daemons. The biod daemons are used in client operation.

4.  The same file in /sbin/rc3.d starts the mountall program, which reads the client's vfstab file and mounts all NFS-type files mentioned there in a manner similar to an explicit mount (described below)

Here is the sequence of events when an administrator mounts a resource during a work session, using the command line:

1.  The administrator enters a command, such as

    ```
    mount -F nfs -o ro,soft dancer:/usr/src \
        /usr/src/dancer.src
    ```

2.  The mount command validates that the administrator has superuser permission, that the mount point is a full pathname, and that there is a file /usr/lib/nfs/mount. If all three conditions are valid, /sbin/mount then passes all the relevant arguments and options to

/usr/lib/nfs/mount, which takes control of the process (when we say mount from now on in this section, we will be referring to this last file.)

3. mount then opens /etc/mnttab and checks that the mount was not done automatically at the start of the work session.

4. mount parses the argument *special* into host dancer and remote directory /usr/src.

5. mount calls dancer's rpcbind to get the port number of dancer's mountd.

6. mount calls dancer's mountd daemon and passes it /usr/src, requesting it to send a file handle fhandle for the directory.

7. The server's mountd daemon handles the client's mount requests. If the directory /usr/src is available to the client (or to the public), the mountd daemon does a NFS_GETFH system call on /usr/src to get the fhandle, and it sends it to the client's mount process.

8. mount checks if /usr/src/dancer.src is a directory.

9. mount does a mount(2) system call with the fhandle and /usr/src/dancer.src.

10. The client kernel looks up the directory /usr/src/dancer.src and, if everything is in order, ties the file handle to the hierarchy in a mount record.

11. The client kernel looks up the directory /usr/src on dancer.

12. The client kernel does a statfs(2) call to dancer's NFS server nfsd.

13. Mount's mount(2) system call returns.

14. mount opens /etc/mnttab and adds an appropriate entry to the end, reflecting the new addition to the list of mounted files.

15. When the client kernel does a file operation, once the resource is mounted, it sends the NFS RPC information to the server, where it is read by one of the nfsd daemons to process the file request.

16. The nfsd daemons know how a resource is shared from the information sent to the server's kernel by share. These daemons allow the client to access the resource according to its permissions.

## Determining Where NFS Service Has Failed

When tracking down an NFS problem, keep in mind that there are three main points of possible failure: the server, the client, or the network itself. The strategy outlined in this section tries to isolate each individual component to find the one that is not working.

The mountd daemon must be present in the server for a remote mount to succeed. Make sure mountd will be available for an RPC call by checking that /sbin/init.d/nfs has lines similar to the following:

```
if [ -x /usr/lib/nfs/mountd ]
then
        /usr/lib/nfs/mountd > /dev/console 2>&1
fi
```

Remote mounts also need a number of nfsd daemons to execute on NFS servers (the default is four). Check the server's file /sbin/init.d/nfs for the following (or similar) lines:

```
if [ -x /usr/lib/nfs/nfsd ]
then
/usr/lib/nfs/nfsd 4 > /dev/console 2>&1
fi
```

To enable these daemons without rebooting, become the superuser and type:

```
/usr/lib/nfs/nfsd 4
```

The client's biod daemons are not necessary for NFS to work, but they improve performance. Make sure the following (or similar) lines are present in the client's file /sbin/init.d/nfs:

```
if [ -x /usr/lib/nfs/biod ]
then
/usr/lib/nfs/biod 4 > /dev/console 2>&1
fi
```

To enable these daemons without rebooting, become the superuser and type:

```
/usr/lib/nfs/biod 4
```

## Clearing Server Problems

When the network or server has problems, programs that access hard mounted remote files will fail differently than those that access soft mounted remote files. Hard mounted remote resources cause the client's kernel to retry the requests until the server responds again. Soft mounted remote resources cause the client's system calls to return an error after trying for a while. mount is like any other program: if the server for a remote resource fails to respond, and the hard option has been used, the kernel retries the mount until it succeeds. When you use mount with the bg option, it retries the mount in the background if the first mount attempt fails.

When a resource is hard mounted, a program that tries to access it hangs if the server fails to respond. In this case, NFS displays the message

```
NFS server hostname not responding, still trying
```

on the console. When the server finally responds, the message

```
NFS server hostname ok
```

appears on the console.

A program accessing a soft mounted resource whose server is not responding may or may not check the return conditions. If it does, it prints an error message in the form

> ...*hostname* `server not responding: RPC: Timed out`

If a client is having NFS trouble, check first to make sure the server is up and running. From the client, type

> `/usr/sbin/rpcinfo` *server_name*

to see if the server is up. If it is up and running, it prints a list of program, version, protocol, and port numbers, similar to the following:

```
program   version   netid       address           service
100000    3         icmp        0.0.0.0.0.111
100000    2         icmp        0.0.0.0.0.111
100000    3         udp         0.0.0.0.0.111
100000    2         udp         0.0.0.0.0.111
100000    3         tcp         0.0.0.0.0.111
100000    2         tcp         0.0.0.0.0.111
100000    3         ticotsord   phpeb.rpc
100000    3         ticots      phpeb.rpc
100000    3         ticlts      phpeb.rpc
100000    1         udp         0.0.0.0.4.8
100000    1         tcp         0.0.0.0.4.133
```

If the server fails to print a list, try to log in at the server's console. If you can log in, check to make sure the server is running `rpcbind`.

If the server is up but your machine cannot communicate with it, check the network connections between your machine and the server.

## Clearing Remote Mounting Problems

This section deals with problems related to mounting. Any step in the remote mounting process can fail, some of them in more than one way. Below are the error messages you may see and detailed descriptions of the failures associated with each error message.

`mount` can get its parameters explicitly from the command line or from `/etc/vfstab`. The examples below assume command line arguments, but the same debugging techniques work if mounting is done automatically through `/etc/vfstab`.

```
mount: ...server not responding: RPC_PMAP_FAILURE - RPC_TIMED_OUT
```

Either the server sharing the resource you are trying to mount is down, at the wrong run level, or its `rpcbind` is dead or hung. You can check the server's run level by entering (at the server) the command

```
who -r
```

If the server is at run level 3, try going to another run level and back, or try rebooting the server to restart `rpcbind`. Try to log in to the server from your machine, using the `rlogin` command. If you can't log in, but the server is up, try to log in to another remote machine to check your network connection. If that connection is working, check the server's network connection.

```
mount: ... server not responding: RPC_PROG_NOT_REGISTERED
```

`mount` got through to `rpcbind`, but the NFS mount daemon `mountd` is not registered. Check the server's run level and make sure its daemons are running.

```
mount: ...: No such file or directory
```

Either the remote directory or the local directory does not exist. Check the spelling of the directory names. Use `ls` on both directories.

```
mount: not in share list for ...
```

Your machine name is not in the list of clients allowed access to the resource you want to mount. From the client, you can display the server's share list by entering

```
dfshares -F nfs server
```

If the resource you want is not in the list, log in to the server and run the `share` command without options.

```
mount: ...: Permission denied
```

This message indicates that the user does not have the appropriate permissions or that some authentication failed on the server. It may be that you are not in the share list (see the preceding error message and explanation), or that the server does not believe you are who you say you are. Check the server's `/etc/dfs/sharetab` file.

```
mount: ...: Not a directory
```

Either the remote path or the local path is not a directory. Check the spelling in your command, and try to run `ls` on both directories.

The `mount` command hangs indefinitely if there are no `nfsd` daemons running on the NFS server. This happens when there is no `/etc/dfs/dfstab` file on the server when it enters run level 3. To clear the problem, restart the `nfsd` daemons by typing

```
/usr/lib/nfs/nfsd 4
```

## Fixing Hung Programs

If programs hang while doing file-related work, your NFS server may be dead. You may see the following message on your console:

```
NFS server hostname not responding, still trying
```

This message indicates that NFS server *hostname* is down, or that there is a problem with the server or with the network.

If your machine hangs completely, check the server(s) from which you mounted the resource. If one or more are down, do not be concerned. When the server comes back up, programs resume automatically. No files are destroyed.

If you soft mount a resource and the server dies, other work should not be affected. Programs that time out trying to access soft mounted remote files will fail with errno ETIMEDOUT, but you should still be able to access other resources.

If all servers are running, ask someone else using these same servers if they are having trouble. If more than one machine is having problems getting service, there is a problem with the server. Log in to the server. Run ps to see if nfsd is running and accumulating CPU time (run ps -ef a few times, letting some time pass between each call). If not, you may be able to kill and then restart nfsd. If this does not work, you have to reboot the server. If nfsd is not running, it may be that the server has been taken to a run level that does not support file sharing. Use who -r to obtain the server's current run level.

If other systems seem to be up and running, check your network connection and the connection of the server.

If programs on the client are hung but the server is up, NFS requests to the server other than reads and writes are succeeding, and messages of the form

```
xdr_opaque: encode FAILED
```

are appearing on either the client or the server console, you may be requesting more data than the underlying transport provider can provide. Try remounting the file system using the -o rsize=*nnn*,wsize=*nnn* options to mount(1M) to restrict the request sizes the client will generate.

## Fixing a Machine That Hangs Part Way Through Boot

If your machine boots normally, then hangs when it tries to mount resources automatically, most likely one or more servers are down. Use init to go to single user mode or to a run level that does not mount remote resources automatically. Then start the appropriate daemons in the background and use the mount command to mount each resource usually mounted automatically through the /etc/vfstab file. By mounting resources one at a time, you can determine which server is down. To restart a server that is down or hung, see the preceding section.

If you cannot mount any of your resources, most likely your network connection is bad.

### Improving Access Time

If access to remote files seems unusually slow, type

```
ps -ef
```

on the server to be sure that it is not being affected adversely by a runaway daemon. If there is nothing unusual in the display, and other clients are getting good response, make sure your biod daemons are running. At the client, type

```
ps -ef | grep biod
```

Look for biod daemons in the display, then enter the command again. If the biods do not accumulate excessive CPU time, they are probably hung. If they are dead or hung, follow these steps:

**Step 1**  Kill the daemon processes by typing:

> kill -9 *pid1 pid2 pid3 pid4*

**Step 2**  Restart the biod daemons by typing:

> /usr/lib/nfs/biod 4

If the biods are running, check your network connection. The command netstat -i can help you determine if you are dropping packets; for more information, see the netstat(1M) manual page.

# ❑ Using the Automounter

Resources shared through NFS can be mounted using a method called "automounting." The automount program mounts and unmounts remote directories on an as-needed basis. Whenever a user on a client running the automounter invokes a command that needs to access a remote file, the shared resource to which that file belongs is mounted automatically. When a certain amount of time has elapsed without the resource being accessed, it is automatically unmounted.

Once the automounter is invoked, an administrator does not have to set up automatic mounting with the `vfstab` file, or use the `mount` and `umount` commands at the command line. All mounting is done automatically and transparently.

 ***Note***   Mounting some resources with `automount` does not exclude the possibility of mounting others with `mount`; in fact, in a diskless machine you *must* mount root (/) and `/usr` with `mount`.

See..... for more about setting up and using the automounter facility. We will discuss failure modes.

## Troubleshooting

The following are error messages you may see if the automounter fails.

```
mapname: Not found
```

The required map cannot be located. This message is produced only when the `-v` (verbose) option is given. Check the spelling and pathname of the map name.

```
dir mountpoint must start with '/'
```

The automounter mount point must be given as full pathname. Check the spelling and pathname of the mount point.

```
mountpoint: Not a directory
```

The *mountpoint* exists but it is not a directory. Check the spelling and pathname of the mount point.

```
hierarchical mountpoint: mountpoint
```

The automounter will not allow itself to be mounted within an automounted directory. You will have to think of another strategy.

---

WARNING: *mountpoint* not empty!

---

The mount point is not an empty directory. This message is produced only when the -v (verbose) option is given, and it is only a warning. All it means is that the previous contents of *mountpoint* will not be accessible.

---

Can't mount *mountpoint*: *reason*

---

The automounter cannot mount itself at *mountpoint*. The *reason* should be self-explanatory.

---

*hostname*:*filesystem* already mounted on *mountpoint*

---

The automounter is attempting to mount a resource on a mount point, but the resource is already mounted on that mount point. This happens if an entry in /etc/vfstab is duplicated in an automounter map (either by accident or because the output of mount -p was redirected to vfstab). Delete one of the redundant entries.

---

WARNING: *hostname*:*filesystem* already mounted on *mountpoint*

---

The automounter is mounting itself on top of an existing mount point.

---

couldn't create *directory*: *reason*

---

The system could not create a directory. The *reason* should be self-explanatory.

```
bad entry in map mapname "map entry"
```

```
map mapname, key map key: bad
```

The map entry is malformed, and the automounter cannot interpret it. Recheck the entry; perhaps there are characters in it that need escaping.

```
hostname: exports: rpc_err
```

There is an error when the automounter tries to get a share list from *hostname*. This indicates a server or network problem.

```
host hostname not responding
```

```
hostname:filesystem server not responding
```

```
Mount of hostname:filesystem on mountpoint: reason
```

You will see these error messages after the automounter attempts to mount from *hostname* but gets no response or fails. This may indicate a server or network problem.

```
mountpoint - pathname from hostname: absolute symbolic link
```

When mounting a resource, the automounter has detected that *mountpoint* is an absolute symbolic link (beginning with /). The content of the link is *pathname*. This may have undesired consequences on the client; for example, the content of the link may be /usr.

```
Cannot create socket for broadcast rpc: rpc_err
```

```
Many_cast select problem: rpc_err
```

```
Cannot send broadcast packet: rpc_err
```

```
Cannot receive reply to many-cast: rpc_err
```

All these error messages indicate problems attempting to "ping" servers for a replicated file system. This may indicate a network problem.

```
trymany: servers not responding: reason
```

No server in a replicated list is responding. This may indicate a network problem.

```
Remount hostname:filesystem on mountpoint: server not responding
```

An attempted remount after an unmount failed. This indicates a server problem.

```
NFS server (pidn@mountpoint) not responding still trying
```

An NFS request made to the automount daemon with PID *n* serving *mountpoint* has timed out. The automounter may be overloaded temporarily, or dead. Wait a few minutes; if the condition persists, the easiest solution is to reboot the client. If you don't want to reboot, exit all processes that make use of automounted resources (or change to a non-automounted resource, in the case of a shell), kill the current automount process, and restart it again from the command line. If this fails, you must reboot.

# 6

# *Monitoring System Activity*

## ❏ Overview

The System Performance Analysis Utilities (SPAU) package, introduced in Chapter 1, contains a set of tools that measure and produce reports on system activities. As various system actions occur, counters in the operating system are incremented to keep track of these activities. System activities that are tracked include:

▲ CPU utilization

▲ paging

▲ system call activity

▲ file access

▲ kernel table usage

▲ interprocess communication

▲ Kernel Memory Allocation (KMA)

▲ buffer usage

▲ terminal device activity

▲ process switching

▲ scheduling queue activity

▲ Remote File Sharing (RFS)

▲ available memory and swap space

▲ disk and tape input/output activity

System activity data can be accessed on a special request basis using the `sar` command or it can be saved automatically on a routine basis using the `sadc` command and the shell scripts `sa1` and `sa2`. Generally, the demand system activity reports are used to pinpoint specific performance problems, and the automatic reports are generated as a means of monitoring system performance. The following sections describe both methods of activity reporting in detail.

# ❏ Automatically Collecting System Activity Data

The `sadc` command can automatically sample system data. The format of this command is as follows:

```
/usr/lib/sa/sadc [t n]  [ofile]
```

The command samples *n* times with an interval of *t* seconds (*t* should be greater than 5 seconds) between samples. It then writes, in binary format, to the file *ofile*, or to standard output. If *t* and *n* are omitted, a default interval is used.

When the performance package is installed, a number of files are automatically created and/or appended to that cause system activity commands to run automatically.

The file `/sbin/init.d/perf`, which is linked to `/sbin/rc2.d/S21perf`, causes the `sadc` command to be invoked to mark usage from when the activity counters are reset to zero. The output of `sadc` is put in the file `/var/adm/sa/` sa*dd* where *dd* is the date. The command entry in the `/sbin/init.d/perf` file that starts the daily activity file and resets the counters is:

```
su sys -c "/usr/lib/sa/sadc /var/adm/sa/sa`date +%d`"
```

Once the SPAU tools are installed, `cron` will execute `/var/spool/cron/crontabs/sys`, which invokes two shell scripts, `sa1` and `sa2`, that automatically collect system activity data. The shell script `sa1` has the following format:

```
/usr/lib/sa/sa1 [t n ]
```

The arguments *t* and *n* cause records to be written *n* times at an interval of *t* seconds. If these arguments are omitted, the records are written only one time. The records are written to the binary file /var/adm/sa/sa*dd*, where *dd* is the current date. The sa1 command is performed automatically by cron using the following entries found in /var/spool/cron/crontab/sys:

```
0 * * * 0-6 /usr/lib/sa/sa1
20,40 8-17 * * 1-5 /usr/lib/sa/sa1
```

The first causes a record to be written to /var/adm/sa/sa*dd* on the hour, every hour, seven days a week. The second entry causes a record to be written to /var/adm/sa/sa*dd* 20 minutes and 40 minutes after each hour from 8:00 a.m. to 5:00 p.m., Monday through Friday, typically considered to be peak working hours. Thus, these two crontab entries cause a record to be written to /var/adm/sa/sa*dd* every 20 minutes from 8:00 a.m. to 5:00 p.m., Monday through Friday, and every hour on the hour otherwise. These defaults can easily be changed to meet your daily needs.

The shell script sa2 has the following format:

```
/usr/lib/sa/sa2 [ -abcdgkmpqruvwxyADSC ] [ -s time ] [ -e time ] \
    [ -i sec ]
```

The sa2 command invokes the sar command with the arguments given and writes the ASCII output to the file /var/adm/sa/sar*dd* where *dd* is the current date. The report starts at -s *time*, ends at -e *time*, and is taken as close to -i *sec* intervals as possible. See the sar command, later in the chapter, for an explanation of the remaining options.

When installed, the performance package includes the following entry in the /var/spool/cron/crontabs/sys file:

```
5 18 * * 1-5 /usr/lib/sa/sa2 -s 8:00 -e 18:01 -i 1200 -A
```

This causes a `sar -A` report to be generated from `/var/adm/sa/sadd`. The report covers twenty-minute intervals in the time period from 8:00 a.m. to 6:01 p.m., Monday through Friday. Note that since `/var/adm/sa/sadd` does not have data for 5:20 and 5:40 if the above `sa1` cron entries are used, the `sar` report will not have data for those times either.

**Figure 6-1**
*Automatically collecting system activity data.*
*Entries in crontab files run* sadc, sa1, *and* sa2 *to initilize a file for collecting the data, to collect the data, and to generate a report at the end of the day.*

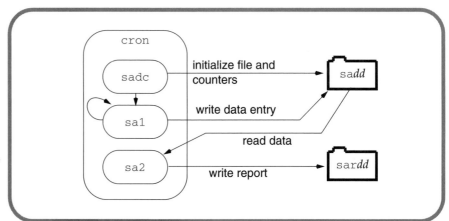

# ❑ Collecting System Activity Data on Demand

The `sar` command can either be used to gather system activity data itself or to extract what has been collected in the daily activity files created by `sa1` and `sa2`.

The `sar` command has the following formats:

```
sar [-abcdgkmpqruvwxyADSC] [-o file] t [n]
sar [-abcdgkmpqruvwxyADSC] [-s time] [-e time] \
    [-i sec] [-f file]
```

In the first format, `sar` samples cumulative activity counters in the operating system at intervals specified by *n* for a time (in seconds) specified by *t* (*t* should be 5 seconds or greater). The default value of *n* is 1. If the `-o` option is specified, samples are saved in *file* in binary format.

In the second format, with no sampling interval specified, sar extracts data from a previously recorded *file*, either the one specified by the -f option or, by default, the standard daily activity file, /var/adm/sa/sar*dd*. The -s and -e options define the starting and ending times for the report. Starting and ending times are of the form *hh[:mm[:ss]]*. The -i option specifies, in seconds, the intervals to select records. If the -i option is not included, all intervals found in the daily activity file are reported.

Figure 6-2 summarizes sar options and their results as well as where to find a detailed explanation of each one.

| Option | Description | Page # of Detailed Description |
|:------:|-------------|:-----------------------------:|
| -a | monitors file access operations | 194 |
| -b | monitors buffer activity | 195 |
| -c | monitors system calls | 196 |
| -d | monitors disk activity | 199 |
| -g | monitors page-out and memory freeing activity | 201 |
| -k | monitors kernel memory use | 202 |
| -m | monitors interprocess communications | 204 |
| -p | monitors page-in and page fault activity | 205 |
| -q | monitors scheduling queue activity | 206 |
| -r | monitors unused memory levels | 207 |
| -u | monitors CPU utilization | 208 |
| -v | monitors system table status | 210 |
| -w | monitors swap space usage | 211 |
| -y | monitors terminal line activity | 213 |
| -x | monitors RFS operations | 212 |
| -A | reports overall system performance; equivalent to entering all the options | 214 |
| -D | monitors remote system calls (if used with -c), remote buffer usage (if used with (-b), and remote CPU utilization (if used with -u) on RFS networks. | 195 (-Db) 196 (-Dc) 208 (-Du) |
| -C | monitors client caching performance (RFS) | 218 |
| -S | monitors RFS server availability and requests | 220 |

**Figure 6-2**
*sar options.*

# ❏ Monitoring File Access

The `sar -a` option reports on the use of file access operations. The UNIX operating system routines reported are as follows:

iget/s        Number of s5 and ufs files located by inode entry per second.

namei/s       Number of file system path searches per second. If namei does not find a directory name in the directory name logic cache, it will call iget to get the directory. Hence, most igets are the result of directory name logic cache misses.

dirbk/s       Number of s5 directory block reads issued per second.

**Figure 6-3**
*Output from*
*sar -a.*
*The sampling*
*interval is one*
*minute.*

```
unix sfxbs 4.0 2 3B2     08/22/89

14:28:12   iget/s namei/s dirbk/s
14:29:12        0       2       1
14:30:12        0       4       1
14:31:12        0       3       1

Average         0       3       1
```

The larger the values reported, the more time the UNIX kernel is spending to access user files. The amount of time reflects how heavily programs and applications are using the file systems. The -a option is helpful for understanding how disk-dependent an application system is; it is not used for any specific tuning step.

# ❏ Monitoring Buffer Activity

The -b option reports on the following buffer activities.

bread/s        Average number of physical block (512 bytes each) reads into the system from the disk per second.

lread/s        Average number of logical reads from system buffers per second.

%rcache        Fraction of logical reads found in the system buffers (100% minus the ratio of breads to lreads).

bwrit/s        Average number of physical writes from the system buffers to disk per second.

lwrit/s        Average number of logical writes to system buffers per second.

%wcache        Fraction of logical writes found in the system buffers (100% minus the ratio of bwrit/s to lwrit/s).

pread/s        Average number of physical read requests per second.

pwrit/s        Average number of physical write requests per second.

The most important entries are the cache hit ratios %rcache and %wcache, which measure the effectiveness of system buffering. If %rcache falls below 90, or if %wcache falls below 65, it may be possible to improve performance by increasing the buffer space by adjusting the tunable BUFHWM in /etc/master.d/kernel.

The -Db option is available to systems that have Remote File Sharing installed. It reports the information described above for local disk reads and writes, plus information on buffer pool usage for locally mounted remote resources.

**Figure 6-4**
*Output from*
`sar -b.`
*In this example,*
*the buffers are not*
*causing any slow-*
*downs; the data is*
*within acceptable*
*limits.*

| 14:28:12 | bread/s | lread/s | %rcache | bwrit/s | lwrit/s | %wcache | pread/s | pwrit/s |
|----------|---------|---------|---------|---------|---------|---------|---------|---------|
| 14:29:12 | 0 | 14 | 100 | 6 | 17 | 67 | 0 | 0 |
| 14:30:12 | 0 | 12 | 99 | 6 | 16 | 65 | 0 | 0 |
| 14:31:12 | 0 | 12 | 100 | 6 | 16 | 65 | 0 | 0 |
| Average | 0 | 12 | 100 | 6 | 16 | 66 | 0 | 0 |

**Figure 6-5**
*Output from*
`sar -Db.`
`pread/s` *and*
`pwrite/s` *are*
*not reported for*
*remote resources.*
*Because*
`%wcache<65,`
*consider increas-*
*ing the buffer*
*space.*

```
#sar -dB
UNIX System V charlie 4.0 2 9/03/89
```

| 14:37:15 | bread/s | lread/s | %rcache | bwrit/s | lwrit/s | %wcache | pread/s | pwrit/s |
|----------|---------|---------|---------|---------|---------|---------|---------|---------|
| 14:37:18 | | | | | | | | |
| local | 2 | 40 | 93 | 1 | 3 | 64 | 0 | 0 |
| remote | 1 | 11 | 92 | 1 | 1 | 0 | | |
| 14:37:21 | | | | | | | | |
| local | 2 | 39 | 92 | 1 | 3 | 63 | 0 | 0 |
| remote | 0 | 10 | 94 | 1 | 1 | 0 | | |
| 14:31:12 | | | | | | | | |
| local | 2 | 40 | 93 | 1 | 3 | 64 | 0 | 0 |
| remote | 1 | 12 | 93 | 1 | 1 | 0 | | |
| Average | | | | | | | | |
| local | 2 | 40 | 93 | 1 | 3 | 64 | 0 | 0 |
| remote | 1 | 11 | 93 | 1 | 1 | 0 | | |

## ❑ Monitoring System Calls

The `-c` option reports on system calls in the following categories:

`scall/s`       All types of system calls per second (generally about 30 per second on a busy four- to six-user system).

`sread/s`       The number of `read` system calls per second.

`swrit/s`       The number of `write` system calls per second.

| | |
|---|---|
| fork/s | The number of fork system calls per second, about 0.5 per second on a four- to six-user system. This number will increase if shell scripts are running. |
| exec/s | The number of exec system calls per second. If (exec/s)/(fork/s) > 3, look for inefficient PATH variables. |
| rchar/s | Characters (bytes) transferred by read system calls per second. |
| wchar/s | Characters (bytes) transferred by write system calls per second. |

Typically, reads plus writes account for about half of the total system calls, although the percentage varies greatly with the activities that are being performed by the system.

The -Dc option is available for systems that have Remote File Sharing installed. The report contains the average number of system calls per second and the average number of reads and writes per second, but not the number of exec system calls per second.

Information is divided into three categories: incoming requests (a remote client requesting access to a local resource), outgoing requests (a local client requesting a remote resource), and strictly local system calls (the output of the -c option).

Some statistics will not reflect the actual number of messages sent across the network, since the client caching feature allows some remote read requests to be satisfied from data in local buffers. Outgoing scall/s, sread/s, and rchar/s fields include statistics for these read "hits" of remote data in the client cache. Though these reads do not result in actual messages to the remote machine, they are still categorized as outgoing, since they access remote data.

If performance on your RFS network is poor, you can use the `sar -Dc` report to see how efficiently system read and write calls to and from your computer are using the RFS network. Divide the number of characters read and written by the number of reads and writes, respectively. If your computer is attempting more than 30 remote system calls per second (in and out `scall/s`), you are probably nearing capacity. Performance problems with undoubtedly result from this much demand.

You may want to consider moving resources to machines where they are most in demand. Use the `fusage` command, described in the next chapter, to determine what resources are being used most heavily.

**Figure 6-6**
*Output from*
*sar -c.*
*The ratio of execs*
*to forks does not*
*indicate any*
*probems with*
*pooly formed*
*PATH variables.*

```
unix sfxbs 4.0 2 3B2      08/22/89

14:28:12   scall/s  sread/s  swrit/s   fork/s   exec/s  rchar/s  wchar/s
14:29:12      17        2        2      0.28     0.28    2527     1542
14:30:12      25        2        1      0.50     0.47    1624      295
14:31:12      21        2        2      0.35     0.35    1812      703

Average       21        2        2      0.38     0.37    1987      847
```

**Figure 6-7**
*Output from*
*sar -Dc.*

```
#sar -Dc
UNIX System V lucy 4.0 2 02/14/89

00:00:04   scall/s  sread/s  swrit/s   fork/s   exec/s  rchar/s  wchar/s
01:00:04
     in        4        1        2               0.00     350      220
    out        3        2        1               0.00     240      300
  local      133       30       12      0.73     1.33   11202     3813
02:00:04
     in        4        1        2               0.00     350      220
    out        3        2        1               0.00     240      300
  local      133       30       12      0.73     1.33   11202     3813
03:00:04
     in        4        1        2               0.00     350      220
    out        3        2        1               0.00     240      300
  local      133       30       12      0.73     1.33   11202     3813

Average
     in        4        1        2               0.00    2527     1542
    out        3        2        1               0.00    2527     1542
  local      133       30       12      0.73     1.33    2527     1542
```

# ❑ Monitoring Disk Activity

The `sar -d` option reports the activities of disk devices.

| | |
|---|---|
| `device` | Name of the disk device(s) monitored. |
| `%busy` | Percentage of time the device spent servicing a transfer request. |
| `avque` | The average number of requests outstanding during the monitored period (measured only when the queue was occupied). |
| `r+w/s` | Number of read and write transfers to the device per second. |
| `blks/s` | Number of 512 byte blocks transferred to the device per second. |
| `avwait` | Average time in milliseconds that transfer requests wait idly in the queue (measured only when the queue is occupied). |
| `avserv` | Average time in milliseconds for a transfer request to be completed by the device (for disks this includes seek, rotational latency, and data transfer times). |

Figure 6-8 and Figure 6-9 illustrate the `sar -d` output. The first example, Figure 6-8, is from a computer with a disk that does not use an SCSI interface. This example illustrates data being transferred from a hard disk (`hdsk-0`) to the floppy disk (`fdsk-0`).

The second example, Figure 6-9, shows data from a computer with disks that use an SCSI interface. The example illustrates data being transferred from one SCSI hard disk (`sd00-0`) to another SCSI integral disk (`sd00-1`).

Note that queue lengths and wait times are measured when there is something in the queue. If %busy is small, large queues and service times probably represent the periodic sync efforts by the system to ensure that altered blocks are written to the disk in a timely fashion.

**Figure 6-8**
*Output from*
*sar -d.*
*This computer has a disk that does not use an SCSI interface. Data is being transferred from a hard disk (hdsk-0) to the floppy disk (fdsk-0).*

```
unix unix 4.0 2 3B2     8/11/89
13:46:28   device %busy avque r+w/s blks/s   avwait   avserv
13:46:58   hdsk-0     6   1.6     3      5     13.8     23.7
           fdsk-0    93   2.1     2      4    467.8    444.0
13:47:28   hdsk-0    13   1.3     4      8     10.8     32.3
           fdsk-0   100   3.1     2      5    857.4    404.1
13:47:58   hdsk-0    17    .7     2     41       .6     48.1
           fdsk-0   100   4.4     2      6   1451.9    406.5
Average    hdsk-0    12   1.2     3     18      8.4     34.7
           fdsk-0    98   3.2     2      5    925.7    418.2
```

**Figure 6-9**
*Output from*
*sar -d.*
*This computer has disks that use an SCSI interface. Data is being transferred from one SCSI hard disk (sd00-0) to another (sd00-1).*

```
unix unix 4.0 2 3B2     8/11/89
14:16:24   device %busy avque r+w/s blks/s   avwait   avserv
14:16:52 sd00-0       2   1.0     1      3      0.0     17.9
         sd00-1       6   1.1     3      5      2.0     23.9
14:17:21 sd00-0       2   1.0     1      2      0.0     19.6
         sd00-1       6   1.1     3      5      0.2     24.3
14:17:48 sd00-0       3   1.0     1      3      0.3     18.3
         sd00-1       7   1.1     3      5      1.3     25.4
14:18:15 sd00-0       3   1.0     1      3      0.0     17.2
         sd00-1       5   1.0     2      5      0.0     21.6
Average  sd00-0       2   1.0     1      3      0.1     18.2
         sd00-1       6   1.0     3      5      0.9     23.8
```

# ❑ Monitoring Page-Out Activity

The `sar -g` option reports page-out and memory freeing activities as follows:

pgout/s        The number of times per second file that systems receive page-out requests.

ppgout/s      The number of pages that are paged-out per second. (A single page-out request may involve paging-out multiple pages.)

pgfree/s      The number of pages per second that are placed on the freelist by the page-stealing daemon. If this value is greater than 5, it may be an indication that more memory is needed. (This is the same as `rclm/s` previously reported by option `-p`.)

pgscan/s      The number of pages per second scanned by the page-stealing daemon. If this value is greater than 5, the page-out daemon is spending a lot of time checking for free memory. This implies that more memory may be needed.

%s5ipf        The percentage of `s5` inodes taken off the freelist by `iget` which had reusable pages associated with them. These pages are flushed and cannot be reclaimed by processes. Thus, this is the percentage of `iget`s with page flushes. If this value is greater than 10 percent, then the freelist of inodes is considered to be page-bound and the number of `s5` inodes should be increased.

```
unix sfxbs 4.0 2 3B2      08/22/89

14:28:12   pgout/s ppgout/s pgfree/s pgscan/s %s5ipf
14:29:12     0.00     0.00     0.35     8.18   0.00
14:30:12     0.00     0.00     0.00     0.00   0.00
14:31:12     0.00     0.00     0.00     0.00   0.00
      .
Average      0.00     0.00     0.12     2.72   0.00
```

sar -g  is a good indicator of whether more memory may be needed. The number of cycles used by the page-stealing daemon can be found using ps -elf. If it has used many cycles then coupled with high pgfree/s and pgscan/s values it is a good indicator of a memory shortage. sar -p, sar -u, sar -r, and sar -w are also good memory shortage indicators.

sar -g also shows whether inodes are being recycled too quickly, causing a loss of reusable pages.

# ❏ Monitoring Kernel Memory Usage

The -k option reports on the following activities of the Kernel Memory Allocator (KMA).

| | |
|---|---|
| sml_mem | The amount of memory in bytes the KMA has available in the small memory request pool (a small request is less than 256 bytes). |
| alloc | The amount of memory in bytes the KMA has allocated from its small memory request pool to small memory requests. |
| fail | The number of requests for small amounts of memory that failed. |
| lg_mem | The amount of memory in bytes the KMA has available |

in the large memory request pool (a large request is from 512 bytes to 4K bytes).

`alloc`      The amount of memory in bytes the KMA has allocated from its large memory request pool to large memory requests.

`fail`      The number of requests for large amounts of memory that failed.

`ovsz_alloc`      The amount of memory allocated for oversized requests (those greater than 4K). These requests are satisfied by the page allocator; thus, there is no pool.

`fail`      The number of requests for oversized amounts of memory that failed.

The KMA allows a kernel subsystem to allocate and free memory as needed. Rather than statically allocating the maximum amount of memory it is expected to require under peak load, the KMA divides requests for memory into three categories: small (less than 256 bytes), large (512 - 4K bytes), and oversized (greater than 4K bytes). It keeps two pools of memory to satisfy small and large requests. The oversized requests are satisfied by allocating memory from the system page allocator.

If your system is being used to write drivers or STREAMS that use KMA resources then `sar -k` will likely prove useful. Otherwise, you will probably not need the information it provides. Any driver or module that uses KMA resources but does not specifically return the resources before it exits can create a memory leak. A memory leak will cause the amount of memory allocated by KMA to increase over time. Thus, if the `alloc` fields of `sar -k` increase steadily over time, then there may be a memory leak. Another indication of a memory leak is failed requests. If this occurs then it is likely that a memory leak has caused KMA to be unable to reserve and allocate memory.

If it appears that a memory leak has occurred, you should check any locally written drivers or STREAMS that may have requested memory from KMA and not returned it. Figure 6-11 shows an example of `sar -k` output.

**Figure 6-11**
*Output from*
***sar -k.***
*There are no obvi-*
*ous memory leaks*
*in this report.*

```
unix sfxbs 4.0 2 3B2    08/22/89

14:28:12 sml_mem    alloc  fail  lg_mem   alloc  fail  ovsz_alloc  fail
14:29:12   95232    73472     0  311296  198656     0      180224     0
14:30:12   95232    75120     0  311296  198656     0      180224     0
14:31:12   95232    73600     0  311296  197632     0      180224     0

Average    95232    74064     0  311296  198314     0      180224     0
```

# ❑ Monitoring Interprocess Communication

The `sar -m` option reports interprocess communication activities. Message and semaphore calls are reported as follows:

msg/s          Number of message operations (sends and receives) per second.

sema/s         Number of semaphore operations per second.

**Figure 6-12**
*Output from*
***sar -m.***
*The reported val-*
*ues will be zero*
*(0.00) unless you*
*are running appli-*
*cations that use*
*messages or sema-*
*phores.*

```
unix sfxbs 4.0 2 3B2     08/22/89

14:28:12   msg/s   sema/s
14:29:12    0.00     0.00
14:30:12    0.00     0.00
14:31:12    0.00     0.00

Average     0.00     0.00
```

# ❏ **Monitoring Page-In Activity**

The `sar -p` option reports paging-in activity, including protection and validity faults.

atch/s          The number of page faults per second that are satisfied by reclaiming a page currently in memory (attaches per second). Instances of this include reclaiming an invalid page from the free list and sharing a page of text currently being used by another process (for example, two or more processes accessing the code for data.)

pgin/s          The number of times per second file systems receive page-in requests. (This encompasses and replaces the old `sar -p` report of `pgfil/s`, which previously reported the number of validity faults per second satisfied by a page-in from the file system.)

ppgin/s         This new field reports the number of pages paged in per second. (A single page-in request, such as a softlock request as described below, or a large block size, may involve paging-in multiple pages.)

pflt/s          The number of page faults from protection errors per second. Instances of protection faults are illegal access to a page and "copy-on-writes." Generally, this number consists primarily of "copy-on-writes." (This field is carried over from the old -p option.)

vflt/s          The number of address translation page faults per second. These are known as validity faults and occur when a valid page is not present in memory. (This field is carried over from the old -p option.)

slock/s         This new field reports the number of faults per second caused by software lock requests requiring physical I/O. An example of the occurrence of a softlock request is the transfer of data from a disk to memory. To ensure that the page which is to receive the data is not claimed and used by another process, it is locked by the system hardware.

**Figure 6-13**
*Output from*
*sar -p.*

```
unix sfxbs 4.0 2 3B2      08/22/89

14:28:12  atch/s  pgin/s ppgin/s  pflt/s  vflt/s slock/s
14:29:12   1.17   12.87   12.87    5.67   11.28    1.15
14:30:12   1.67    7.08    7.08    9.12    6.33    0.67
14:31:12   1.37   12.48   12.48    6.83   10.78    1.03

Average    1.40   10.81   10.81    7.21    9.46    0.95
```

If vflt/s becomes much higher than 15, then sar -g should be looked at to determine if there is a memory shortage or if the s5 inode freelist is page bound. (See sar -g for more details). In addition, sar -u, sar -w, and sar -r can help verify that memory is a bottleneck.

## ❏ Monitoring Scheduling Queue Activity

The sar -q option reports the average queue length while the queue is occupied and the percentage of time that the queue is occupied.

runq-sz
:   The number of processes waiting, in memory, to run. Typically, this should be less than 2. Consistently higher values mean you are CPU-bound.

%runocc
:   The percentage of time the run queue is occupied. The larger this value, the better.

swpq-sz, %swpocc
:   Values for these headings are no longer reported due to the removal of swap queues.

```
unix sfxbs 4.0 2 3B2     08/22/89

14:28:12 runq-sz %runocc swpq-sz %swpocc
14:29:12    1.2      53
14:30:12    1.3      38
14:31:12    1.1      37

Average     1.2      43
```

**Figure 6-14**
*Output from*
*sar -q.*
*This CPU can*
*handle the load.*

If %runocc > 90% and runq-sz > 2, the CPU is heavily loaded and response is degraded. In this case, additional CPU capacity may be required to obtain acceptable system response. If sar -p shows a large number of validity faults and sar -g shows high page-out activity, then more memory may be required.

# ❏ Monitoring Unused Memory Status

The -r option records the number of memory pages and swap file disk blocks that are currently unused.

freemem     Average number of 2K pages of memory available to user processes over the intervals sampled by the command.

freeswap    Number of 512-byte disk blocks available for page swapping.

**Figure 6-15**
*Output from*
*sar -r.*

```
unix sfxbs 4.0 2 3B2      08/22/89

14:28:12 freemem freeswp
14:29:12      268    3034
14:30:12      351    3009
14:31:12      297    3033

Average       306    3025
```

# ❏ Monitoring CPU Utilization

The CPU utilization is listed by sar -u. At any given moment the processor is either busy or idle. When busy, the processor is in either user or system mode. When idle, the processor is either waiting for input/output completion or "sitting still" with no work to do. sar -u lists the percentage of time that the processor is in system mode (%sys), in user mode (%user), waiting for input/output completion (%wio), and idle (%idle).

In typical timesharing use, %sys and %usr are about the same value. In special applications, either of these may be larger than the other without anything being abnormal. A high %wio generally means a disk slowdown has occurred. A high %idle, with degraded response time, may mean memory constraints are present; time spent waiting for memory is attributed to %idle.

If your computer is equipped with a co-processor, the sar -u report contains additional information, including an extra column showing the number of system calls per second being executed on the co-processor. The %wio column is empty for the co-processor because the co-processor does not perform I/O. The sar data in Figure 6-17 was collected on a co-processor system at intervals of 20 seconds.

The -Du option is available for systems on which Remote File Sharing is installed. It lists the total CPU time spent on system calls from remote computers, as shown in Figure 6-18. If the percent of CPU time spent servicing remote system calls is high, your local users may be suffering. On server machines, of course, you would expect %sys remote to be high.

To reduce the amount of time spent servicing requests, you may want to place high demand resources on another computer (see the discussion of fusage in the next chapter for details) or limit access to resources by changing some of the tunable parameters (see Chapter 8, *Configuring UNIX*). You may also want to ensure that clients are doing I/O in an efficient way (see sar -Dc).

```
unix sfxbs 4.0 2 3B2      08/22/89

14:28:12     %usr     %sys     %wio     %idle
14:29:12      22       27       18       32
14:30:12       6       24       13       57
14:31:12       8       28       19       45

Average       12       27       17       45
```

**Figure 6-16**
*Output from*
*sar -u.*

```
sf600 sf600 4.0 3 3B2     08/12/89

10:02:07     %usr     %sys     %wio     %idle
10:02:27      82       18        0        0
10:02:47      39       35       16       10
10:03:07       7       28       16       50
10:03:27       1       16        0       83

Average       32       24        8       36

10:02:07 %co-usr %co-sys          %co-idle scall/s
10:02:27     98       0              2        0
10:02:47     65       0             35        0
10:03:07     11       0             89        1
10:03:27      0       0            100        0

Average       44       0             56        0
```

**Figure 6-17**
*sar -u output*
*on a co-proces-*
*sor system.*

**Figure 6-18**
*Output from*
*sar -Du.*

```
#sar -Du
UNIX System V lucy 4.0 202/14/89
00:00:04  %usr   %sys    %sys    %wio   %idle
                 local   remote
01:00:04    7     21      10      28      44
02:00:04   11      9      10       4      76
03:00:02    8     18      10      17      57
04:00:02    2      4      10       1      93
05:00:03    1      4      10       1      93
06:00:02    2      5      10       2      91
07:00:02    1      4      10       1      94
08:00:02    2      5      10       2      91
08:20:02   26     16      10      11      48
08:40:02   18     11      10       9      62
09:00:17   25     21      10      13      41
09:20:18   23     21      10      11      45
09:40:20   21     24      10      15      39
10:00:09   21     29      10      17      33
10:20:14   29     28      10      13      31
10:40:18   19     20      10       7      54

Average     9     12      10       8      71
#
```

## ❏ Monitoring System Table Status

The -v option reports the status of the process, inode, file, and shared memory record table. From this report you know when the system tables need to be modified.

proc-sz     Number of process table entries currently being used or allocated in the kernel.

inod-sz     Number of inode table entries currently being used or allocated in the kernel.

file-sz     Number of file table entries currently being used in the kernel. The sz is given as 0 since space is allocated dynamically for the file table.

ov                Number of times a table has overflowed (reported for the three tables listed above).

lock-sz           Number of shared memory record table entries currently being used or allocated in the kernel. The sz is given as 0 because space is allocated dynamically for the shared memory record table.

```
unix sfxbs 4.0 2 3B2     08/22/89

14:28:12 proc-sz ov inod-sz ov file-sz ov lock-sz
14:29:12  28/200   0 297/300  0  63/  0  0   6/  0
14:30:12  30/200   0 297/300  0  65/  0  0   6/  0
14:31:12  28/200   0 296/300  0  63/  0  0   6/  0
```

**Figure 6-19**
*Output from*
*sar -v.*
*All tables are large enough to have no over-flows. Consider reducing the sizes of the tables as a way of saving space in main memory.*

## ❑ Monitoring Swapping Activity

The -w option reports swapping and switching activity. The following are some target values and observations.

swpin/s           Number of transfers into memory per second.

bswin/s           Number of 512-byte blocks transferred for swap-ins (including initial loading of some programs) per second.

swpot/s           Number of transfers from memory to the disk swap area per second. If greater than 1, you may need to increase memory or decrease the amount of buffer space.

bswot/s           Number of blocks transferred for swap-outs per second.

pswch/s           Process switches per second. This should be 30 to 50 on a busy 4- to 6-user system.

**Figure 6-20**
*Output from*
***sar -w.***
*Because no swap-*
*ping is occurring,*
*there is sufficient*
*memory for the*
*currently active*
*users.*

```
unix sfxbs 4.0 2 3B2      08/22/89

14:28:12 swpin/s pswin/s swpot/s pswot/s pswch/s
14:29:12   0.00     0.0    0.00     0.0      22
14:30:12   0.00     0.0    0.00     0.0      12
14:31:12   0.00     0.0    0.00     0.0      18


Average    0.00     0.0    0.00     0.0      18
```

# ❑ Monitoring RFS Operations

The -x option reports activity on an RFS file system. The reported operations are:

| | |
|---|---|
| open/s | the number of open operations per second. |
| create/s | the number of create operations per second. |
| lookup/s | the number of lookup operations per second. The number of outgoing lookups can be compared to name/s given by sar -a to see if a large percentage of the lookups are due to remote requests. |
| readdir/s | the number of readdir operations per second. |
| getpage/s | the number of getpage operations per second. These are the page fault operations the server sees from the client. |
| putpage/s | the number of putpage operations per second. A putpage operation flushes pages to file systems on the server. |

other/s          the number of other operations per second. This count
                 does not include the above operations or the close,
                 read, and write operations. sar -Dc reports the read
                 and write system calls.

High outgoing values indicate that your machine is accessing files on server
machines frequently. If they are especially high, you may want to copy files
you are using remotely to your local machine.

High incoming values indicate that your machine is spending a large amount
of its resources servicing clients. If you computer is a server machine, this is to
be expected. However, if your computer is not primarily a server, the local
users could be experiencing degraded response time. sar -S and sar -Du
can verify whether a machine is spending too much of its resources servicing
clients. To reduce the time spent servicing remote requests, you may want to
move resources that are in demand to another computer. See the fusage(1M)
command in the next chapter for more details.

```
# sar -x
UNIX System V ginger 4.0 2 09/13/89
18:03:38     open/s create/s lookup/sreaddir/sgetpage/sputpage/s other/s
18:04:38
      in     0.67    0.20    5.48     0.27     0.05     0.00     18.50
     out     0.32    0.07    3.08     0.10     0.12     0.00      1.13
18:05:38
      in     0.57    0.20    5.72     0.27     0.08     0.00     11.61
     out     0.77    0.27    4.99     0.23     0.00     0.00      4.12
18:05:38
      in     0.23    0.00    1.00     0.34     0.00     0.00      7.23
     out     0.58    0.13    5.56     0.53     0.00     0.00      4.18

Average
      in     0.48    0.13    4.03     0.29     0.04     0.00     12.39
     out     0.56    0.16    4.54     0.29     0.04     0.00      3.14
```

**Figure 6-21**
*Output from*
*sar -x.*

# ❑ Monitoring Terminal Activity

The -y option monitors terminal device activities. If you have a lot of terminal I/O, you can use this report to determine if there are any bad lines. The
activities recorded are defined as follows:

| | |
|---|---|
| rawch/s | input characters (raw queue) per second |
| canch/s | input characters processed by canon (canonical queue) per second |
| outch/s | output characters (output queue) per second |
| rcvin/s | receiver hardware interrupts per second |
| xmtin/s | transmitter hardware interrupts per second |
| mdmin/s | modem interrupts per second |

The number of modem interrupts per second (mdmin/s) should be close to 0, and the receive and transmit interrupts per second (xmtin/s and rcvin/s) should be less than or equal to the number of incoming or outgoing characters, respectively. If this is not the case, check for bad lines.

**Figure 6-22**
*Output from*
*sar -y.*

```
unix sfxbs  4.0 2 3B2      08/22/89

14:28:12 rawch/s canch/s outch/s rcvin/s xmtin/s mdmin/s
14:29:12       0       1     157       1       3       0
14:30:12       0       2      34       2       2       0
14:31:12       0       1      11       1       2       0

Average        0       1      67       1       2       0
```

## ❏ Monitoring Overall System Performance

The -A option provides a view of overall system performance. Use it to get a more global perspective. If data from more than one time slice is shown, the report includes averages.

Figure 6-23 give an example of `sar -A` output. The figure covers three pages: `sar -A` reports information as if all of the other options had been invoked.

```
unix sfxbs 4.0 2 3B2      08/22/89

14:28:12    %usr     %sys     %sys     %wio    %idle
                     local    remote
14:29:12     22       27        0       18      32
14:30:12      6       24        0       13      57

Average      14       26        0       16      44



14:28:12   device   %busy    avque    r+w/s   blks/s   avwait   avserv

14:29:12   hdsk-0      34     10.8       20       39    170.2     17.4

14:30:12   hdsk-0      24     13.6       13       26    236.4     18.8

Average    hdsk-0      29     12.0       16       32    196.6     17.9

14:28:12 runq-sz %runocc swpq-sz %swpocc
14:29:12    1.2      53
14:30:12    1.3      38

Average     1.2      11

14:28:12 bread/s lread/s %rcache bwrit/s lwrit/s %wcache pread/s pwrit/s
14:29:12
   local     0      14     100       6      17      67       0       0
   remote    0       0       0       0       0       0
14:30:12
   local     0      12      99       6      16      65       0       0
   remote    0       0       0       0       0       0

Average
   local     0      13     100       6      17      66       0       0
   remote    0       0       0       0       0       0

14:28:12 swpin/s pswin/s swpot/s pswot/s pswch/s
14:29:12    0.00     0.0    0.00     0.0      22
14:30:12    0.00     0.0    0.00     0.0      12

Average     0.00     0.0    0.00     0.0      17

14:28:12 scall/s sread/s swrit/s  fork/s  exec/s rchar/s wchar/s
14:29:12
   in        0       0       0             0.00       0       0
   out       0       0       0             0.00       0       0
   local    17       2       2      0.28   0.28    2527    1542
14:30:12
   in        0       0       0             0.00       0       0
   out       0       0       0             0.00       0       0
   local    25       2       1      0.50   0.47    1624     295

Average
   in        0       0       0             0.00       0       0
   out       0       0       0             0.00       0       0
   local    21       2       2      0.39   0.38    2075     918
```

(continued on the next page)

```
14:28:12   iget/s  namei/s  dirbk/s
14:29:12        0        2        1
14:30:12        0        4        1

Average         0        3        1

14:28:12   rawch/s  canch/s  outch/s  rcvin/s  xmtin/s  mdmin/s
14:29:12         0        1      157        1        3        0
14:30:12         0        2       34        2        2        0

Average          0        1       95        1        3        0

14:28:12   proc-sz ov inod-sz ov file-sz ov lock-sz
14:29:12   28/200   0 297/300  0  63/  0  0   6/100
14:30:12   30/200   0 297/300  0  65/  0  0   6/100


14:28:12     msg/s   sema/s
14:29:12      0.00     0.00
14:30:12      0.00     0.00

Average       0.00     0.00

14:28:12   atch/s   pgin/s  ppgin/s   pflt/s   vflt/s  slock/s
14:29:12     1.17    12.87    12.87     5.67    11.28     1.15
14:30:12     1.67     7.08     7.08     9.12     6.33     0.67

Average      1.42     9.97     9.97     7.40     8.81     0.91

14:28:12   pgout/s  ppgout/s  pgfree/s  pgscan/s  %s5ipf
14:29:12     0.00      0.00      0.35      8.18    0.00
14:30:12     0.00      0.00      0.00      0.00    0.00

Average      0.00      0.00      0.18      4.09    0.00

14:28:12   freemem  freeswp
14:29:12       268     3034
14:30:12       351     3009

Average        310     3022

14:28:12   sml_mem     alloc  fail   lg_mem    alloc  fail  ovsz_alloc  fail
14:29:12     95232     73472     0   311296   198656     0      180224     0
14:30:12     95232     75120     0   311296   198656     0      180224     0

Average      95232     74296     0   311296   198656     0      180224     0
```

(continued on the next page)

```
14:28:12 open/s create/s lookup/s readdir/s getpage/s putpage/s other/s
14:29:12
  in      0.00     0.00     0.00      0.00      0.00      0.00    0.08
  out     0.00     0.00     0.00      0.00      0.00      0.00    0.00
14:30:12
  in      0.00     0.00     0.00      0.00      0.00      0.00    0.08
  out     0.00     0.00     0.00      0.00      0.00      0.00    0.00

Average
  in      0.00     0.00     0.00      0.00      0.00      0.00    0.08
  out     0.00     0.00     0.00      0.00      0.00      0.00    0.00

14:28:12   snd-inv/s   snd-msg/s   rcv-inv/s   rcv-msg/s dis-bread/s   blk-
inv/s
14:29:12      0.0         0.0         0.0         0.0         0.0         0.0
14:30:12      0.0         0.0         0.0         0.0         0.0         0.0

Average       0.0         0.0         0.0         0.0         0.0         0.0

14:28:12 serv/lo - hi   request    request    server    server
              3 -  6     %busy     avg lgth    %avail   avg avail
14:29:12        0         0.0          0        0.0          0
14:30:12        0         0.0          0        0.0          0

Average         0         0.0          0        0.0          0

14:28:12 evpoll/s evpost/s evtrap/s
14:29:12    0.00     0.00     0.00
14:30:12    0.00     0.00     0.00

Average     0.00     0.00     0.00
```

# ❑ Monitoring RFS Client Caching

The client caching feature of RFS improves RFS performance by reducing the
number of times data is retrieved across the network. With client caching, the
first read of data will bring the data into local buffers. Once the data is in the
local buffer, it will remain there so that subsequent reads can get the data
locally.

Client caching is enabled in the default system configuration, using the RCHACHETIME parameter, described in Chapter 8, *Configuring UNIX*. It can be disabled for a specific remote resource using the mount(1M) command. You will almost always want to take advantage of the improved performance of client caching. There are only two very rare occasions when you may want to turn it off:

▲   If the buffer space is limited on your system, you may choose to turn of client caching for some resources or for the entire system.

▲   If you are using programs that do their own private network buffering, you may not want to use client caching.

Information on the overhead related to maintaining cache consistency is listed with sar -C. Figure 6-24 shows some sample output. The fields in the report are:

snd-inv/s       *the number of invalidation messages sent by the server per second*. These messages inform client machines about changes to server files.

snd-msg/s       the total number of outgoing RFS messages sent per second.

rcv-inv/s       *the number of invalidation messages received per second.* Each message informs the client that the contents of one or more of its cache buffers may have been modified by a write on the server. The client machine reacts by invalidating data in the affected buffers.

rcv-msg/s       the total number of incoming RFS messaged received per second.

dis-bread/s     *the number of buffer reads per second while caching is disabled.* When an invalidation message is received, caching is turned off until the writing process closes or until a time interval has elapsed (see the RCACHETIME parameter in Chapter 8). This counter tracks the number of buffer reads that normally would be eligible for caching in a resource with caching turned on, but that are not cached because it is temporarily turned off. It indicates the penalty of running uncached and provides a basis for tuning the RCACHETIME parameter.

blk-inv/s    The number of buffers removed from the client cache on receiving an invalidation message while a remote file is open or re-opening a remote file that has been modified since the last close on the client.

**Figure 6-24**
*Output from*
*sar -C.*

```
# sar -C
UNIX System V charlie 4.0 2 09/03/89
14:36:56  snd-inv/s snd-msg/s rcv-inv/s rcv-msg/s dis-bread/s blk-inv/s
14:36:59      0.0       1.1       0.0       1.5        0.0        0.2
14:37:02      0.0       0.6       0.0       0.5        0.0        0.4
14:37:05      0.3       0.6       0.0       0.5        0.0        0.1

Average       0.1       0.9       0.0       0.8        0.0        0.2
```

## ❑ Monitoring RFS Server Activity

Every request from a remote computer to access your resources is handled by a server process. When there are too many requests for the servers to handle, the requests are queued. Requests leave the queue when servers are available. Information on server availability and the request queue are listed sar -S. A sample of the output is shown in Figure 6-26.

As a system administrator, you can control the number of server processes with two tunable parameters, MINSERVE and MAXSERVE. MINSERVE is the number of servers that are initially available to service remote requests. Servers are created dynamically as needed up to a total of MAXSERVE processes.

Information from sar -S can be used to establish sensible values for MINSERVE and MAXSERVE. If the receive queue is almost always busy (a consistently high value in the request %busy column), consider increasing the number of servers:

▲ Increase MAXSERVE if the average value in the serv column is high.

▲ Increase MINSERVE if the average value for the serv column is low.

Alternatively, if servers are almost always available (a high value in the server %avail column), consider reducing the number of servers:

▲ Decrease MAXSERVE if the average value in the server avg avail column is near MAXSERVE.

▲ Decrease MINSERVE if the average value for the serv column is near MINSERVE.

```
# sar -S
UNIX System V lucy 4.0 2 02/14/89
00:00:04 serv/lo-hi  request   request   server      server
             3-6      %busy    avg lgth  %avail   avg avail
01:00:04       3        0         0        100         3
02:00:04       3        0         0        100         3
03:00:04       4       80         8         20         2
04:00:04       6      100        24          0         0

Average        4       45         8         55         2
#
```

**Figure 6-25**
*Output from*
*sar -S.*

## ❏ Displaying System Activity Data

sag graphically displays the system activity data stored in a binary data file created by a sar run. Any sar data items may be plotted separately. sag invokes sar and matches strings in the data column header. Figure 6-26 shows a typical sag display. Run sar to see what data is available.

**Figure 6-26**
*Example of* sag
*Output.*
*The processor is*
*completely uti-*
*lized over three*
*time intervals:*
*9-10 A.M., 1-2*
*P.M., and 3:30-*
*5:30 P.M.*

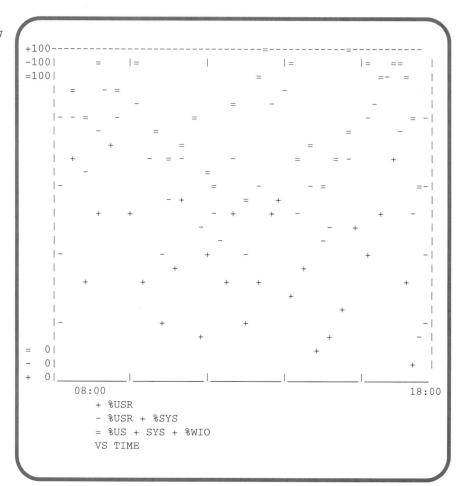

In Figure 6-26, the processor is completely utilized over three time intervals: 9-10 A.M., 1-2 P.M., and 3:30-5:30 P.M. Remember the actual fraction of time that the processor is busy is the sum of user (%usr) mode time and system (%sys) mode time. When this sum approaches 100 percent, the processor is running at its maximum capacity as configured. The sum of %usr + %sys + %wio is about the same as the sum of %usr + %sys (%wio is low). This means that the disk subsystem is able to handle requests from the processor with little delay. In this example, the best way to minimize the slowdown is to reduce the processor load.

The sag command is useful only if you have a standard output device that can read plotting instructions. Refer to your computer documentation to see if your console terminal has this ability.

## ❏ Summary: Using System Monitoring To Detect And Correct Performance Problems.

The table in Figure 6-27 lists some performance problems (and a few solutions) that can be detected by examining the system activity reports produced by sar. If you think one of the problems may apply to your system, use the indicated sar option to produce a report, and then examine the report for the symptom listed in the table.

**Figure 6-27**
*Using sar reports to detect performance problems.*

| Problem: Solution | sar Option | Symptom |
|---|---|---|
| **not enough buffer space:** increase BUFHWM and/or NBUF. See the *"Buffer Cache"* section in Chapter 8. | -b -Db | %rcache<90 or %wcache<65 |
| **inefficient PATH variables:** find and fix them, as described in the *"Processes, Schedules, and Work-loads"* section of Chapter 1 | -c | (exec/s)/(fork/s)>3 |
| **not enough s5 inodes:** increase NINODES. See the *"s5 File System Type"* section in Chapter 8. | -g -p | %s5ipf>10 vfet/s >>15 |
| **not enough memory:** consider buying more | -g -p -u | pgscan>5 or pgfree>5 vfet/s >>15 %idle high |
| **memory leak in a home-grown driver:** fix the bug | -k | alloc values increasing over time or fail>0 |
| **CPU bound:** consider buying another computer or lightening the load on this one | -q | runq-sz>2 and %runocc>90 |
| **disk slowdown:** use fsck(1) to check for file consistency and correct any problems. Use sadp to evaluate your disk layout and correct it as necessary. See *"Reporting Disk Access Location and Seek Distance"* in Chapter 7. | -u | %wio high |
| **system tables too small:** increase NPROC (see *"General Kernel Tunables"* in Chapter 8) and/or NINODES (see *"s5 File System Type"* in Chapter 8) | -v | proc-sz overflows inode-sz overflows |
| **system tables too large:** consider decreasing NPROC (see *"General Kernel Tunables"* in Chapter 8) and/or NINODES (see *"s5 File System Type"* in Chapter 8) to make the system smaller | -v | proc-sz mostly unused inode-sz mostly unused |
| **thrashing:** decrease buffer size or increase memory | -w | swpot/s>1 |

| **Problem**: Solution | `sar` Option | Symptom |
|---|---|---|
| **bad terminal lines**: fix them | `-y` | `mdmin` close to 0<br>`xmtin/srawch/s`<br>`rcvin/souch/s` |
| **heavy use of RFS shared resources on other machines**: consider moving the resources to your machine | `-x` | high outgoing values |
| **heavy use of RFS shared resources by remote users**: consider moving resources to other servers | `-Du`<br>`-x` | `%sys remote` high<br>high incoming values |
| **too many RFS server processes**: decrease `MAXSERVE`. See "*RFS Parameters*" in Chapter 8. | `-S` | `server %avail` is high and value of `server avg avail` is near `MAXSERVE` |
| **not enough RFS server processes**: increase `MAXSERVE`. See "*RFS Parameters*" in Chapter 8. | `-S` | `request %busy` is high and average value of `serv` is high |
| **too many RFS server processes**: decrease `MINSERVE`. See "*RFS Parameters*" in Chapter 8. | `-S` | `server %avail` is high and value of `serv` is near `MINSERVE` |
| **not enough RFS server processes**: increase `MINSERVE`. See "*RFS Parameters*" in Chapter 8. | `-S` | `request %busy` is high and average value of `serv` is low |

*Figure 6-27
Continued*

# 7

# *Performance Tools*

## ❑ Overview

This chapter discusses the SPAU tools not covered in the preceding chapter and a few other system tools that you can use to identify system problems. We describe tools for:

▲ timing the execution of commands: `timex`

▲ monitoring resource usage by remote users: `fusage`

▲ profiling the kernel: `prfdc`, `prfld`, `prfpr`, `prfsnap`, and `prfstat`

▲ measuring disk activity: `sadp`

▲ taking memory dumps: `errdump` and `sysdump`

# ❏ Timing Application Program Execution

The timex command records the amount of time taken by a command to execute, and reports the system activities that occurred during the time the command was executing. If no other programs are running, then timex can give you a good idea of which resources a specific command uses during its execution. A record of system consumption can be collected for each application program and then used for tuning the heavily loaded resources. In the following example, the date command is used.

**Figure 7-1**
*A timex example.*
*While date, for its simplicity, is used in this example, the timex statistics it produces are not representative: most commands use more system resources.*

```
$ timex -s date
Tue Aug 22 15:07:09 EDT 1989
real        0.17
user        0.00
sys         0.13


unix sfxbs 4.0 2 3B2      08/22/89

15:07:09     %usr      %sys      %sys     %wio     %idle
                       local    remote
15:07:09        8        90         0        2         0


15:07:09 bread/s lread/s %rcache bwrit/s lwrit/s %wcache pread/s pwrit/s
15:07:09
   local      0       4      100       1       1       0       0       0
   remote     0       0        0       0       0       0

15:07:09   device   %busy    avque    r+w/s   blks/s  avwait  avserv

15:07:09   hdsk-0       2      1.0        1        2     0.0    20.0

15:07:09 rawch/s canch/s outch/s rcvin/s xmtin/s mdmin/s
15:07:09       0       0      31       0       1       0

15:07:09 scall/s sread/s swrit/s  fork/s   exec/s rchar/s wchar/s
15:07:09
   in         0       0       0             0.00       0       0
   out        0       0       0             0.00       0       0
   local    157      23       2      3.23     3.23   67918     775

15:07:09 swpin/s pswin/s swpot/s pswot/s pswch/s
15:07:09    0.00     0.0    0.00     0.0      14

15:07:09  iget/s namei/s dirbk/s
15:07:09       0      23       0
```

(continued on the next page)

```
15:07:09 runq-sz %runocc swpq-sz %swpocc
15:07:09    1.0     100

15:07:09 proc-sz ov inod-sz ov file-sz ov lock-sz
15:07:09 28/200  0 300/300  0  61/  0  0   6/100

15:07:09   msg/s  sema/s
15:07:09   0.00    0.00

15:07:09 atch/s pgin/s ppgin/s  pflt/s  vflt/s slock/s
15:07:09 49.46   0.00   0.00   24.73   44.09    2.15

15:07:09  pgout/s ppgout/s pgfree/s pgscan/s %s5ipf
15:07:09    0.00     0.00     0.00     0.00   0.00

15:07:09 sml_mem   alloc  fail  lg_mem   alloc  fail  ovsz_alloc  fail
15:07:09  95232   73344     0  311296  200704     0      180224     0


15:07:09 freemem freeswp
15:07:09    428    3044

15:07:09 open/s create/s lookup/s readdir/s getpage/s putpage/s other/s
15:07:09
  in      0.00    0.00    0.00     0.00     0.00     0.00    0.00
  out     0.00    0.00    0.00     0.00     0.00     0.00    0.00

15:07:09   snd-inv/s   snd-msg/s   rcv-inv/s   rcv-msg/s dis-bread/s  blk-
inv/s
15:07:09       0.0         0.0         0.0        0.0        0.0        0.0

15:07:09 serv/lo - hi   request   request   server    server
            3 -  6    %busy    avg lgth  %avail  avg avail
15:07:09       0        0.0        0       0.0        0
```

timex can be used as follows:

timex [ -p [ -fkjmrt ]] [ -o ] [ -s ] *command*

The given *command* executes normally; the elapsed time, user, time, and system time spent in execution are reported in seconds. This can be extremely interesting; you get a precise record of the system resources used while your program was executing.

The -s option reports total system activity (not just that due to *command*) that occurred during the execution interval. All the data items listed in a sar -A report are given (see the previous chapter for more on sar -A).

If process accounting is installed and running (see Chapter 2), then `timex` can present the accounting information as well. The following options can be used with the existence of accounting:

-p List process accounting records for command and all of its children. The following secondary options govern what is reported:

  -f Print the `fork/exec` flag and system exit status columns

  -h Instead of mean memory size, show the fraction of total available CPU time consumed by the process during its execution. This "hog factor" is computes as (total CPU time)/(elapsed time).

  -k Instead of memory size, show total kcore-minutes.

  -m Show mean core size (the default).

  -r Show CPU factor (user time/(system-time + user-time)).

  -t Show separate system and user CPU times. The number of blocks read or written and the number of characters transferred are always reported.

-o Report the total number of blocks read or written and total characters transferred by *command* and all of its children.

Process records associated with *command* are selected from the accounting file `/var/adm/pacct` by inference: background processes with the same user ID, terminal ID, and execution interval will be spuriously included. (It should be real easy for you to avoid this situation: don't run anything in the background while you are generating `timex` statistics in the foreground!)

# ❑ Monitoring Resource Usage by Remote Clients

You can find out how extensively remote computers are using your resources with the fusage(1M) command. It reports how many kilobytes were read and written from your resources by each remote computer that mounted the resource. The counts ar cumulative since the time of the mount. The form of the fusage command for reporting resource usage is:

    fusage *advertizedResource*

where *advertizedResource* is the resource you have shared. Calling fusage with no arguments produces a full report of data usage for all disks and shared directories on your system, as shown in Figure 7-5.

The report includes one section for each file system and advertized resource and has one entry for each machine that has the resource mounted, ordered by decreasing usage. Sections are ordered by device name; advertized resources that are not complete files systems immediately follow the sections for the file systems they are in.

If a remote computer's requests for your resources are high, it may be causing performance problems on your computer. With the output from fusage, you can see which resources are being heavily utilized. Consider moving them to the computers that access them the most.

**Figure 7-2**
*Output from*
***fusage.***
*The report
includes one sec-
tion for each file
system and
advertized
resource and has
one entry for each
machine that has
the resource
mounted, ordered
by decreasing
usage. Sections
are ordered by
device name;
advertized
resources that are
not complete files
systems immedi-
ately follow the
sections for the
file systems they
are in.*

```
# fusage
FILE USAGE REPORT FOR charlie
          /dev/root     /dev/root
                        /
                            charlie     292 KB

              /proc     /proc
                        /proc
                            charlie       0 KB

           /dev/fd      /dev/fd
                        /dev/fd
                            charlie       0 KB
     /dev/dsk/cld0s3    /dev/dsk/cld0s3
                        /stand
                            charlie    1039 KB

     /dev/dsk/cld0s8    /dev/dsk/cld0s8
                        /var
                            charlie       0 KB

     /dev/dsk/cld0s2    /dev/dsk/cld0s2
          CHUCKUSER     /usr
                        peanuts.linus    649 KB
                        peanuts.lucy      51 KB
                            Sub Total    700 KB
                        /usr
                            charlie     988 KB

     /dev/dsk/cld0s9    /dev/dsk/cld0s9
                        /home
                            charlie       0 KB
#
```

## ❑ Kernel Profiling

Kernel profiling is a mechanism that allows you to determine where the operating system is spending its time during operation. It consists of commands
that control the profiling process and generate reports (see `profiler`(1M) for
a description of these commands). The system profiler samples the program
counter on every clock interrupt and increments the counter corresponding to
the function shown by that value of the program counter.

The system profiler initializes the sampling mechanism, then generates a table containing the starting address of each subroutine in the UNIX kernel. To operate the system profiler, you must follow the following procedure:

**Step 1**   Use the `prfld` command to initialize or load the profiler.

**Step 2**   Use the `prfstat` command to turn on the sampling mechanism.

**Step 3**   Use the `prfdc` or `prfsnap` command to collect and enter the data into a file.

**Step 4**   Use the `prfpr` command to print the contents of the data, collected by either `prfdc` or `prfsnap`.

**Step 5**   Use the `prfstat` command to turn off the sampling mechanism.

The system profiler must be loaded and turned on after every boot. If you want the profiler to begin automatically when you boot the system to multi-user mode, you can add the following lines to the `/sbin/init.d/perf` file:

```
/usr/sbin/prfld
/usr/sbin/prfstat on
```

The `prf` shell script will be executed during system initialization and the following messages will be displayed:

```
profiling enabled

xxx kernel text addresses
```

where *xxx* states how many kernel text addresses are in the current UNIX system kernel.

The following sections describe kernel profiling commands in detail.

## Loading the System Profiler

The `prfld` command initializes, or loads, the system profiler mechanism. The command has the following format:

```
/usr/sbin/prfld [namelist]
```

This command generates a table, in memory, containing the starting address of each subroutine as extracted from *namelist*. The default of *namelist* is /stand/unix. If *namelist* is not indicated, the starting address of each subroutine is recorded. If the number of kernel text addresses is greater than PRFMAX defined in /etc/master.d/prf, then PRFMAX should be increased and the system rebuilt.

## Enabling/Disabling the Sampling Mechanism

The prfstat command enables or disables the sampling mechanism of the system profiler initialized by prfld. The prfstat command has the following format:

```
/usr/sbin/prfstat [on | off]
```

Profiler overhead is less than 3 percent as calculated for 2000 text addresses. If neither of the optional parameters is entered, the status of the profiler is displayed. If the on parameter is supplied, the sampling mechanism is turned on. The opposite happens if off is indicated.

## Collecting Profiling Data

The prfdc command performs the data collection function of the profiler by copying the current value of all the text address counters to a file where the data can be analyzed. The prfdc command has the following format:

```
/usr/sbin/prfdc file [period [off_hour]]
```

This command stores the contents of the counters in a *file* every *period* minutes and turns off at *off_hour*. Valid values for *off_hour* are 0 through 24.

For example, the following copies the current value of all the text address counters into a file called temp every five minutes and turns off at 4:00 P.M.:

```
/usr/sbin/prfdc temp 5 16
```

The prfsnap command also performs data collection, but takes a snapshot of the system at the time it is called. The format of this command is as follows:

```
/usr/sbin/prfsnap [file]
```

where the command appends the counter values to *file*.

## Formatting the Collected Data

The `prfpr` command formats the contents of *file* (data that was collected by `prfdc` or `prfsnap`). The `prfpr` command has the following format:

```
/usr/sbin/prfpr file [cutoff [namelist]]
```

Each text address is converted to a system function name and the percentage of time used by that function is printed if the activity percentage is greater than the *cutoff* number that you specify. The range of *cutoff* is 0 percent to 99 percent where 0 prints all contents. The default *cutoff* is 1 percent. The default *namelist* is /stand/unix.

```
# /usr/sbin/prfpr temp 0

07/20/89 18:02
07/20/89 18:03

_waitloc 91.0
fsflush 0.3
bdwrite 0.1
brelse 0.1
getblk 0.1
dma_access 0.1
wakeprocs 0.2
systrap 0.1
mon_enter 0.1
ts_setdq 0.1
iupdat 0.3
idstrategy 0.2
idsetup 0.4
idint 0.2
idldcmd 0.1
user      0.7
```

**Figure 7-3**
*Output from*
**prfpr.**
*These are the function calls in the kernel. For detailed information on function calls, refer to your computer installation manual, source code, or experienced user.*

# ❑ Reporting Disk Access Location and Seek Distance

The `sadp` command has the following format:

    sadp  [-th]  [-d device[-drive]]  s  [n]

`sadp` reports disk access locations and seek distance in tabular (`-t`) or histogram (`-h`) form. If neither option is designated, the two reports will be in tabular form.

Valid names for *device* are `hdsk` for non-SCSI integral disks, `sdsk` for SCSI integral disks, and `fdsk` for an integral floppy disk.

*drive* specifies the disk drives and it may be a single drive number, two numbers separated by a dash to show an inclusive range, or a list of drive numbers separated by commas.

Disk activity is sampled once every second during a specified interval of length $n$. Cylinder usage and seek distance are recorded in units of 20 cylinders. The `s` option specifies the duration of the sampling interval in seconds. The sampling interval must be 10 seconds or greater. The $n$ argument specifies the number of reports to be generated during the sampling interval. The default of $n$ is 1.

An example of `sadp` output for hard disk drive 0 follows.

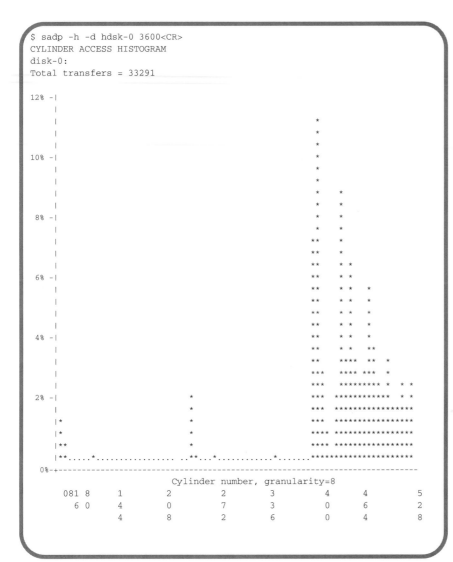

```
$ sadp -h -d hdsk-0 3600<CR>
CYLINDER ACCESS HISTOGRAM
disk-0:
Total transfers = 33291

12% -|
      |
      |
      |                                              *
      |                                              *
10% -|                                               *
      |                                              *
      |                                              *
      |                                              *
      |                                              *   *
      |                                              *   *
 8% -|                                               *   *
      |                                              *   *
      |                                             **   *
      |                                             **   *
      |                                             **   * *
 6% -|                                              **   * *
      |                                             **   * *   *
      |                                             **   * *   *
      |                                             **   * *   *
      |                                             **   * *   *
 4% -|                                              **   * *   *
      |                                             **   * *  **
      |                                             **   **** **  *
      |                                             ***  **** *** *
      |                                             *** ********* *   * *
 2% -|                      *                       *** ************  * *
      |                     *                       *** *****************
      |*                    *                       *** *****************
      |*                    *                       **** *****************
      |**                   *                       **** *****************
      |**.....*.................. ..**...*...........*.......*****************
 0%-+-------------------------------------------------------------------------
                   Cylinder number, granularity=8
        081 8      1       2       2       3       4       4       5
          6 0      4       0       7       3       0       6       2
            4      8       2       6       0       4       8
```

**Figure 7-4**
*Output from* **sadp**: *A Cylinder Access Histogram*
This graph shows proper block partitioning. Blocks can be referenced by the disk head (for reading or writing) within a small region of the disk. Most references (as shown by the percentage of times referenced) point to files near cylinders 450 to 600; a few references point to files around cylinder 250. There are a few references to other files on the disk, but they appear only a small percentage of the time. The most-often used files are grouped together in the same general region of cylinders on the disk; the more clustered the stars on the histogram, the better. The disk has an excellent file system configuration.

**Figure 7-5**
*Output from*
***sadp:*** *A Seek*
*Distance Histo-*
*gram*
*This graph shows*
*another aspect of*
*an excellent file*
*system configur-*
*ation: the head*
*seek distance, or*
*the distance the*
*disk head has to*
*move from the*
*current cylinder*
*to the cylinder of*
*the next block ref-*
*erenced. Most*
*physical seeks*
*were under ten*
*cylinders. Specifi-*
*cally, some 14 per-*
*cent of the seeks*
*occurred within a*
*distance of 0 to 8*
*cylinders, and*
*some 17 percent of*
*the seeks occurred*
*within a distance*
*of 8 to 16 cylin-*
*ders. Approxi-*
*mately one-third*
*of the disk activ-*
*ity, the disk head*
*was forced to*
*move no more*
*than 16 cylinders*
*to reference a*
*given block; the*
*further left the*
*stars are grouped,*
*the better.*

```
SEEK DISTANCE HISTOGRAM
disk-0:
Total seeks = 30308
       |
 20% -|
       |
       |
       |
       |
       |
       | *
       | *
 16% -| *
       | *
       | *
       | *
       |**
       |**
       |**
       |**
 12% -|**
       |**
       |**
       |**
       |**
       |**
       |**
       |**
  8% -|**
       |**
       |**
       |**
       |***
       |***
       |***    *
       |**** **
  4% -|*********
       |*********
       |*********
       |************
       |**************
       |******************
       |***********************
       |*************************...*.................................*..............
  0% -+-------------------------------------------------------------------------------
        =<< <        <     <     <     <     <     <     <
        081 8        1     2     2     3     4     4     5
          6 0        4     0     7     3     0     6     2
                     4     8     2     6     0     4     8
```

Using the `sadp` output, along with the output of `/sbin/mount`, or `/usr/sbin/prtvtoc`, and a table of disk sections, you can identify the file systems with a large amount of I/O activity. In general, try to move files with high activity close together. This will reduce the number of seeks over large distances.

The first graph (Figure 7-4) shows proper block partitioning. This partitioning allows the block to be referenced by the disk head (for reading or writing), within a small region of the disk. In the example, most references (as shown by the percentage of times referenced) point to files near cylinders 450 to 600; a few references point to files around cylinder 250. There are a few references to other files on the disk, but they appear only a small percentage of the time. This graph shows, then, that the most-often used files are grouped together in the same general region of cylinders on the disk; the more clustered the stars on the histogram, the better. Another way to say this is that the disk has an excellent file system configuration.

The second graph (Figure 7-5) shows another aspect of an excellent file system configuration:   the head seek distance. This refers to the distance the disk head has to move from the current cylinder to the cylinder of the next block referenced. In the example, most physical seeks were under ten cylinders. Specifically, some 14 percent of the seeks occurred within a distance of 0 to 8 cylinders, and some 17 percent of the seeks occurred within a distance of 8 to 16 cylinders. This means that for approximately one-third of the disk activity, the disk head was forced to move no more than 16 cylinders to reference a given block, and the further left the stars are grouped, the better.

These two graphs show how finely you can tune your system. If, after a working period of weeks or months, you can identify which file systems are consistently the most active, you might consider repartitioning your disks to achieve the maximum from disk access activity (see Chapter 4, *Storage Devices*, and Chapter 3, *File Systems*, for more information).

# ❑ Recovering from System Trouble

This section provides instructions for handling hardware problems and software errors and describes how to return the system to a usable state.

A system experiencing trouble may be in any of the following conditions:

▲ The system is running, but throughput is degraded.

▲ The system is running after an automatic reboot.

▲ The system is halted or in an unknown state.

◆ *Note*     You must log in as `root` at the console terminal before proceeding.

## Identifying System Trouble

Consult the information about troubleshooting in your computer installation manual for problems that occurred during the first-time setup of your computer. If you need additional information, call your service representative.

If the operating system is running, use the `/usr/sbin/errdump` command to display the error history file, which includes the contents of various system registers and the last five error messages received. Enter

```
errdump
```

If possible, send the output of this command to a printer, as follows:

```
errdump | pr | lp
```

## Example of `errdump`

Use the `errdump` command when there is system trouble but the operating system is still running. The command lines and system responses shown in Figure 7-6 give an example of `errdump`.

```
# errdump
nvram status:    sane

csr:    0x0258   (unassigned) (clock) (pir9) (uart)

psw:    rsvd CSH_F_D QIE CSH_D OE NZVC TE IPL CM PM R I ISC TM FT
(hex)    0       0    0    0    0    0   0  f   0  0 1 0  5  0  3

r3:     0xffffffff
r4:     0x400d554c
r5:     0x866f6300
r6:     0xc002001e
r7:     0x0021413f
r8:     0x866f62cc
oap:    0x400806e0
opc:    0x40010d3f
osp:    0x40080708
ofp:    0x40080708
isp:    0x40080004
pcbp:   0x40041a9c

fltar:  0x866f62cc

fltcr:  reqacc   xlevel   ftype
        0xb      0x0      0x3

        srama              sramb
[0]     0x02083000         0x0000011f
[1]     0x02083900         0x00000030
[2]     0x0209b860         0x00000074
[3]     0x0209bc00         0x00000015

        Panic log

[0]     Thu Oct 20 07:37:11 1988
        KERNEL MMU FAULT (F_STDLEN)

[1]     Sun Oct 23 15:43:59 1988
        SYSTEM BUS TIME OUT INTERRUPT

[2]     Wed Nov  2 15:47:50 1988
        KERNEL BUS TIMEOUT

[3]     Sat Dec 31 18:59:59 1988
        D,LxTV

[4]     (0xffffffff,0xffffffff,0xffffffff,0xffffffff)

#
```

**Figure 7-6**
*Using err-dump.*

# ❏ Performing a System Dump

You should perform a system dump when a SYSTEM FAILURE message appears on the screen of the console terminal. To perform a system dump from firmware state (system state 5), complete the following procedure:

**Step 1**   If the operating system crashes, it automatically enters firmware state (system state 5). After the SYSTEM FAILURE message appears, you will see the following prompt:

  FIRMWARE MODE

Enter the firmware password (the default password is mcp).

**Step 2**   When you see the prompt

    Enter name of program to execute [unix]:

enter sysdump. This program dumps the system core image to diskettes. Because it runs in system state 5, it does not depend on the integrity of the root file system.

**Step 3**   Gather the appropriate number of formatted diskettes for the dump. Use this rule of thumb: you need one diskette for each 0.75 megabytes of memory in your configuration.

| with... | use... |
|---------|--------|
| 1 MB | 2 diskettes |
| 2 MB | 3 diskettes |
| 3 MB | 4 diskettes |
| 4 MB | 6 diskettes |

Allow about 4.5 minutes per diskette.

**Step 4**   Follow the instructions displayed on the screen, which prompt you to insert diskettes into the diskette drive.

**Step 5**   When the dump is finished, the program exits and gives you the option of executing another program.

    Enter name of program to execute [unix]:

◆*Note*  You may run diagnostics after you do the dump. Before
you can run diagnostics from the hard disk, however, the
root file system must be undamaged.

**Step 6**  To return to multi-user state (system state 2) execute the boot program. When you see the prompt

```
Enter name of program to execute [unix]:
```

enter

```
/stand/unix
```

In general, once you have performed the system dump, be sure to
boot your system by running the /stand/unix program. If you boot
your system by running the /stand/system program, the resulting
/stand/unix that is generated may not match the previous version.

**Step 7**  It is good practice to make a copy of the current version of
/stand/unix (the version that was current at the time of the system
crash) on an additional diskette. Making this copy of /stand/unix
allows the dump to be analyzed properly by /usr/sbin/crash. To
make a copy of /stand/unix, use the  cpio command.

You may want to contact your service representative for help in ana-
lyzing a system dump.

## Example of sysdump

If there is system trouble and the operating system is not running, run the
sysdump command. The command line entries and system responses in Figure 7-7 show how to run sysdump.

**Figure 7-7**
*Using sysdump.*
*Things you*
*should type are*
*shown in bold.*

```
SYSTEM FAILURE
<mcp>

Enter name of program to execute [ ]: sysdump

Do you want to dump the system image to the floppy diskette?
Enter 'c' to continue, 'q' to quit: c

Insert first sysdump floppy.
Enter 'c' to continue, 'q' to quit: c

Dumping main store
...........................................................
...........................................................
.................

If you wish to dump more of main store,
insert new floppy.

Enter 'c' to continue, 'q' to quit: c

Dumping more main store
...........................................................
...........................................................
.................

If you wish to dump more of main store,
insert new floppy.

Enter 'c' to continue, 'q' to quit: c

Dumping more main store
...........................................................
..........................................................
Dump completed.
three floppies written

Returning to firmware

SELF-CHECK

FIRMWARE MODE

Enter name of program to execute [  ]: /stand/unix
```

# 8

---

# *Configuring UNIX*

## ❏ Overview

During the boot procedure, the boot program reads from disk a program called unix, loads it into memory, and executes it. This file, unix (often referred to as the bootable operating system), defines the running UNIX system on your machine.

The absolute path name of this file is /stand/unix.

◆ *Note*    /unix is symbolically linked to /stand/unix for compatibility with earlier releases.

For simplicity, we will refer to this file as the bootable operating system, or unix.

The unix that runs on your machine is specifically configured for the hardware and software currently on your machine.

All software changes that need to be incorporated into the bootable operating system are specified in the `/stand/system` file, or in one of the `/etc/master.d` files. For simplicity, we refer to `/stand/system` as the `system` file, and to files found in `/etc/master.d` as `master` files.

There are two reasons that the bootable operating system would need to be reconfigured:

▲ software changes were made to the system that need to be incorporated into the bootable operating system

▲ hardware resources were added to or removed from the system

The software changes that could be made to a system include the following:

▲ changing the definition of a driver in the `/etc/master.d` directory

▲ changing tunable parameters found in a `master` file

▲ adding or deleting a driver or module definition in a `master` file

▲ making changes to the `system` file

▲ adding or removing driver modules from `/boot`

While the `system` file is read directly by the configuration software, changes to `master` files require execution of the `mkboot`(1M) command before the configuration process is begun. First, you must change the appropriate file(s) in the directory `/etc/master.d`, and then execute a separate `mkboot` command for each changed `master` file. The `mkboot` command will read the `master` file and create a new object file in the `/boot` directory.

The `/boot` directory contains object files for use in the configuration process; these object files contain configuration information necessary for various hardware and software drivers on your system. The `system` file is used to specify which of the object files in `/boot` must be configured into `unix`, and which are to be excluded.

Some modules in `/boot` are included in the bootable operating system even if they are not explicitly included in the `system` file. If you want to explicitly exclude a driver in `/boot`, it is best to do so with an `EXCLUDE` statement in `/stand/system` (see `system`(4)). Do not move the driver to a new file name in `/boot` or some other directory to exclude it from the bootable operating system.

Hardware changes always require the configuration of a new `unix`. These changes include adding or removing a board, a tape drive, and so on.

One topic we have not considered is the installation of a new software package. Usually, the installation procedure for installing a new software package that requires a modification of the bootable operating system includes some modification of the `system` file and drivers in `/boot`; this is usually done directly by the installation software provided with the software package. The system is then rebooted at the end of the installation process, and a new bootable operating system is built, loaded, and executed.

Standard procedures for installing new hardware are given in the documentation that accompanied your computer.

## ❑ Configuration Scenarios

The configuration of a new `unix` can occur in one of five ways:

▲ on powerup, the system detects that the `system` file is newer than the `unix` file

▲ a `shutdown -i6` or `init 6` is executed at the shell prompt and the `system` file is newer than `unix`

▲ the name of the `system` file (or another text file) is entered at the firmware prompt

▲ the `cunix` command is executed at the shell prompt

▲ a hardware change is made that makes the current `unix` inoperable

Of all the above methods, using the `cunix` command provides the most flexibility, and has the added advantages of allowing you to build a new bootable operating system without rebooting the machine, and without overwriting the currently running bootable operating system. The `cunix` command is particularly useful in development environments where the possibility exists of creating a bootable operating system that will not execute properly, or not at all, because of bad changes made to the `system` file, a bad change made to a `master` file, or symbol-referencing problems.

The remaining sections in this chapter describe configuring a new operating system through a reboot, recovering from an attempt to boot an unbootable operating system, and the use of cunix. A procedure for configuring a new mUNIX (a version of the UNIX operating system that runs during the configuration process) is also given.

## ❏ Reconfiguring the System Through a Reboot

This section tells you how to configure a new bootable operating system through a system reboot. The procedure includes the modification of system tunable parameters as an example, though any change in the hardware or software configuration of your system could be substituted for that part of the procedure.

There are four things to remember when reconfiguring the operating system:

1.  Always copy the existing bootable operating system (/stand/unix) to another file; it is recommended that you copy it to a file in the root directory and not to another file in the /stand directory. This way, in the event you create an unbootable unix, you can boot mUNIX from firmware and copy the existing bootable operating system from the root directory back to /stand/unix.

2.  For each driver or module that you modified in /etc/master.d, execute a separate mkboot command.

3.  When reconfiguring the operating system do not arbitrarily change the node name (NODE) of the computer. If basic networking has been established, a change in node name must be coordinated with all interfacing systems.

4.  Take detailed notes of everything you do so that you can identify and correct any mistakes you may make. In the event that you need to contact a service representative for your computer, your notes will be an invaluable aid in resolving your problem.

To reconfigure the operating system, you must change the system configuration and then rebuild the operating system. These steps are described in the procedures as follows.

## Modifying the Tunable Parameters

**Step 1**  Log in as root.

**Step 2**  Copy the existing /stand/unix to /oldunix.

```
# cp /stand/unix /oldunix
```

**Step 3**  Change the present working directory to /etc/master.d.

```
# cd /etc/master.d
```

**Step 4**  Edit the applicable master files to modify the tunable parameters. Keep a record of all changes you make; this is important in case you make a mistake that results in the configuration of an unbootable operating system or the failure of the configuration process.

## Configuring a New Bootable Operating System

**Step 5**  Change the present working directory to /boot.

```
# cd /boot
```

**Step 6**  Execute the mkboot command to create a bootable object file for each of the files modified in /etc/master.d. For example, if some of the tunable parameters in the /etc/master.d/kernel were modified, you would enter:

```
# /usr/sbin/mkboot -k KERNEL
```

If the tunables that you changed were in another file (for example, /etc/master.d/sem), the mkboot command does not take the -k option:

```
# /usr/sbin/mkboot SEM
```

**Step 7**  Execute the cunix command to make a new unix:

```
# cunix -o /newunix
```

If cunix works successfully, move newunix to /stand/unix:

```
# mv /newunix /stand/unix
```

and reboot, otherwise fix the problems and try again. (For more information about cunix, see cunix(1M).)

◆ *Note*    Using the touch command on the file stand/system and then rebooting will also remake your system, as in previous releases, but will not allow you to check for errors before you shut down.

See "Sample System Configuration" in the next section for an example of the prompts that appear during the reboot and configuration process.

**Step 8**  Reboot the system:

```
# shutdown -i6
```

If the system will not boot, you must boot /stand/mUNIX to bring up a system so that you can repair problems.

If you cannot determine and/or fix the problem, you must undo the changes made to the files in /etc/master.d in Step 4; then, repeat Steps 5 and 6. After completing Step 6, move /oldunix back to /stand/unix and reboot.

## Sample System Reconfiguration

The following is an illustration of a typical scenario for reconfiguring an AT&T 3B2 Computer because of adding more memory.

Because of the additional memory, many tunable parameters should be increased. Most of them are in the /etc/master.d/kernel file. The command line entries and system responses in the illustration below show the reconfiguration and rebooting of the operating system to support these new parameters. The illustration also indicates that tunable parameters for semaphores are being modified. The editing of the /etc/master.d/kernel and /etc/master.d/sem files is not shown.

**Figure 8-1**
*A sample sys-
tem reconfigura-
tion.*

```
# cp /stand/unix /oldunix
# cd /etc/master.d
# ed kernel
```

NOTE:   *Editing of* /etc/master.d/kernel *is not shown.*

```
q
# cd /boot
# mkboot -k KERNEL
# cd /etc/master.d
# ed sem
```

NOTE:   *Editing of* /etc/master.d/sem *is not shown.*

```
q
# cd /boot
# mkboot SEM
```

NOTE:   *If parameters in other* /etc/master.d *files are changed,
execute* mkboot *on the uppercase name for each changed file.
Only the KERNEL file requires the* -k *option.
See* mkboot(1M).

```
# cd
# touch /stand/system
# shutdown -i6
```

NOTE:   *A series of messages are displayed ending with the following:*

```
INIT: New Run level: 6
The system is coming down. Please wait.
System services are now being stopped.
A new unix is being built

/stand/unix is being created

CONFIGURATION SUMMARY
=====================
     ----driver---- #devices major
     LOG               1    50
     CLONE             1    63
     PRF               1    49
     SXT               1    48
     GENTTY            1    20
     PORTS             2     1,   2
     MEM               1    18
     IUART             1     0
     IDISK             1    17
     HDELOG            1    16

     ----module---
     INTP
     ELF
     COFF
```

(continued on the next page)

```
     FIFOFS
     BFS
     .
     .
     .

     ----device info----
majorminor
     rootdev     17     0
     swapdev     17     1
```

NOTE:   *A series of messages is displayed ending with the following:*

```
The system is down.

SELF-CHECK

UNIX System V Release 4.0 AT&T 3B2 Version 2
Node ptrph
Total real memory  = 2087157
Available memory   = 1236992


************************************************************


Copyright (c) 1984, 1986, 1987, 1988, 1989 AT&T  - All Rights Reserved

THIS IS UNPUBLISHED PROPRIETARY SOURCE CODE OF AT&T INC.
The copyright notice above does not evidence any actual or
intended publication of such source code.

************************************************************
The system is coming up.  Please wait.

AT&T 3B2 SYSTEM CONFIGURATION:

Memory size: 2 Megabytes
System Peripherals:
        Device Name        Subdevices              Extended Subdevices
        SBD

                           Floppy Disk
                           30 Megabyte Disk
                           72 Megabyte Disk

        PORTS
        MAU
The system is ready.

Console Login:
```

# ❑ Recovering from an Unbootable Operating System

If your attempt at configuring a new bootable operating system is unsuccessful, resulting in an unbootable operating system or the failure of the configuration process, you can get a viable version of the system running using the procedure outlined below. This procedure can also be used if you configure a new bootable operating system that performs poorly and you want to recover the previously used /stand/unix.

It is assumed that you previously saved a copy of /stand/unix as /old-unix.

**Step 1**  If the system is in the firmware state, skip to Step 2.

If you are in single- or multi-user mode, bring the system to the firmware state:

```
# shutdown -i5
```

Note that if you are in multi-user mode, you must be logged in as root.

If you are in the shell spawned during an error in the configuration process, use exit or ⟨ctrl⟩⟨D⟩ to go to firmware mode.

If for some reason the system is not able to come up at all, see the hardware documentation for your computer for instructions on getting the system to firmware mode in this case (most computers are equipped with some form of hardware reset switch).

**Step 2**  Enter the firmware password. When prompted, enter /stand/mU-NIX:

```
Enter name of program to execute [ ]: /stand/mUNIX
```

The system boots mUNIX, a version of the operating system that always resides in /stand.

**Step 3**  After the system has rebooted and you have logged in as root, move /oldunix back to /stand/unix:

```
# mv /oldunix /stand/unix
```

This returns the previous working version of the operating system to /stand/unix.

**Step 4**  If you made any changes to files in /etc/master.d or to the /stand/system file before a configuration attempt that failed, undo all the changes made at this time (if you have not done so already) so that these system files match the current bootable operating system in /stand/unix. If you had saved copies of these files before changing them, simply move the old files back to /etc/master.d. Then, execute a separate mkboot for each module corresponding to the master files as shown in the section *"Configuring a New Bootable Operating System."*

**Step 5**  Reboot the system:

```
# shutdown -i6
```

**Step 6**  When the Console Login: prompt appears you can log in to your system.

Try to determine what you did to cause the configuration process to fail so that you can avoid the problem in the future. If you are unable to determine what went wrong, and repeated attempts at configuring a new operating system fail, retain all notes and other documentation that you kept during the attempt(s) (including changes made to master files and/or the /stand/-system file), and contact your computer service representative.

## ❑ User-Level Configuration of the UNIX System

Configuring unix at the user-level has several major advantages over configuring unix automatically through a reboot:

▲  no reboot of the system is necessary (i.e., system remains available to all users)

▲  the reconfigured operating system can be placed in a file other than /stand/unix, leaving the current bootable operating system intact

▲  an alternate system file and /boot directory can be specified

Typically, the cunix command will be used as in the following example:

```
cunix [-f system] [-o new_unix]
```

The -f option specifies the pathname of the system file to be used for the configuration of the new bootable operating system. By default, this is /stand/system, but can be any text file in system(4) format.

There are also other options to cunix that allow you to further customize your configuration environment. See the cunix(1M) manual page for more information.

# ❑ Configuring a New mUNIX

As previously described, mUNIX is a version of the UNIX system that runs during the configuration process. It was configured originally using the /stand/mini_system file as the system file.

You may want to configure a new mUNIX to account for your particular operating environment. To do this, just make changes to the /stand/mini_system file as necessary and execute the cunix command, as in the following example:

```
cunix -f /stand/mini_system -o new_mUNIX
```

This command will build new_mUNIX (in the current directory) using the mini_system file as the system file. Do not make any changes to master files unless you also intend to reconfigure unix along with mUNIX.

Once the configuration process is complete, you should move the new mUNIX to /stand, optionally saving the old one before doing so, as in the following:

```
mv /stand/mUNIX old_mini_unix
mv new_mUNIX /stand/mini_unix
```

This causes your newly configured mUNIX to be the one used for future configurations of the operating system, and retains a copy of the old mUNIX in the current directory. Of course, you can keep an old copy of mUNIX in any directory, including the root directory.

# ❏ Tunable Parameters

Tunable system parameters are used to set various table sizes and system thresholds to handle the expected system load. Caution should be used when changing these variables since such changes can directly affect system performance. For the most part, the initial tunable parameter values for a new 3B2 computer are acceptable for most configurations and applications. If your application has special performance needs, you may have to experiment with different combinations of parameter values to find an optimal set.

Note that whenever a parameter's value is being changed from the default value to a much higher value, you should read the `master.d` file to determine the type of parameter data that affects its maximum value.

The tunables for the core package can be found in the following `/etc/master.d` files delivered with the core package:

| | |
|---|---|
| kernel | Kernel Tunables |
| hrt | High Resolution Timers |
| ports | Ports Board--STREAMS Version |
| log | STREAMS Log Driver |
| sad | STREAMS Administrative Driver |
| ts | Time Sharing Scheduler |
| s5 | System V File System Type |

Figure 8-2 shows the default values for the tunable parameters found in these files for systems equipped with 4 megabytes of random access memory (RAM).   Also included in Figure 8-2 are the default values for the tunable parameters found in the in the `/etc/master.d` files of the following packages:

UFS Utilities
    `/etc/master.d/ufs`       4.2BSD Fast File System

System Performance Analysis Utilities
    `/etc/master.d/prf`       Kernel Profiler

Interprocess Communication Utilities
    `/etc/master.d/msg`       Messages

| | |
|---|---|
| `/etc/master.d/shm` | Shared Memory |
| `/etc/master.d/sem` | Semaphores |

The following packages also have tunable parameters found in `/etc/master.d` files. The files associated with the package and where the respective tunables are found are also given.

Internet Utilities *(Network User's and Administrator's Guide)*

| | |
|---|---|
| `/etc/master.d/arp` | Address Resolution Protocol |
| `/etc/master.d/ip` | Internet Protocol |
| `/etc/master.d/tcp` | Transmission Control Protocol |
| `/etc/master.d/udp` | User Datagram Protocol |
| `/etc/master.d/llcloop` | Loopback Driver |

Network File System Utilities *(Network User's and Administrator's Guide)*

| | |
|---|---|
| `/etc/master.d/nfs` | Network File System |

Remote File Sharing Utilities *(Network User's and Administrator's Guide)*

| | |
|---|---|
| `/etc/master.d/rfs` | Remote File Sharing |

XENIX Compatibility Package *(BSD/XENIX® Compatibility Guide)*

| | |
|---|---|
| `/etc/master.d/xnamfs` | XENIX Semaphores |

The following notes apply to Figure 8-2:

■ The parameters are set to specific values, as defined in the appropriate `/etc/master.d` file. The default value and the size in bytes for each entry are shown in the figure.

■ A dash (-) is used in the size information to indicate parameters that do not affect the size of the kernel when the values are changed. These parameters instead act as flags, limits, or provide a naming function.

**Figure 8-2**
*Suggested Parameter Values.*

| master.d File | Tunable Type | Parameter | Default Value | Size per Entry (bytes) |
|---|---|---|---|---|
| kernel | General. Kernel Tunables | NCALL | 60 | 16 |
| | | ARG_MAX | 5120 | - |
| | | FLCKREC | 300 | - |
| | | MAXUP | 25 | - |
| | | NCLIST | 0 | - |
| | | NPROC | 200 | 212 |
| | | PUTBFSZ | 2000 | 1 |
| | | ROOTFSTYPE | "s5" | - |
| | System Information | SYS | "UNIX Sys. V" | - |
| | | NODE | "unix" | - |
| | | REL | "4.0" | - |
| | | VER | "2" | - |
| | | SRPC_DOMAIN | " " | - |
| | Hardware Information | ARCHITECTURE | "M32100" | - |
| | | HW_SERIAL | " " | - |
| | | HW_PROVIDER | "AT&T" | - |
| | Buffer Cache | NBUF | 100 | 88 |
| | | NHBUF | 64 | 12 |
| | | NPBUF | 20 | 52 |
| | | BUFHWM | 200 | - |

| master.d File | Tunable Type | Parameter | Default Value | Size per Entry (bytes) | |
|---|---|---|---|---|---|
| kernel | Paging | FSFLUSHR | 1 | - | *Figure 8-2 Continued* |
| | | NAUTOUP | 60 | - | |
| | | SPTMAP | 100 | 8 | |
| | | MAXPMEM | 0 | | |
| | | GPGSLO | 25 | - | |
| | | MINARMEM | 25 | - | |
| | | MINASMEM | 25 | - | |
| | Per Process Limits | SHLBMAX | 2 | - | |
| | | SCPULIM | 0x7fffffff | - | |
| | | HCPULIM | 0x7fffffff | - | |
| | | SFSZLIM | 0x100000 | - | |
| | | HFSZLIM | 0x100000 | - | |
| | | SDATLIM | 0x1000000 | - | |
| | | HDATLIM | 0x1000000 | - | |
| | | SSTKLIM | 0x1000000 | - | |
| | | HSTKLIM | 0x1000000 | - | |
| | | SCORLIM | 0x100000 | - | |
| | | HCORLIM | 0x1000000 | - | |
| | | SFNOLIM | 0x18 | - | |
| | | HFNOLIM | 0x400 | - | |
| | | SVMMLIM | 0x1000000 | - | |
| | | HVMMLIM | 0x1000000 | - | |
| | File Access Features | RSTCHOWN | 0 | - | |
| | | NGROUPS_MAX | 16 | - | |

*Figure 8-2 Con-*
*tinued*

| master.d File | Tunable Type | Parameter | Default Value | Size per Entry (bytes) |
|---|---|---|---|---|
| kernel | STREAMS | NSTRPUSH | 9 | - |
| | | STRCTLSZ | 1024 | - |
| | | STRMSGSZ | 0 | - |
| | | STRTHRESH | 2000000 | - |
| log | STREAMS Logging | NLOG | 16 | 12 |
| sad | STREAMS Admin. Driver | NSTRPHASH | 64 | 4 |
| | | NAUTOPUSH | 32 | 44 |
| | Scheduler Information | MAXCLSYSPRI | 99 | - |
| | | SYS_NAME | "SYS" | - |
| | | INITCLASS | "TS" | - |
| | XENIX Shared Data | XSDSEGS | 25 | 12 |
| | | XSDSLOTS | 3 | 20*XSDSEGS |
| hrt | High Resolution Timers | HRTIME | 50 | 60 |
| | | HRVTIME | 50 | 60 |
| ports | Ports Board | SAVEXP | 125 | 1 |
| ts | Time Sharing | TSMAXUPRI | 20 | - |
| s5 | s5 File System Type | NINODE | 400 | 132 |
| ufs | ufs File System Type | UFSNINODE | 150 | 268 |
| | | NDQUOT | 200 | 60 |
| prf | Profiler | PRFMAX | 2048 | 1 |

| master.d File | Tunable Type | Parameter | Default Value | Size per Entry (bytes) |
|---|---|---|---|---|
| msg | IPC Messages | MSGMAP | 100 | 8 |
| | | MSGMAX | 2048 | - |
| | | MSGMNB | 4096 | - |
| | | MSGMNI | 50 | 53 |
| | | MSGSSZ | 8 | 1024 |
| | | MSGTQL | 40 | 12 |
| | | MSGSEG | 1024 | 8 |
| sem | IPC Semaphores | NBPW | 4 | - |
| | | SEMMAP | 10 | 8 |
| | | SEMMNI | 10 | 34 |
| | | SEMMNS | 60 | 12 |
| | | SEMMNU | 30 | 8x(SEMUME+2) |
| | | SEMMSL | 25 | - |
| | | SEMOPM | 10 | 8 |
| | | SEMUME | 10 | 8x(SEMMNU) |
| | | SEMVMX | 32767 | - |
| | | SEMAEM | 16384 | - |
| shm | IPC Shared Memory | SHMMAX | 131072 | - |
| | | SHMMIN | 1 | - |
| | | SHMMNI | 100 | 112 |
| | | SHMSEG | 6 | 12xNPROC |

*Figure 8-2 Continued*

*Figure 8-2 Continued*

| master.d File | Tunable Type | Parameter | Default Value | Size per Entry (bytes) |
|---|---|---|---|---|
| rfs | RFS Parameters | NSRMOUNT | 20 | 28 |
| | | MAXGDP | 24 | 144 |
| | | NRCVD | 150 | 40 |
| | | NRDUSER | 250 | 36 |
| | | NSNDD | 150 | 144 |
| | | MINSERVE | 3 | 284 |
| | | MAXSERVE | 6 | 284 |
| | | RCACHETIME | 10 | |
| | | RF_MAXKMEM | 0 | |

## ❑ General Kernel Tunables

The following general kernel parameters are defined in the /etc/master.d/kernel file.

ARG_MAX    *the maximum number of characters allowed in the argument and environment strings* passed to an exec system call, including NULL characters. This can be increased to allow larger argument lists, but it should not be less than 5120. If it is increased, it should be no more than about SSTKLIM/8 (see *"Per Process Limits"* below) so that there is room for both the pointer arrays and the ordinary stack frames.

FLCKREC    *the number of records that can be locked* by the system. The default is 300.

MAXUP    *the number of concurrent processes a nonsuperuser is allowed to run.* The entry is normally in the range of 15 to 25. This value should not exceed the value of NPROC (NPROC should be at least 10 percent more than MAXUP). This value is per user identification number, not per terminal. For example, if twelve people are logged in with the same user identification, the default limit would be reached very quickly.

NCALL         *the number of callout table entries.* Each entry represents a function to be invoked at a later time by the clock handler portion of the kernel. This value must be greater than 2 and is normally in the range of 10 to 70. The default value is 60. Each entry contains 16 bytes.

Software drivers may use call entries to check hardware device status. When the call-out table overflows, the system crashes and outputs the following message on the system console:

```
PANIC: Timeout table overflow
```

NCLIST       NCLIST is no longer used by 3B2 UNIX systems. Other machine architectures may use clist, however.

NPROC        *the number of process table entries.* Each table entry represents an active process. The swapper is always the first entry and /sbin/init is always the second entry. The number of entries depends on the number of terminal lines available and the number of processes spawned by each user. The average number of processes per user is in the range of 2 to 5 (also see MAXUP, default value 25). When full, the fork(2) system call returns the error EAGAIN. The default value of NPROC is 200. It should probably be no less than 50.

PUTBUFSZ    *the size, in bytes, of the circular buffer* putbuf, used to record various system messages, including PANIC messages. The messages in putbuf can be seen in a system dump by using the crash command to print the contents of putbuf as ASCII characters. There should be no reason to change this value unless you are doing operating system development.

ROOTFSTYPE   *the file system type of the root file system.* This is used to determine the format of the file system.

# ❑ System Information

The following system information tunables are defined in the `/etc/master.d/kernel` file.

SYS                 *the system name.* The default system name is `UNIX_System_V`.

NODE                *the node name* of the system. The default node name is `unix`.

REL                 *the UNIX system release.*

VER                 *the version* of UNIX. This value may be 1 or 2.

SRPC_DOMAIN         *the name of the "Secure RPC Domain,"* the realm in which a uid space is unique. When using secure RPC, each user is assigned a "netname" which is of the form

```
Operating System.UserId@Realm
```

So, if the user id of each user is the same for machines A, B, and C, then SRPC_DOMAIN should be set to the same name on A, B, and C. Thus, if the SRPC_DOMAIN name for machines A, B, and C is "documentation," then user 1701 from any one of those machines would have the netname

```
unix.1701@documentation
```

See "RPC Administration" in the *Programmer's Guide: Networking Interfaces* for more information on secure domain.

# ❑ Hardware Information

The following parameters are defined in the `/etc/master.d/kernel` file.

ARCHITECTURE  *the machine architecture information.*

HW_SERIAL          *the serial number* of your machine. Its value, of course, must be filled in by the administrator.

HW_PROVIDER        *the hardware provider's name.*

## ❑ Buffer Cache

The following parameters are defined in the /etc/master.d/kernel file.

NBUF               *the number of buffer headers.* Block I/O uses both buffers and buffer headers. Whenever a buffer header is needed, but no free ones are available, the system dynamically allocates more buffer headers in chunks of NBUF at a time. There is no limit to the total number of buffer headers in the system, however, the tunable BUFHWM limits the number of kilobytes that may be used by buffers. This effectively limits the number of buffer headers that will be allocated.

Once allocated, buffer header space cannot be freed for other uses. Thus, care should be taken when raising the value of NBUF. A higher value of NBUF will decrease the number of times the Kernel Memory Allocator must be called to allocate space for buffer headers, but this could also result in the allocation of headers that are not used.

NHBUF              *the number of "hash buckets"* to allocate for 1K buffers. These are used to search for a buffer given a device number and block number, rather than a linear search through the entire list of buffers. This value must be a power of 2. Each entry contains 12 bytes. NHBUF must be specified in /etc/master.d/kernel.

NPBUF              *the number of physical I/O buffers* to allocate. One I/O buffer is needed for each physical read or write active. Each entry contains 52 bytes. The default value is 20.

BUFHWM             *the amount of space that is reserved for buffers,* in kilobytes. If sar -b shows the buffer hit ratio to be low, then BUFHWM and/or NBUF should be increased.

# ❑ Paging

A paging daemon, `pageout`, exists in the system. Its sole responsibility is to free memory as the need arises. It uses a ``least recently used'' algorithm to approximate process working sets and writes those pages that have not been touched during some period of time out to disk. The page size is 2048 bytes. When memory is exceptionally tight, the working sets of entire processes may be swapped out.

The first two tunables are for file system hardening. The remaining tunable parameters determine how often `pageout` runs and under what conditions. The default values in `/etc/master.d/kernel` should be adequate for most applications.

FSFLUSHR    *the file system flush rate*. It specifies the rate in seconds for checking the need to write the file system buffers, modified inodes, and mapped pages to disk. The default is one second. (This has replaced `BDFLUSHR` of previous releases.)

NAUTOUP    *the buffer age* in seconds for automatic file system updates. System buffers and other cached file attributes (such as inodes) are written to the hard disk when they have been memory-resident for the interval specified by the `NAUTOUP` parameter. Specifying a smaller limit increases system reliability by writing the buffers to disk more frequently and decreases system performance. Specifying a larger limit increases system performance at the expense of reliability.

SPTMAP    *the number of map entries for free space accounting* for the dynamic portion of the kernel virtual address space. The dynamic kernel space is used by drivers and `kmem_alloc` for execution time allocation of kernel memory. It should never be made smaller. It should be made larger if the following warning message is seen:

```
rmfree map overflow SPTMAPADDR.
Lost N items at LOSTADDRESS.
```

where `SPTMAPADDR` is the hexadecimal address of the `sptmap` array and `LOSTADDRESS` is a kernel virtual address in the dynamic allocation address interval. (On the 3B2, 0x40300000  LOSTADDRESS < 0x40500000.)

MAXPMEM          *the maximum amount of physical memory to use in pages.* The default value of 0 specifies that all available physical memory be used.

GPGSLO           *the low water mark of free memory* in pages for `pageout` to start stealing pages from processes. The default is 25. Increase the value to make the daemon more active; decrease the value to make the daemon less active (must be an integer 0.)

MINARMEM         *the minimum number of memory pages reserved for the text and data segments of user processes.*

MINASMEM         *the number of memory and swap pages reserved for system purposes* (unavailable for the text and data segments of user processes).

PAGES_UNLOCK     Unused.

## ❑ Per Process Limits

SHLBMAX          *the maximum number of shared libraries* that can be attached to a process at one time. This applies only to COFF shared executables.

The following tunables are soft and hard limit pairs on process resource limits. These limits are given to process 0; thereafter child processes inherit the parent process's hard and soft limits. However, whenever a process `exec`s a file whose set-user-id or set-group-id bit has been set, the resource limits of that process are reinitialized to the default system limits.

Processes can change their own values of these limits using `setrlimit` (see `getrlimit`(2)). Soft limits may be changed but must remain less than or equal to the hard limits. Only processes whose effective user ID is equal to 0 (`root`) may raise their hard limits. Any process may lower its hard limit.

A value equal to RLIMIT_INFINITY (0x7fffffff on the 3B2) indicates a resource without limitation.

See getrlimit(2) for more information on hard and soft limits.

SCPULIM          *the soft limit of the maximum combined user and system CPU time, in seconds, that a process is allowed.* A SIGXCPU signal will be sent to processes whose CPU time exceeds this value.

HCPULIM          *the maximum value of SCPULIM.*

SFSZLIM          *the soft limit specifying the largest offset, in bytes, of any single file that may be created by the process.* A SIGXFSX signal will be sent to processes that attempt to write a file whose offset is greater than this value. In addition, the write will fail with an EFBIG error.

HFSZLIM          *the maximum value of SFSZLIM.*

SDATLIM          *the soft limit specifying the maximum size, in bytes, of a process's heap.* If a process attempts to extend its heap beyond this limit using brk(2), the attempt will fail and errno will be set to ENOMEM.

HDATLIM          *the maximum value of SDATLIM.*

SSTKLIM          *the soft limit specifying the maximum size, in bytes, of the stack segment for a process.* This defines the limit of automatic stack growth by the system. A SIGSEGV signal will be sent to processes that attempt to grow the stack beyond this value. Unless the process has arranged to catch this signal on a separate stack (see signalstack(2)) this will terminate the process.

HSTKLIM          *the maximum value of SSTKLIM.*

SCORLIM          *the soft limit specifying the largest size, in bytes, of a core file that may be created.* A soft limit of 0 will prevent the creation of core files.

HCORLIM             *the maximum value of* SCORLIM.

SFNOLIM             *the soft limit specifying the maximum number of open files the process may have.* When this limit is exceeded, attempts to open files will fail and errno will be set to EMFILE.

HFNOLIM             *the maximum value of* SFNOLIM.

SVMMLIM             *the soft limit specifying the maximum address space that may be mapped to a process.* Attempts to increase a process's address space beyond this value (i.e., brk(2), shmat(2), mmap(2)) will fail with a ENOMEM error.

HVMMLIM             *the maximum value of* SVMMLIM.

# ❏ File Access Features

RSTCHOWN            *the restricted file ownership changes flag.* Only 0 and 1 are valid values for RSTCHOWN. A value of 0 is the System V Release 3 compatibility mode. As in Release 3, the owner of a file can change user ID and group ID of the file to any value, including nonexistent user IDs and group IDs. RSTCHOWN set to 1 designates the FIPS/BSD compatibility mode. This restricts the ability to change ownership of the file. Only the superuser or root processes (those whose UID is 0) are able to change the ownership of a file. The owner of the file may only change the group ID of the file to one of the groups in which the owner has membership (see getgroups(1)). Superuser and root processes may change the group ID of any file to any value. (RSTCHOWN set to 1 is FIPS/BSD compatibility mode.)

NGROUPS_MAX         *the maximum number of groups in which a process can have membership.* See getgroups(1).

# ❏ STREAMS

The following tunable parameters are associated with STREAMS processing. These parameters are defined in the /etc/master.d/kernel file.

NSTRPUSH          *the maximum number of modules that may be pushed onto a Stream.* This is used to prevent an errant user process from consuming all of the available queues on a single Stream. By default this value is 9, but in practice, existing applications have pushed, at most, four modules on a Stream.

STRMSGSZ          *the maximum allowable size of the data portion of any STREAMS message.* This should usually be set just large enough to accommodate the maximum packet size restrictions of the configured STREAMS modules. If it is larger than necessary, a single write or putmsg can consume an inordinate number of message blocks. A value of zero indicates no upper bound. A value of 4096 is sufficient for existing applications.

STRCTLSZ          *the maximum allowable size of the control portion of any STREAMS message.* The control portion of a putmsg message is not subject to the constraints of the minimum/maximum packet size, so the value entered here is the only way of providing a limit for the control part of a message. The recommended value of 1024 is more than sufficient for existing applications.

STRTHRESH         *the maximum total of bytes streams are normally allowed to allocate.* When the threshold is passed, users without the appropriate privilege will not be allowed to open streams, push streams modules, or write to streams devices; they will fail with ENOSR (out of streams resources). Users with appropriate privilege will always be allowed to do anything. Note also that the threshold applies to the output side only, thus data coming into the system (for example, the console) is not affected and will continue to work properly. A value of zero means there is no threshold. STRTHRESH should be set to about 1/4 to 1/2 of the total system memory. The default of 2000000 (approximately 2 megabytes) is a good maximum for a 4 megabyte system.

The configurable parameter for the STREAMS log driver is found in the file `/etc/master.d/log`. It is:

NLOG                    *the number of minor devices* that are available through the clone interface of the log driver (`/dev/log`). If an open of `/dev/log` fails with `errno` set to `ENXIO`, this number may need to be increased.

The configurable parameters for the STREAMS Administrative Driver (SAD) are found in the file `/etc/master.d/sad`. They are:

NSTRPHASH               *the size of the internal hash table.* This will probably never need to be changed unless the number of drivers on the system gets very, very large.

NAUTOPUSH               *the number of devices that can be configured to be autopushed.* If the `SAD_SAP ioctl` fails with `errno` set to `ENOSR`, then this number should be increased.

# ❑ Scheduler Information

The following parameters are defined in the `/etc/master.d/kernel` file.

MAXCLSYSPRI             *the maximum global priority* used by the SYS scheduling class for scheduling kernel processes. Changing this changes the range of priorities used to schedule kernel processes and can have a significant effect on the performance of the system. In general, there is no need to change this unless you are adding new scheduling classes or reconfiguring the priorities of other currently configured classes. If it is set to a value below 39, the kernel will automatically set it to 39 at boot time because it needs a range of 40 priorities for the SYS class. (See Chapter 2, *Users, Processes, and Workloads*, for detailed information.)

SYS_NAME                *the character string name of the system scheduling class.* There is no need to change the default unless you are configuring a different scheduling class with the name SYS.

INITCLASS          *the scheduling class assigned to the* `init` *process.* This class will be inherited by all processes on the system except descendents of a process whose class has been reset using `priocntl`(2). Should not be changed without good reason.

## ❏ XENIX Shared Data

The following parameters are defined in the `/etc/master.d/kernel` file.

XSDSEGS            *the number of shared data segments* in the system. The minimum value is 1, and the default and maximum value is 25.

XSDSLOTS           *the scale factor for* *XSDSEGS*. (XSDSEGS× XSDSLOTS) specifies the maximum number of shared data segment attachments allowed in the system. The minimum value of XSDSLOTS is 1, and the default and value of XSDSLOTS is 1, and the default and maximum value is 3.

## ❏ High Resolution Timers

The configuration parameters for High Resolution Timers are found in the `/etc/master.d/hrt` file. They are:

HRTIME            *the size of the* `hrtimes` *array.* The `hrtimes` array is used for keeping track of sleep and alarm requests for the standard, real-time clock.

HRVTIME           *the size of the* `itimes` *array.* The `times` array is used for keeping track of the alarm requests for the clocks measuring user process virtual time and a process's virtual time.

# ❏ Ports Board

The configurable parameter for the Ports Board is found in the `/etc/master.d/ports` file. It is:

SAVEXP       *the number of saved express jobs on the ports and high-ports boards.* SAVEXP should be increased if the message

```
PORTS: EXPRESS QUEUE OVERLOAD:
One entry lost, bin = N, pid = M
```

is printed (where $N$ is the board number and $M$ is the port number). It probably will not need to be changed.

# ❏ Time Sharing Scheduler

The following parameter for the Time Sharing Scheduler is found in the `/etc/master.d/ts` file.

TSMAXUPRI     *the range within which users may adjust the user priority* of a time-sharing process is -TSMAXUPRI to +TSMAXUPRI. Configuring higher values gives users more control over the priority of their processes (note that only super-user can raise priority in any case). The default value of 20 provides a degree of control equivalent to what has been available in the past through the `nice`(2) interface.

# ❏ s5 File System Type

The following parameter for the System V File System is found in the `/etc/master.d/s5` file.

NINODE            *the number of inode entries in the S5 inode table.* If `sar -v` shows that table overflows are occurring or if `sar -g` shows `%s5ipf > 10` percent, then the value should be raised. On the other hand, if `sar -v` consistently shows that the inode table is underutilized, then the value could be lowered. NINODE should be greater than `ncsize` which is specified in `/etc/master.d/kernel`. `ncsize` determines the number of inodes used by the directory lookup cache. A general guideline for the value of NINODE is 100 s5 inode entries for each megabyte of memory or `ncsize + 100`, whichever is greater.

## ❏ `ufs` File System Type

The following parameters are associated with the Fast File System and are found in the `/etc/master.d/ufs` file.

UFSNINODE         *the number of `ufs` inode table entries.* If the main file system is `ufs`, then 100 inode entries per megabyte of memory should be allocated and the number should be greater than the value NCSIZE in `/etc/master.d/kernel`.

NDQUOT            *the size of the kernel quota table.* There is one entry for each user, thus, NDQUOT should be more than the maximum number of users that can be logged onto the system. If quotas are in effect, the table entries limit the amount of disk space a user can use. If there are no available entries, the message

```
dquot table full
```

will be printed on the console. If this occurs, the value of NDQUOT should be increased.

# ❑ Profiler

The following parameter is associated with the profiler and is found in the
/etc/master.d/prf file.

PRFMAX              *the maximum expected number of kernel addresses*. This value
                   should be increased if the message

                        too many text symbols

                   is printed when /usr/sbin/prfld is run.


# ❑ Interprocess Communication

The following tunable parameters are associated with interprocess communication messages. These parameters are defined in the /etc/master.d/msg
file. The order in which they are described follows the order in which they are
defined in the output of the /usr/sbin/sysdef command.

MSGMAP             *the size of the control map* used to manage message segments.
                   Default value is 100. Each entry contains 8 bytes.

MSGMAX             *the maximum size of a message*. The default value is 2048. The
                   maximum size is 65,535 bytes (64 KB -1).

MSGMNB             *the maximum length of a message queue*. The default value is
                   4096.

MSGMNI             *the maximum number of message queues* systemwide (id struc-
                   ture). The default value is 50.

MSGSSZ             *the size, in bytes, of a message segment*. Messages consist of a
                   contiguous set of message segments large enough to fit the
                   text. The default value is 8. The value of MSGSSZ times the
                   value of MSGSEG must be less than or equal to 131,072 bytes
                   (128 KB).

MSGTQL          *the number of message headers* in the system and, thus, the number of outstanding messages. The default value is 40. Each entry contains 12 bytes.

MSGSEG          *the number of message segments* in the system. The default value is 1024. The value of MSGSSZ times the value of MSG-SEG must be less than or equal to 131,072 bytes (128 KB).

The following tunable parameters are associated with interprocess communication semaphores. These parameters are defined in the /etc/master.d/sem file. The order in which they are described follows the order in which they are defined in the output of the /usr/sbin/sysdef command.

NBPW            *the number of bytes per word*. This should not be changed since it is used to calculate the sizes of some tunables.

SEMMAP          *the size of the control map* used to manage semaphore sets. The default value is 10. Each entry contains 8 bytes.

SEMMNI          *the number of semaphore identifiers* in the kernel. This is the number of unique semaphore sets that can be active at any given time. The default value is 10. Each entry contains 34 bytes.

SEMMNS          *the number of semaphores* in the system. The default value is 60. Each entry contains 12 bytes.

SEMMNU          *the number of undo structures* in the system. The default value is 30. The size is equal to 8 x (SEMUME + 2) bytes.

SEMMSL          *the maximum number of semaphores per semaphore identifier*. The default value is 25.

SEMOPM          *the maximum number of semaphore operations* that can be executed per semop(2) system call. The default value is 10. Each entry contains 8 bytes.

SEMUME          *the maximum number of undo entries per undo structure*. The default value is 10. The size is equal to 8*(SEMMNU) bytes.

SEMVMX
*the maximum value a semaphore can have.* The default value is 32,767. The default value is the maximum value for this parameter.

SEMAEM
*the adjustment on exit for maximum value,* alias `semadj`. SEMAEM is used when a semaphore value becomes greater than or equal to the absolute value of `semop`(2), unless the program has set its own value. The default and maximum value is 16,384.

The following tunable parameters are associated with interprocess communication shared memory. These parameters are defined in the `/etc/master.d/shm` file. The order in which they are described follows the order in which they are defined in the output of the `/usr/sbin/sysdef` command.

SHMMAX
*the maximum shared memory segment size.* The default value is 131,072.

SHMMIN
*the minimum shared memory segment size.* The default value is 1.

SHMMNI
*the maximum number of shared memory identifiers* system wide. The default value is 100. Each entry contains 112 bytes.

SHMSEG
*the maximum number of shared memory segments that can be attached per process.* There is no maximum value enforced for this tunable (it was 15 in the past). SHMSEG is dependent on the available unused space the process has. So even if a process has fewer than SHMSEG shared memory segments, it may not be able to attach another because of its limited space.

# ❑ RFS Parameters

RFS parameters define the extent remote computers can use your resources. They also control your own access to remote resources. If the values are too small, you may not be providing enough resources to properly handle your RFS load. Requests for mounts, shares, or even a file could fail if either of those values reach the maximum number allowed for your machine. If these parameters are too large, you could be allocating more system resources than you need to use.

Default values for the parameters described below are in `/etc/conf/pack.d/rfs/space.c` and in Figure 8-3.

NRCVD
: *the maximum number of receive descriptors.* There is one receive descriptor for each file or directory being referenced by remote users and one for each local process with a remote request pending. By limiting the number of receive descriptors, you limit the number of local files and directories that can be accessed at a given time by remote users. Remote user commands will receive error messages if the limit is exceeded.

NSNDD
: *the maximum number of send descriptors.* One send descriptor is created for each remote file or directory that is referenced by a local client. A send descriptor is also allocated for each server process and for each message waiting on a the receive queue. By limiting the number of send descriptors, you limit how many remote files and directories your machine can access at one time, effectively limiting the amount of RFS activities your users can perform. Attempts to exceed the limit produce error messages to the offending user command.

NSRMOUNT
: *the number of server mount table entries.* Each time a remote machine mounts one of your resources, an entry is added to your server mount table. This number limits the total number of your resources that can be mounted by a remote machine at any given time.

MAXGDP | *the maximum number of virtual circuits.* A virtual circuit, or connection, is set up for each computer whose resources you mount, and for each computer that mounts your resources. The virtual circuit from client to host is created when the client mounts the first resource on a host, and is taken down when the last resource is unmounted.

This parameter limits the number of RFS virtual circuits your computer can have open on the network at any one time, thereby limiting the number of remote computers you can share resources with at one time. Note that the limits can be different on each computer on the network.

MINSERVE | *the minimum number of active server processes.* Server processes handle remote requests for local resources. This parameter sets the number of server processes that are always active on your system. Use sar -S to monitor server process activity.

MAXSERVE | *the maximum number of active server processes.* When there are more remote requests for shared resources than the minimum number of server processes can handle, more servers can be created. This parameter sets the maximum number of server processes allowed at a given time. If MAXSERVE>MINSERVE, the number of active servers will change dynamically with the load.

NRDUSER | *the maximum number of receive descriptor user entries.* Each user entry corresponds to a user on a remote client machine that is accessing one of your resources. There is one receive descriptor per shared resource, and one user entry per user sharing the resource. These entries are used during recovery when the network or a client go down, and should be set at about one and half times the value of NRCVD.

RCACHETIME | *control network caching.* To turn off network caching, set RCACHETIME to -1. To turn it off for a few seconds while a file is modified, set RCACHETIME to a small positive integer.

When a write to a server file occurs, the server machine sends invalidation messages to all client machines that have that file open. The client machines remove data affected by the write from their caches. Caching of that file's data is not resumed until the writing process close the file or until RCACHETIME seconds have elapsed.

This algorithm is based on the assumption that write traffic is "bursty": the first write may be closely followed by other writes. Turning off caching avoids the overhead of sending invalidation messages for subsequent writes.

RF_MAXKMEM        *limit persistent use of kernel memory.* The default value of this parameter is 0, or no limit. It cannot be applied to allocations that are otherwise limited (NRCVD, NSNDD, NRDUSER, MAXGDP, NSRMOUNT), to stream messages that are not persistent, or to certain allocations that are directly controlled by an administrator (for example, the number of resource advertisements allowed.) A suggested value for a moderately used RFS server machine would be 10000. This means that 10000 bytes of kernel memory could be devoted to persistent use by RFS.

Figure 8-3 lists the RFS parameters and the recommended values for different uses of RFS. The Client Only column applies to situations where your machine will only be using remote resources, not sharing any from your own machine. Similarly, Server Only configurations offer resources to other machines but never access remote resources. Client+Server machines offer shared resources and access shared resources on other machines.

**Figure 8-3**
*Suggested RFS tunable parameter settings.*

| Parameter | Client Only | | | Server Only | | | Client+Server | | | Default Value | Size per entry (bytes) |
|---|---|---|---|---|---|---|---|---|---|---|---|
| | 2M | 3M | 4M | 2M | 3M | 4M | 2M | 3M | 4M | | |
| NSRMOUNT | 20 | 20 | 20 | 20 | 20 | 20 | 20 | 20 | 20 | 20 | 28 |
| MAXGDP | 10 | 15 | 20 | 24 | 32 | 32 | 24 | 32 | 32 | 24 | 144 |
| NRCVD | 40 | 60 | 80 | 160 | 250 | 350 | 300 | 400 | 500 | 150 | 40 |
| NRDUSER | 0 | 0 | 0 | 225 | 375 | 525 | 450 | 600 | 700 | 250 | 36 |
| NSNDD | 150 | 250 | 350 | 30 | 30 | 30 | 150 | 250 | 300 | 150 | 144 |
| MINSERVE | 0 | 0 | 0 | 3 | 3 | 3 | 3 | 3 | 3 | 3 | 284 |
| MAXSERVE | 0 | 0 | 0 | 6 | 6 | 6 | 6 | 6 | 6 | 6 | 284 |
| RCACHETIME | 10 | 10 | 10 | 10 | 10 | 10 | 10 | 10 | 10 | 10 | |

# Quick Reference Guide to Performance Management

The following table lists many of the tasks a system administrator might do to identify and correct a performance problem. Some routine maintenance activities that will help you avoid performance degradation are also included. In each case, relevant tools or procedures are mentioned along with a pointer to the chapters in this book that address the issue. The list in arranged alphabetically by task.

| Task | Tool or Procedure | Chapter |
|------|-------------------|---------|
| to collect kernel profiling data | `prfdc` | 7 |
| to collect kernel profiling data at the time of invocation only | `prfsnap` | 7 |
| to collect system activity data automatically | `sadc` | 6 |
| to collect system activity data on demand | `sar` | 6 |
| to compress a single directory | `mkdir` *copy*<br>`mv` *dir copy*<br>`chmod 777` *copy*<br>`cd` *copy*<br>`find . -print \| cpio -plm`<br>`../`*copy*<br>`cd ..`<br>`rm -rf` *copy* | 1, 3 |
| to compress an entire file system | `/usr/sbin/dcopy` *fs1 fs2* | 3 |
| to create a `bfs` files system | `mkfs -F bfs` | 3 |
| to create a `s5` file system | `mkfs -F s5` | 3 |
| to create a `ufs` file system | `mkfs -F ufs` | 3 |

| Task | Tool or Procedure | Chapter |
|---|---|---|
| to detect and identify noisy terminal lines | `sar -y`<br>`acctcon -1` *file* `</var/adm/wtmp` | 2, 6 |
| to detect and repair file system inconsistencies | `fsck` | 3 |
| to detect the existence of inefficient PATH variables | `sar -c` | 1, 6 |
| to determine the elapsed time, user time, and system time spent in execution of a command | `timex` *command* | 7 |
| to enable, disable, or check the status of the kernel profiling sampling mechanism | `prfstat` | 7 |
| to enforce disk quotas | edit `/etc/vfstab`<br>set quotas with `edquota`<br>turn on and off with `quotaon` and `quotaoff` | 3 |
| to examine paging performance and memory size | `sar -pgrwu` | 1, 6 |
| to find inactive files | `find / -mtime +90 -atime +90 \`<br>`    -print >` *filename* | 1, 3 |
| to find large, inefficient directories | `find / -type d -size +10 -print` | 1, 3 |
| to format a diskette | `fmtflop` | 4 |
| to format a SCSI disk | `format` | 4 |
| to format the data collected by `prfdc` or `prfsnap` | `prfpr` | 7 |
| to identify runaway processes | `ps` | 1 |
| to initialize the kernel-recording mechanism | `prfld` | 7 |

| Task | Tool or Procedure | Chapter |
|------|-------------------|---------|
| to limit the size of files that grow through normal use | `tail -50` *file* `>/tmp/`*file*<br>`mv /tmp/`*file* *file* | 3 |
| to list scheduler class parameters | `dispadmin -g [-r` *res*`] -c` *class* | 2 |
| to list shared resources by NFS server | `dfmounts -F nfs` | 5 |
| to list the current scheduler classes | `dispadmin -l` | 2 |
| to list the set of shared resources | `dfshares` | 5 |
| to monitor buffer activity | `sar -b` | 6 |
| to monitor CPU utilization | `sar -u` | 6 |
| to monitor disk activity | `sar -d` | 6 |
| to monitor file access operations | `sar -a` | 6 |
| to monitor interprocess communication | `sar -m` | 6 |
| to monitor kernel memory allocation | `sar -k` | 6 |
| to monitor overall system performance | `sar -A` | 6 |
| to monitor page-in and fault rates | `sar -p` | 6 |
| to monitor page-out and memory freeing activity | `sar -g` | 6 |
| to monitor queue activity | `sar -q` | 6 |
| to monitor remote buffer usage | `sar -Db` | 6 |
| to monitor remote CPU utilization | `sar -Du` | 6 |
| to monitor remote system calls | `sar -Dc` | 6 |
| to monitor RFS client caching performance | `sar -C` | 6 |

| Task | Tool or Procedure | Chapter |
|------|-------------------|---------|
| to monitor RFS server availability and usage | `sar -S` | 6 |
| to monitor shared resource usage | `fusage` | 5, 7 |
| to monitor system calls | `sar -c` | 6 |
| to monitor system table status | `sar -v` | 6 |
| to monitor terminal activity | `sar -y` | 6 |
| to monitor the swapping and switching volume | `sar -w` | 6 |
| to monitor unused memory | `sar -r` | 6 |
| to mount a shared resource | `mount` | 5 |
| to move user directories | `cd /fs1`<br>`find user1 user2 -print | \`<br>`    cpio -pdm /fs2`<br>`rm -rf /fs1/user1 /fs1/user2` | 1, 3 |
| to partition a disk | `fmthd` | 4 |
| to print out the number of free file blocks and inodes | `df` | 3 |
| to print out the total number of allocated blocks and files as well as free blocks and inodes | `df -t` | 3 |
| to print the VTOC on a disk or diskette | `prtvtoc` | 4 |
| to report disk access location and seek distance | `sadp` | 7 |
| to select a file system type | | 1, 3 |
| to set scheduler class parameters | `dispadmin -s config -c class` | 2 |

| Task | Tool or Procedure | Chapter |
|------|-------------------|---------|
| to set up non-prime time discounts | edit `/etc/acct/holidays` | 2 |
| to share a resource | `share` | 5 |
| to shift workload to off-peak hours | `nice` and `batch` | 1 |
| to summarize file system usage | `du` | 1, 3 |
| to take a memory dump after a system failure | `sysdump` | 7 |
| to take a system dump while the system is running | `errdump` | 7 |
| to terminate a runaway process | `kill -9` | 1 |
| to update the timestamp on the `/stand/system` file | `touch /stand/system` | 4, 8 |
| to use a shell script to collect and store data in the binary file `/var/adm/sa/sa`*dd* | `sa1` | 6 |
| to use a shell script to collect and store data in the ASCII file `/var/adm/sa/sar`*dd* | `sa2` | 6 |

# Appendix A

# *Checking s5 File Systems*

The `fsck` program runs in phases. Each phase reports any errors that it detects. Figure A-1 lists the abbreviations that are used in the `fsck` error messages. If the error is one that `fsck` can correct, the user is asked if the correction should be made. This appendix describes the messages that are produced by each phase.

The following abbreviations that appear in the messages have the meaning indicated by the text following them:

| | |
|---|---|
| BLK | block number |
| DUP | duplicate block number |
| DIR | directory name |
| MTIME | time file was last modified |
| UNREF | unreferenced |
| CG | cylinder group |

The following single-letter abbreviations are replaced by specific values, described by the text associated with each name, when the message appears on your screen:

| | |
|---|---|
| *B* | block number |
| *F* | file (or directory) name |
| *I* | inode number |
| *M* | file mode |
| *O* | user-ID of a file's owner |
| *S* | file size |
| *T* | time file was last modified |
| *X* | link count, *or* |
| | number of BAD, DUP, or MISSING blocks, *or* |
| | number of files (depending on context) |
| *Y* | corrected link count number, *or* |
| | number of blocks in file system (depending on context) |
| *Z* | number of free blocks |

**Figure A-1**
*Abbreviations used in `fsck` error messages.*

# ❏ Initialization Phase

Command line syntax is checked. Before the file system check can be performed, fsck sets up some tables and opens some files. The fsck program terminates when it encounters errors during the initialization phase.

# ❏ General Errors

The following three error messages may appear in any phase after initialization. While they offer the option to continue, it is generally best to regard them as fatal, end the run, and try to determine what caused the problem.

```
CAN NOT SEEK: BLK B (CONTINUE?)
```

A request to move to a specified block number $B$ in the file system failed. This message indicates a serious problem, probably a hardware failure.

```
CAN NOT READ: BLK B (CONTINUE?)
```

A request to read a specified block number $B$ in the file system failed. The message indicates a serious problem, probably a hardware failure.

```
CAN NOT WRITE: BLK B (CONTINUE?)
```

A request to write a specified block number $B$ in the file system failed. The disk may be writeprotected.

An n (no) response to the CONTINUE? prompt means terminate fsck; this is the recommended response.

A y (yes) response to the CONTINUE? prompt tells fsck to continue to check the file system. Note that the problem will often recur. This error condition prevents a complete check of the file system. A second run of fsck should be made to recheck the file system.

# ❑ Phase 1: Check Blocks and Sizes

This phase checks the inode list. It reports error conditions encountered while:

- ▲ checking inode types
- ▲ setting up the zero-link-count table
- ▲ examining inode block numbers for bad or duplicate blocks
- ▲ checking inode size
- ▲ checking inode format

Phase 1 produces four types of error messages:

- ▲ informational messages
- ▲ messages with a CONTINUE? prompt
- ▲ messages with a CLEAR? prompt
- ▲ messages with a RECOVER? prompt

There is a connection between some informational messages and messages with a CONTINUE? prompt. The CONTINUE? prompt generally indicates that some limit has been reached. An n (no) response to the CONTINUE? prompt means terminate the program. In Phase 1, a y (yes) response to the CONTINUE? prompt means continue with the program. When this error occurs a complete check of the file system is not possible. A second run of fsck should be made to recheck the file system.

An n (no) response to the RECOVER? prompt means recover all the blocks to which the inode points. A no response is only appropriate if the user intends to delete the excess blocks.

An n (no) response to the CLEAR? prompt means ignore the error condition. A no response is only appropriate if the user intends to take other measures to fix the problem. A y (yes) response to the CLEAR? prompt means deallocate the inode *I* by zeroing out its contents. This may generate the UNALLOCATED error condition in Phase 2 for each directory entry pointing to this inode.

## Phase 1 Error Messages

> UNKNOWN FILE TYPE I= *I* (CLEAR?)

The mode word of the inode *I* indicates that the inode is not a pipe, special character inode, regular inode, or directory inode. If the -p option is specified the inode will be cleared.

> LINK COUNT TABLE OVERFLOW (CONTINUE?)

An internal table for fsck containing allocated inodes with a link count of zero has no more room. If the -p option is specified the program will exit and fsck will have to be completed manually.

> *B* BAD I= *I*

Inode *I* contains block number *B* with a number lower than the number of the first data block in the file system or greater than the number of the last block in the file system. This error condition may generate the EXCESSIVE BAD BLKS error message in Phase 1 if inode *I* has too many block numbers outside the file system range. This error condition generates the BAD/DUP error message in Phases 2 and 4.

> EXCESSIVE BAD BLOCKS I= *I* (CONTINUE?)

There are too many (usually more than 10) blocks with a number lower than the number of the first data block in the file system or greater than the number of the last block in the file system associated with inode *I*. If the -p option is specified the program will terminate.

> *B* DUP I= *I*

Inode *I* contains block number *B*, which is already claimed by the same or another inode or by a free-list. This error condition may generate the EXCESSIVE DUP BLKS error message in Phase 1 if inode *I* has too many block numbers claimed by the same or another inode or by a free-list. This error condition invokes Phase 1B and generates the BAD/DUP error messages in Phases 2 and 4.

> EXCESSIVE DUP BLKS I= *I* (CONTINUE?)

There are too many (usually more than 10) blocks claimed by the same or another inode or by a free-list. If the -p option is specified the program will terminate.

> DUP TABLE OVERFLOW (CONTINUE?)

An internal table in fsck containing duplicate block numbers has no more room. If the -p option is specified the program will terminate.

> DIRECTORY MISALIGNED I= *I*

The size of a directory inode is not a multiple of 16. If the -p option is used, the directory will be recovered automatically.

> PARTIALLY ALLOCATED INODE I= *I* (CLEAR?)

Inode *I* is neither allocated nor unallocated. If the -p option is specified the inode will be cleared.

> DIR/FILE SIZE ERROR

The file references more or less data than is indicated by the inode.

```
DELETE OR RECOVER EXCESS DATA
```

The user has the choice of deleting or recovering the excess blocks
pointed to by the inode.

```
RECOVER?
```

The file references more data than is indicated by the inode. The user
is given the choice of correcting the inode information. If the -p
option is specified the data will be recovered.

```
DELETE?
```

The file references more data than is indicated by the inode. The user
is given the choice of deleting the referenced blocks and leaving the
inode data intact.

# ❑ Phase 1B: Rescan for More DUPS

When a duplicate block is found in the file system, the file system is rescanned to find the inode that previously claimed that block. When the duplicate block is found, the following informational message is printed:

```
DUP I= I
```

Inode *I* contains block number *B* that is already claimed by the same
or another inode or by a free-list. This error condition generates the
BAD/DUP error message in Phase 2. Inodes that have overlapping
blocks may be determined by examining this error condition and the
DUP error condition in Phase 1.

# ❏ Phase 2: Check Pathnames

This phase removes directory entries pointing to bad inodes found in Phases 1 and 1B. It reports error conditions resulting from

▲ incorrect root inode mode and status

▲ directory inode pointers out of range

▲ directory entries pointing to bad inodes

Phase 2 has four types of error messages:

▲ informational messages

▲ messages with a FIX? prompt

▲ messages with a CONTINUE? prompt

▲ messages with a REMOVE? prompt

An n (no) response to the FIX? prompt means terminate the program because fsck will be unable to continue. A y (yes) response to the FIX? prompt means change the root inode type to "directory." If the root inode data blocks are not directory blocks, a very large number of error messages are generated.

An n (no) response to the CONTINUE? prompt means terminate the program. A y (yes) response to the CONTINUE? prompt means ignore the DUPS/BAD IN ROOT INODE error message and continue to run the file system check. If the root inode is not correct, a large number of other error messages may be generated.

An n (no) response to the REMOVE? prompt means ignore the error condition. A no response is only appropriate if the user intends to take other measures to fix the problem. A y (yes) response to the REMOVE? prompt means remove duplicate or unallocated blocks.

# Phase 2 Error Messages

> ROOT INODE UNALLOCATED. TERMINATING

The root inode (usually inode number 2) of the file system has no allocate mode bits. This error message indicates a serious problem that causes the program to stop. Call your service representative.

> ROOT INODE NOT DIRECTORY (FIX?)

The root inode (usually inode number 2) of the file system is not directory inode type. If the -p option is specified the program will terminate.

> DUPS/BAD IN ROOT INODE (CONTINUE?)

Phase 1 or 1B found duplicate blocks or bad blocks in the root inode (usually inode number 2) of the file system. If the -p option is specified the program will terminate.

> I OUT OF RANGE I= $I$ NAME= $F$ (REMOVE?)

A directory entry $F$ has an inode number $I$ that is greater than the end of the inode list. If the -p option is specified the inode will be removed automatically.

> UNALLOCATED I= $I$ OWNER= $O$ MODE= $M$ SIZE= $S$ MTIME= $T$ NAME= $F$ (REMOVE?)

A directory entry $F$ has an inode $I$ without allocate mode bits. The owner $O$, mode $M$, size $S$, modify time $T$, and filename $F$ are printed. If the file system is not mounted and the -n option was not specified, the entry is removed automatically if the inode it points to is character size 0. The entry is removed if the -p option is specified.

```
DUP/BAD I= I OWNER= O MODE= M SIZE= S MTIME= T DIR= F (REMOVE?)
```

Phase 1 or Phase 1B found duplicate blocks or bad blocks associated with directory entry $F$, directory inode $I$. The owner $O$, mode $M$, size $S$, modify time $T$, and directory name $F$ are printed. If the -p option is specified the duplicate/bad blocks are removed.

```
DUP/BAD I= I OWNER= O MODE= M SIZE= S MTIME= T FILE= F (REMOVE?)
```

Phase 1 or Phase 1B found duplicate blocks or bad blocks associated with file entry $F$, inode $I$. The owner $O$, mode $M$, size $S$, modify time $T$, and filename $F$ are printed. If the -p option is specified the duplicate/bad blocks are removed.

```
BAD BLK B IN DIR I= I OWNER= O MODE= M SIZE= S MTIME= T
```

This message only occurs when the -D option is used. A physically damaged block was found in directory inode $I$. Error conditions looked for in directory blocks are nonzero padded entries, inconsistent "." and ".." entries, and embedded slashes in the name field. This error message means that the user should at a later time either remove the directory inode if the entire block looks bad or change (or remove) those directory entries that look bad.

# ❑ Phase 3: Check Connectivity

This phase checks the directories examined in Phase 2. It reports error conditions resulting from

▲   unreferenced directories

▲   missing or full lost+found directories

Phase 3 has two types of error messages:

▲ informational messages

▲ messages with a RECONNECT? prompt

An n (no) response to the RECONNECT? prompt means ignore the error condition. This response generates UNREF error messages in Phase 4. A no response is only appropriate if the user intends to take other measures to fix the problem.

A y (yes) response to the RECONNECT? prompt means reconnect directory inode *I* to the file system in the directory for lost files (usually the lost+-found directory). This may generate lost+found error messages if there are problems connecting directory inode *I* to the lost+found directory. If the link is successful, a CONNECTED informational message appears.

## Phase 3 Error Messages

```
UNREF DIR I= I OWNER= O MODE= M SIZE= S MTIME= T (RECONNECT?)
```

The directory inode *I* was not connected to a directory entry when the file system was traversed. The owner *O*, mode *M*, size *S*, and modify time *T* of directory inode *I* are printed. The fsck program forces the reconnection of a nonempty directory. If the -p option is specified the nonempty directory is reconnected.

```
SORRY. NO lost+found DIRECTORY
```

There is no lost+found directory in the root directory of the file system; fsck ignores the request to link a directory to the lost+found directory. This generates the UNREF error message in Phase 4. The access modes of the lost+found directory may be incorrect.

```
SORRY. NO SPACE IN lost+found DIRECTORY
```

There is no space to add another entry to the lost+found directory in the root directory of the file system; fsck ignores the request to link a directory to the lost+found directory. This generates the

UNREF error message in Phase 4. Clear out unnecessary entries in the lost+found directory or make it larger.

```
DIR I= I1 CONNECTED. PARENT WAS I= I2
```

This is an advisory message indicating a directory inode *I1* was successfully connected to the lost+found directory. The parent inode *I2* of the directory inode *I1* is replaced by the inode number of the lost+found directory.

# ❏ Phase 4: Check Reference Counts

This phase checks the link count information obtained in Phases 2 and 3. It reports error conditions resulting from:

▲   unreferenced files

▲   a missing or full lost+found directory

▲   incorrect link counts for files, directories, or special files

▲   unreferenced files and directories

▲   bad or duplicate blocks in files and directories

▲   incorrect total free-inode counts

Phase 4 has five types of error messages:

▲   informational messages

▲   messages with a RECONNECT? prompt

▲   messages with a CLEAR? prompt

▲   messages with an ADJUST? prompt

▲   messages with a FIX? prompt

An n (no) response to the RECONNECT? prompt means ignore this error condition. This response generates a CLEAR error message later in Phase 4. A y (yes) response to the RECONNECT? prompt means reconnect inode *I* to the file system in the directory for lost files (usually the lost+found directory). This can generate a lost+found error message in this phase if there are problems connecting inode *I* to the lost+found directory.

An n (no) response to the CLEAR? prompt means ignore the error condition. This response is only appropriate if the user intends to take other measures to fix the problem. A y (yes) response to the CLEAR? prompt means deallocate the inode by zeroing out its contents.

An n (no) response to the ADJUST? prompt means ignore the error condition. This response is only appropriate if the user intends to take other measures to fix the problem. A y (yes) response to the ADJUST? prompt means replace the link count of file inode *I* by *Y*.

An n (no) response to the FIX? prompt means ignore the error condition. This response is only appropriate if the user intends to take other measures to fix the problem. A y (yes) response to the FIX? prompt means replace the count in superblock by the actual count.

## Phase 4 Error Messages

```
UNREF FILE I= I OWNER= O MODE= M SIZE= S MTIME= T (RECONNECT?)
```

Inode *I* was not connected to a directory entry when the file system was traversed. The owner *O*, mode *M*, size *S*, and modify time *T* of inode *I* are printed. If the -n option is omitted and the file system is not mounted, empty files are cleared automatically. Nonempty files are not cleared. If the -p option is specified the inode is reconnected.

```
SORRY. NO lost+found DIRECTORY
```

There is no lost+found directory in the root directory of the file system; fsck ignores the request to link a file to the lost+found directory. This generates the CLEAR error message later in Phase 4. The access modes of the lost+found directory may be incorrect.

SORRY. NO SPACE IN lost+found DIRECTORY

There is no space to add another entry to the lost+found directory in the root directory of the file system; fsck ignores the request to link a file to the lost+found directory. This generates the CLEAR error message later in Phase 4. Check the size and contents of the lost+found directory.

(CLEAR)

The inode mentioned in the UNREF error message immediately preceding cannot be reconnected.

LINK COUNT FILE I=$I$ OWNER=$O$ MODE=$M$ SIZE=$S$ MTIME=$T$ COUNT=$X$ SHOULD BE Y (ADJUST?)

The link count for file inode $I$, is $X$ but should be $Y$. The owner $O$, mode $M$, size $S$, and modify time $T$ are printed. If the -p option is specified the link count is adjusted.

LINK COUNT DIR I=$I$ OWNER=$O$ MODE=$M$ SIZE=$S$ MTIME=$T$ COUNT=$X$ SHOULD BE Y (ADJUST?)

The link count for directory inode $I$, is $X$ but should be $Y$. The owner $O$, mode $M$, size $S$, and modify time $T$ of inode $I$ are printed. If the -p option is specified the link count is adjusted.

UNREF FILE I=$I$ OWNER=$O$ MODE=$M$ SIZE=$S$ MTIME=$T$ (CLEAR?)

File inode $I$, was not connected to a directory entry when the file system was traversed. The owner $O$, mode $M$, size $S$, and modify time $T$ of inode $I$ are printed. If the -n option is omitted and the file system is not mounted, empty files are cleared automatically. Nonempty directories are not cleared. If the -p option is specified the file is cleared if it can not be reconnected.

UNREF DIR I=$I$ OWNER=$O$ MODE=$M$ SIZE=$S$ MTIME=$T$ (CLEAR?)

Directory inode $I$, was not connected to a directory entry when the file system was traversed. The owner $O$, mode $M$, size $S$, and modify time $T$ of inode $I$ are printed. If the -n option is omitted and the file system is not mounted, empty directories are cleared automatically. Nonempty directories are not cleared. If the -p option is specified the directory is cleared if it can not be reconnected.

```
BAD/DUP FILE I= I OWNER= O MODE= M SIZE= S MTIME= T (CLEAR?)
```

Phase 1 or Phase 1B found duplicate blocks or bad blocks associated with file inode $I$. The owner $O$, mode $M$, size $S$, and modify time $T$ of inode $I$ are printed. If the -p option is specified the file is cleared.

```
BAD/DUP DIR I= I OWNER= O MODE= M SIZE= S MTIME= T (CLEAR?)
```

Phase 1 or Phase 1B found duplicate blocks or bad blocks associated with directory inode $I$. The owner $O$, mode $M$, size $S$, and modify time $T$ of inode $I$ are printed. If the -p option is specified the directory is cleared.

```
FREE INODE COUNT WRONG IN SUPERBLK (FIX?)
```

The actual count of the free inodes does not match the count in the superblock of the file system. If the -q or -p option is specified, the count in the superblock will be fixed automatically.

# ❑ Phase 5: Check Free List

This phase checks the free list. It reports error conditions resulting from:

▲ bad blocks in the free list

▲ a bad free block count

▲ duplicate blocks in the free list

▲ unused blocks from the file system that are not in the free list

▲ an incorrect total free block count

Phase 5 has four types of error messages:

▲ informational messages

▲ messages that have a CONTINUE? prompt

▲ messages that have a FIX? prompt

▲ messages that have a SALVAGE? prompt

An n (no) response to the CONTINUE? prompt means terminate the program. A y (yes) response to the CONTINUE? prompt means ignore the rest of the free list and continue the execution of fsck. This generates the BAD BLKS IN FREE LIST error message later in Phase 5.

An n (no) response to the FIX? prompt means ignore the error condition. This response is only appropriate if the user intends to take other measures to fix the problem. A y (yes) response to the FIX? prompt means replace the count in the superblock by the actual count.

An n (no) response to the SALVAGE? prompt means: ignore the error condition. This response is only appropriate if the user intends to take other measures to fix the problem. A y (yes) response to the SALVAGE? prompt means replace the actual free list by a new free list. The new free list will be ordered according to the gap and cylinder specifications of the -s or -S option to reduce the time spent waiting for the disk to rotate into position.

## Phase 5 Error Messages

```
EXCESSIVE BAD BLKS IN FREE LIST (CONTINUE?)
```

The free list contains too many blocks with a value less than the first data block in the file system or greater than the last block in the file system. If the -p option is specified the program terminates.

```
EXCESSIVE DUP BLKS IN FREE LIST (CONTINUE?)
```

The free list contains too many blocks claimed by inodes or earlier parts of the free block list. If the -p option is specified the program terminates.

BAD FREEBLK COUNT

> The count of free blocks in a free-list block is greater than 50 or less than 0. This condition generates the BAD FREE LIST message later in Phase 5.

X BAD BLKS IN FREE LIST

> $X$ blocks in the free list have a block number lower than the first data block in the file system or greater than the last block in the file system. This condition generates the BAD FREE LIST message later in Phase 5.

X DUP BLKS IN FREE LIST

> $X$ blocks claimed by inodes or earlier parts of the free-list block were found in the free list. This condition generates the BAD FREE LIST message later in Phase 5.

X BLK(S) MISSING

> $X$ blocks unused by the file system were not found in the free list. This condition generates the BAD FREE LIST message later in Phase 5.

FREE BLK COUNT WRONG IN SUPERBLOCK (FIX?)

> The actual count of free blocks does not match the count of free blocks in the superblock of the file system. If the -p option was specified, the free block count in the superblock is fixed automatically.

BAD FREE LIST (SALVAGE?)

> This message is always preceded by one or more of the Phase 5 informational messages. If the -q or -p option was specified, the free list will be salvaged automatically.

# ❑ Phase 6: Salvage Free List

This phase reconstructs the free list. It may display an advisory message about the blocks-to-skip or blocks-per-cylinder values.

## Phase 6 Error Messages

```
DEFAULT FREEBLOCK LIST SPACING ASSUMED
```

This is an advisory message indicating that the blocks-to-skip (gap) is greater than the blocks-per-cylinder, the blocks-to-skip is less than 1, the blocks-per-cylinder is less than 1, or the blocks-per-cylinder is greater than 500. The default values of 10 blocks-to-skip and 162 blocks-per-cylinder are used.

Because the default values used may not be accurate for your system, care must be taken to specify correct values with the -s option on the command line. See the fsck(1M) and mkfs(1M) manual pages for further details.

# ❑ Cleanup Phase

Once a file system has been checked, a few cleanup functions are performed. The cleanup phase displays advisory messages about the file system and the status of the file system.

## Cleanup Phase Messages

```
X files Y blocks Z free
```

This is an advisory message indicating that the file system checked contained X files using Y blocks, and that there are Z blocks free in the file system.

```
***** FILE SYSTEM WAS MODIFIED *****
```

This is an advisory message indicating that the file system was modified by fsck.

# Appendix B

# *Checking* ufs *File Systems*

fsck is a multi-pass file system check program. Each file system pass invokes a different phase of the fsck program. After initialization, fsck performs successive passes over each file system, checking blocks and sizes, path names, connectivity, reference counts, and the map of free blocks (possibly rebuilding it), and performs some cleanup.

At boot time fsck is normally run with the -y option, non-interactively. (fsck can also be run interactively by the administrator at any time.) fsck can also be run non-interactively to "preen" the file systems after an unclean halt. While preening a file system, it will only fix corruptions that are expected to result from an unclean halt. These actions are a subset of the actions that fsck takes when it is running interactively. When an inconsistency is detected, fsck generates an error message. If a response is required, fsck prints a prompt and waits for a response. When preening most errors are fatal. For those that are expected, the response taken is noted. This section explains the meaning of each error message, the possible responses, and the related error conditions.

The error conditions are organized by the phase of the fsck program in which they can occur. The error conditions that may occur in more than one phase are discussed under initialization.

## ❑ Initialization Phase

Before a file system check can be performed, certain tables have to be set up and certain files opened. The messages in this section relate to error conditions resulting from command line options, memory requests, the opening of files, the status of files, file system size checks, and the creation of the scratch file.

```
cannot alloc NNN bytes for blockmap
cannot alloc NNN bytes for freemap
cannot alloc NNN bytes for statemap
cannot alloc NNN bytes for lncntp
```

fsck's request for memory for its virtual memory table s failed. This should never happen. When it does, fsck terminates. This is a serious system failure and should be handled immediately. Contact your service representative or another qualified person.

```
Can't open checklist file: F
```

The file system checklist or default file F (usually /etc/vfstab) cannot be opened for reading. When this occurs, fsck terminates. Check the access modes of F.

```
Can't stat root
```

fsck's request for statistics about the root directory failed. This should never happen. When it does, fsck terminates. Contact your service representative or another qualified person.

```
Can't stat F
Can't make sense out of name F
```

fsck's request for statistics about the file system F failed. When running interactively, it ignores this file system and continues checking the next file system given. Check the access modes of F.

```
Can't open F
```

fsck's attempt to open the file system F failed. When running interactively, it ignores this file system and continues checking the next file system given. Check the access modes of F.

```
F: (NO WRITE)
```

Either the −n flag was specified or fsck's attempt to open the file
system *F* for writing failed. When fsck is running interactively, all
the diagnostics are printed out, but fsck does not attempt to fix anything.

```
file is not a block or character device; OK
```

The user has given fsck the name of a regular file by mistake. Check
the type of the file specified.

Possible responses to the OK prompt are:

YES     Ignore this error condition.

NO      Ignore this file system and continue checking the next file
        system given.

```
UNDEFINED OPTIMIZATION IN SUPERBLOCK (SET TO DEFAULT)
```

The superblock optimization parameter is neither OPT_TIME nor
OPT_SPACE.

Possible responses to the SET TO DEFAULT prompt are:

YES     Set the superblock to request optimization to minimize run-
        ning time of the system. (If optimization to minimize disk
        space use is desired, it can be set using tunefs(1M).)

NO      Ignore this error condition.

```
IMPOSSIBLE MINFREE=D IN SUPERBLOCK (SET TO DEFAULT)
```

The superblock minimum space percentage is greater than 99 percent
or less then 0 percent.

Possible responses to the SET TO DEFAULT prompt are:

YES     Set the minfree parameter to 10 percent. (If some other per-
        centage is desired, it can be set using tunefs(1M).)

NO      Ignore this error condition.

```
MAGIC NUMBER WRONG
NCG OUT OF RANGE
CPG OUT OF RANGE
NCYL DOES NOT JIVE WITH NCG*CPG
SIZE PREPOSTEROUSLY LARGE
TRASHED VALUES IN SUPER BLOCK
...
F: BAD SUPER BLOCK: B
USE -b OPTION TO FSCK TO SPECIFY LOCATION OF AN ALTERNATE
SUPER-BLOCK TO SUPPLY NEEDED INFORMATION; SEE fsck(1M).
```

The superblock has been corrupted. An alternative superblock must
be selected from among the available copies. Choose an alternative
superblock by calculating its offset or call your service representative
or another qualified person. Specifying block 32 is a good first choice.

```
INTERNAL INCONSISTENCY: M
```

fsck has had an internal panic, whose message is M. This should
never happen. If it does, contact your service representative or
another qualified person.

```
CAN NOT SEEK: BLK B (CONTINUE)
```

fsck's request to move to a specified block number B in the file system failed. This should never happen. If it does, contact your service
representative or another qualified person.

Possible responses to the CONTINUE prompt are:

YES     Attempt to continue to run the file system check. (Note that
        the problem will often persist.) This error condition prevents
        a complete check of the file system. A second run of fsck
        should be made to recheck the file system. If the block was

part of the virtual memory buffer cache, fsck will terminate
with the message

```
Fatal I/O error
```

NO      Terminate the program.

```
CAN NOT READ: BLK B (CONTINUE)
```

fsck's request to read a specified block number $B$ in the file system
failed. This should never happen. If it does, contact your service representative or another qualified person.

Possible responses to the CONTINUE prompt are:

YES     Attempt to continue to run the file system check. fsck will
        retry the read and print out the message:

```
THE FOLLOWING SECTORS COULD NOT BE READ: N
```

where $N$ indicates the sectors that could not be read. If fsck
ever tries to write back one of the blocks on which the read
failed it will print the message:

```
WRITING ZERO'ED BLOCK N TO DISK
```

where $N$ indicates the sector that was written with zero's. If
the disk is experiencing hardware problems, the problem will
persist. This error condition prevents a complete check of the
file system. A second run of fsck should be made to recheck
the file system. If the block was part of the virtual memory
buffer cache, fsck will terminate with the message

```
Fatal I/O error
```

NO      Terminate the program.

```
CAN NOT WRITE: BLK B (CONTINUE)
```

fsck's request to write a specified block number $B$ in the file system failed. The disk is write-protected; check the write-protect lock on the drive. If that is not the problem, contact your service representative or another qualified person.

Possible responses to the CONTINUE prompt are:

YES    Attempt to continue to run the file system check. The write operation will be retried. Sectors that could not be written will be indicated by the message:

```
THE FOLLOWING SECTORS COULD NOT BE WRITTEN: N
```

where $N$ indicates the sectors that could not be written. If the disk is experiencing hardware problems, the problem will persist. This error condition prevents a complete check of the file system. A second run of fsck should be made to recheck this file system. If the block was part of the virtual memory buffer cache, fsck will terminate with the message:

```
Fatal I/O error
```

NO    Terminate the program.

```
bad inode number DDD to ginode
```

An internal error was caused by an attempt to read non-existent inode $DDD$. This error causes fsck to exit. If this occurs, contact your service representative or another qualified person.

# ❏ Phase 1: Check Blocks and Sizes

This phase checks the inode list. It reports error conditions encountered while:

▲  checking inode types

▲  setting up the zero-link-count table

▲  examining inode block numbers for bad or duplicate blocks

▲  checking inode size

▲  checking inode format

All the errors in this phase except INCORRECT BLOCK COUNT and PAR-TIALLY TRUNCATED INODE are fatal if the file system is being preened.

## Phase 1 Messages

```
UNKNOWN FILE TYPE I=I (CLEAR)
```

The mode word of the inode *I* indicates that the inode is not a special block inode, special character inode, socket inode, regular inode, symbolic link, FIFO file, or directory inode.

Possible responses to the CLEAR prompt are:

YES    De-allocate inode *I* by zeroing out its contents. This will always generate the UNALLOCATED error message in Phase 2 for each directory entry pointing to this inode.

NO     Ignore this error condition.

```
PARTIALLY TRUNCATED INODE I=I (SALVAGE)
```

fsck has found inode *I* whose size is shorter than the number of blocks allocated to it. This condition should only occur if the system crashes while truncating a file. When preening the file system, fsck completes the truncation to the specified size.

Possible responses to the SALVAGE prompt are:

YES     Complete the truncation to the size specified in the inode.

NO      Ignore this error condition.

LINK COUNT TABLE OVERFLOW (CONTINUE)

An internal table for fsck containing allocated inodes with a link count of zero has no more room.

Possible responses to the CONTINUE prompt are:

YES     Continue with the program. This error condition prevents a complete check of the file system. A second run of fsck should be made to recheck the file system. If another allocated inode with a zero link count is found, the error message is repeated.

NO      Terminate the program.

B BAD I=I

Inode *I* contains block number *B* with a number lower than the number of the first data block in the file system or greater than the number of the last block in the file system. This error condition may generate the EXCESSIVE BAD BLKS error message in Phase 1 if inode *I* has too many block numbers outside the file system range. This error condition generates the BAD/DUP error messages in Phases 2 and 4.

EXCESSIVE BAD BLKS I=I (CONTINUE)

There are too many (usually more than 10) blocks with a number lower than the number of the first data block in the file system or greater than the number of the last block in the file system associated with inode *I*.

Possible responses to the CONTINUE prompt are:

YES    Ignore the rest of the blocks in this inode and continue check-
       ing with the next inode in the file system. This error condi-
       tion prevents a complete check of the file system. A second
       run of `fsck` should be made to recheck this file system.

NO     Terminate the program.

---

BAD STATE *DDD* TO BLKERR

An internal error has scrambled `fsck`'s state map to have the impossible value *DDD*. `fsck` exits immediately. If this occurs, contact your
service representative or another qualified person.

---

*B* DUP I=*I*

Inode *I* contains block number *B* that is already claimed by another
inode. This error condition may generate the EXCESSIVE DUP BLKS
error message in Phase 1 if inode *I* has too many block numbers
claimed by other inodes. This error condition invokes Phase 1B and
generates the BAD/DUP error message in Phases 2 and 4.

---

BAD MODE: MAKE IT A FILE?

This message is generated when the status of a given inode is set to
all ones, indicating file system damage. This message does not indicate disk damage, unless it appears repeatedly after `fsck -y` has
been run. A response of `y` causes `fsck` to reinitialize the inode to a
reasonable value.

---

EXCESSIVE DUP BLKS I=*I* (CONTINUE)

There are too many (usually more than 10) blocks claimed by other
inodes.

Possible responses to the CONTINUE prompt are:

YES    Ignore the rest of the blocks in this inode and continue check-
       ing with the next inode in the file system. This error condi-

tion prevents a complete check of the file system. A second run of `fsck` should be made to recheck the file system.

NO     Terminate the program.

---

`DUP TABLE OVERFLOW (CONTINUE)`

---

An internal table in `fsck` containing duplicate block numbers has no more room.

Possible responses to the `CONTINUE` prompt are:

YES    Continue with the program. This error condition prevents a complete check of the file system. A second run of `fsck` should be made to recheck the file system. If another duplicate block is found, this error message will repeat.

NO     Terminate the program.

---

`PARTIALLY ALLOCATED INODE I=`*I*` (CLEAR)`

---

Inode *I* is neither allocated nor unallocated.

Possible responses to the `CLEAR` prompt are:

YES    De-allocate inode *I* by zeroing out its contents.

NO     Ignore this error condition.

---

`INCORRECT BLOCK COUNT I=`*I*` (`*X*` should be `*Y*`) (CORRECT)`

---

The block count for inode *I* is *X* blocks, but should be *Y* blocks. When preening, the count is corrected.

Possible responses to the `CORRECT` prompt are:

YES    Replace the block count of inode *I* by *Y*.

NO     Ignore this error condition.

# ❑ Phase 1B: Rescan for More DUPS

When a duplicate block is found in the file system, the file system is rescanned to find the inode that previously claimed that block. When the duplicate block is found, the following informational message appears:

```
B DUP I=I
```

Inode *I* contains block number *B* that is already claimed by another inode. This error condition generates the BAD/DUP error message in Phase 2. You can determine which inodes have overlapping blocks by examining this error condition and the DUP error condition in Phase 1.

# ❑ Phase 2: Check Pathnames

This phase removes directory entries pointing to bad inodes found in Phases 1 and 1B. It reports error conditions resulting from:

▲  incorrect root inode mode and status

▲  directory inode pointers out of range

▲  directory entries pointing to bad inodes

▲  directory integrity checks

All errors in this phase are fatal if the file system is being preened, except for directories not being a multiple of the block size and extraneous hard links.

## Phase 2 Messages

```
ROOT INODE UNALLOCATED (ALLOCATE)
```

The root inode (usually inode number 2) has no allocate mode bits. This should never happen.

Possible responses to the ALLOCATE prompt are:

YES     Allocate inode 2 as the root inode. The files and directories usually found in the root will be recovered in Phase 3 and put into the lost+found directory. If the attempt to allocate the root fails, fsck will exit with the message

```
CANNOT ALLOCATE ROOT INODE
```

NO      Terminate the program.

```
ROOT INODE NOT DIRECTORY (REALLOCATE)
```

The root inode (usually inode number 2) of the file system is not a directory inode.

Possible responses to the REALLOCATE prompt are:

YES     Clear the existing contents of the root inode and reallocate it. The files and directories usually found in the root will be recovered in Phase 3 and put into the lost+found directory. If the attempt to allocate the root fails, fsck will exit with the message:

```
CANNOT ALLOCATE ROOT INODE
```

NO      fsck will then prompt with FIX

Possible responses to the FIX prompt are:

YES     Change the type of the root inode to directory. If the root inode's data blocks are not directory blocks, many error messages will be generated.

NO      Terminate the program.

```
DUPS/BAD IN ROOT INODE (REALLOCATE)
```

Phase 1 or Phase 1B has found duplicate blocks or bad blocks in the root inode (usually inode number 2) of the file system.

Possible responses to the REALLOCATE prompt are:

YES  Clear the existing contents of the root inode and reallocate it.
The files and directories usually found in the root will be
recovered in Phase 3 and put into the lost+found directory.
If the attempt to allocate the root fails, fsck will exit with
the message:

> CANNOT ALLOCATE ROOT INODE

NO  fsck will then prompt with CONTINUE.

Possible responses to the CONTINUE prompt are:

YES  Ignore the DUPS/BAD error condition in the root inode and
try to continue running the file system check. If the root
inode is not correct, this may generate many other error messages.

NO  Terminate the program.

> NAME TOO LONG $F$ ·

An excessively long path name has been found. This usually indicates loops in the file system name space. This can occur if a privileged user has made circular links to directories. These links must be
removed.

> I OUT OF RANGE I=$I$ NAME=$F$ (REMOVE)

A directory entry $F$ has an inode number $I$ that is greater than the end
of the inode list.

Possible responses to the REMOVE prompt are:

YES  Remove the directory entry $F$.

NO  Ignore this error condition.

```
UNALLOCATED I=I OWNER=O MODE=M SIZE=S MTIME=T TYPE=F (REMOVE)
```

A directory or file entry *F* points to an unallocated inode *I*. The owner *O*, mode *M*, size *S*, modify time *T*, and name *F* are printed.

Possible responses to the REMOVE prompt are:

YES     Remove the directory entry *F*.

NO      Ignore this error condition.

```
DUP/BAD I=I OWNER=O MODE=M SIZE=S MTIME=T TYPE=F (REMOVE)
```

Phase 1 or Phase 1B has found duplicate blocks or bad blocks associated with directory or file entry *F*, inode *I*. The owner *O*, mode *M*, size *S*, modify time *T*, and directory name *F* are printed.

Possible responses to the REMOVE prompt are:

YES     Remove the directory entry *F*.

NO      Ignore this error condition.

```
ZERO LENGTH DIRECTORY I=I OWNER=O MODE=M SIZE=S MTIME=T DIR=F (REMOVE)
```

A directory entry *F* has a size *S* that is zero. The owner *O*, mode *M*, size *S*, modify time *T*, and directory name *F* are printed.

Possible responses to the REMOVE prompt are:

YES     Remove the directory entry *F*; this will generate the BAD/DUP error message in Phase 4.

NO      Ignore this error condition.

```
DIRECTORY TOO SHORT I=I OWNER=O MODE=M SIZE=S MTIME=T DIR=F (FIX)
```

A directory *F* has been found whose size *S* is less than the minimum size directory. The owner *O*, mode *M*, size *S*, modify time *T*, and directory name *F* are printed.

Possible responses to the FIX prompt are:

YES    Increase the size of the directory to the minimum directory size.

NO    Ignore this directory.

```
DIRECTORY F LENGTH S NOT MULTIPLE OF B (ADJUST)
```

A directory *F* has been found with size *S* that is not a multiple of the directory block size *B*.

Possible responses to the ADJUST prompt are:

YES    Round up the length to the appropriate block size. When preening the file system only a warning is printed and the directory is adjusted.

NO    Ignore the error condition.

```
DIRECTORY CORRUPTED I=I OWNER=O MODE=M SIZE=S MTIME=T DIR=F (SALVAGE)
```

A directory with an inconsistent internal state has been found.

Possible responses to the SALVAGE prompt are:

YES    Throw away all entries up to the next directory boundary (usually a 512-byte boundary). This drastic action can throw away up to 42 entries, and should be taken only after other recovery efforts have failed.

NO    Skip to the next directory boundary and resume reading, but do not modify the directory.

```
BAD INODE NUMBER FOR `.' I=I OWNER=O MODE=M SIZE=S MTIME=T DIR=F (FIX)
```

A directory *I* has been found whose inode number for "." does not equal *I*.

Possible responses to the `FIX` prompt are:

YES     Change the inode number for "." to be equal to *I*.

NO      Leave the inode number for "." unchanged.

```
MISSING `.' I=I OWNER=O MODE=M SIZE=S MTIME=T DIR=F (FIX)
```

A directory *I* has been found whose first entry is unallocated.

Possible responses to the `FIX` prompt are:

YES     Build an entry for "." with inode number equal to *I*.

NO      Leave the directory unchanged.

```
MISSING `.' I=I OWNER=O MODE=M SIZE=S MTIME=T DIR=F
CANNOT FIX, FIRST ENTRY IN DIRECTORY CONTAINS F
```

A directory *I* has been found whose first entry is *F*. `fsck` cannot resolve this problem. The file system should be mounted and entry *F* moved elsewhere. The file system should then be unmounted and `fsck` should be run again.

```
MISSING `.' I=I OWNER=O MODE=M SIZE=S MTIME=T DIR=F
CANNOT FIX, INSUFFICIENT SPACE TO ADD `.'
```

A directory *I* has been found whose first entry is not ".". This should never happen. `fsck` cannot resolve the problem. If this occurs, contact your service representative or another qualified person.

```
EXTRA `.' ENTRY I=I OWNER=O MODE=M SIZE=S MTIME=T DIR=F (FIX)
```

A directory *I* has been found that has more than one entry for ".".

Possible responses to the `FIX` prompt are:

YES        Remove the extra entry for ".".

NO         Leave the directory unchanged.

```
BAD INODE NUMBER FOR `..' I=I OWNER=O MODE=M SIZE=S MTIME=T DIR=F(FIX)
```

A directory *I* has been found whose inode number for ".." does not equal the parent of *I*.

Possible responses to the `FIX` prompt are:

YES        Change the inode number for ".." to be equal to the parent
           of *I*. (Note that ".." in the root inode points to itself.)

NO         Leave the inode number for ".." unchanged.

```
MISSING `..' I=I OWNER=O MODE=M SIZE=S MTIME=T DIR=F (FIX)
```

A directory *I* has been found whose second entry is unallocated.

Possible responses to the `FIX` prompt are:

YES        Build an entry for ".." with inode number equal to the par-
           ent of *I*. (Note that ".." in the root inode points to itself.)

NO         Leave the directory unchanged.

```
MISSING `.' I=I OWNER=O MODE=M SIZE=S MTIME=T DIR=F
CANNOT FIX, SECOND ENTRY IN DIRECTORY CONTAINS F
```

A directory *I* has been found whose second entry is *F*. `fsck` cannot resolve this problem. The file system should be mounted and entry *F* moved elsewhere. The file system should then be unmounted and fsck should be run again.

```
MISSING `.' I=I OWNER=O MODE=M SIZE=S MTIME=T DIR=F
CANNOT FIX, INSUFFICIENT SPACE TO ADD `..'
```

A directory *I* has been found whose second entry is not "..." (the parent directory). fsck cannot resolve this problem. The file system should be mounted and the second entry in the directory moved elsewhere. The file system should then be unmounted and fsck should be run again.

```
EXTRA `..' ENTRY I=I OWNER=O MODE=M SIZE=S MTIME=T DIR=F (FIX)
```

A directory *I* has been found that has more than one entry for "..." (the parent directory).

Possible responses to the FIX prompt are:

YES     Remove the extra entry for "..." (the parent directory).

NO      Leave the directory unchanged.

```
N IS AN EXTRANEOUS HARD LINK TO A DIRECTORY D (REMOVE)
```

fsck has found a hard link *N* to a directory *D*. When preening the extraneous links are ignored.

Possible responses to the REMOVE prompt are:

YES     Delete the extraneous entry *N*.

NO      Ignore the error condition.

```
BAD INODE S TO DESCEND
```

An internal error has caused an impossible state *S* to be passed to the routine that descends the file system directory structure. fsck exits.

If this occurs, contact your service representative or another qualified person.

> BAD RETURN STATE *S* FROM DESCEND

An internal error has caused an impossible state *S* to be returned from the routine that descends the file system directory structure. fsck exits. If you encounter this error, contact your service representative or another qualified person.

> BAD STATE *S* FOR ROOT INODE

An internal error has caused an impossible state *S* to be assigned to the root inode. fsck exits. If this occurs, contact your service representative or another qualified person.

# ❑ Phase 3: Check Connectivity

This phase checks the directories examined in Phase 2. It reports error conditions resulting from:

- ■ unreferenced directories
- ■ missing or full lost+found directories

## Phase 3 Messages

> UNREF DIR I=*I* OWNER=*O* MODE=*M* SIZE=*S* MTIME=*T* (RECONNECT)

The directory inode *I* was not connected to a directory entry when the file system was traversed. The owner *O*, mode *M*, size *S*, and modify time *T* of directory inode *I* are printed. When preening, the directory is reconnected if its size is non-zero; otherwise it is cleared.

Possible responses to the RECONNECT prompt are:

YES       Reconnect directory inode *I* to the file system in the directory
          for lost files (usually the lost+found directory). This may
          generate the lost+found error messages in Phase 3 if there
          are problems connecting directory inode *I* to the lost+-
          found directory. It may also generate the CONNECTED error
          message in Phase 3 if the link was successful.

NO        Ignore this error condition. This generates the UNREF error
          message in Phase 4.

```
NO lost+found DIRECTORY (CREATE)
```

There is no lost+found directory in the root directory of the file system; When preening fsck tries to create a lost+found directory.

Possible responses to the CREATE prompt are:

YES       Create a lost+found directory in the root of the file system.
          This may produce the message:

```
NO SPACE LEFT IN / (EXPAND)
```

          See below for the possible responses. Inability to create a
          lost+found directory generates the message:

```
SORRY. CANNOT CREATE lost+found DIRECTORY
```

          and aborts the attempt to link up the lost inode. This in turn
          generates the UNREF error message in Phase 4.

NO        Abort the attempt to link up the lost inode. This generates the
          UNREF error message in Phase 4.

```
lost+found IS NOT A DIRECTORY (REALLOCATE)
```

The entry for lost+found is not a directory.

Possible responses to the REALLOCATE prompt are:

YES   Allocate a directory inode, and change lost+found to refer-
      ence it. The previous inode referenced by the lost+found
      directory is not cleared. Thus it will either be reclaimed as an
      UNREF'ed inode or have its link count ADJUST'ed later in
      this phase. Inability to create a lost+found directory gener-
      ates the message:

```
SORRY. CANNOT CREATE lost+found DIRECTORY
```

      and aborts the attempt to link up the lost inode. This in turn
      generates the UNREF error message in Phase 4.

NO    Abort the attempt to link up the lost inode. This generates the
      UNREF error message in Phase 4.

```
NO SPACE LEFT IN /lost+found (EXPAND)
```

There is no space to add another entry to the lost+found directory
in the root directory of the file system. When preening the lost+-
found directory is expanded.

Possible responses to the EXPAND prompt are:

YES   Expand the lost+found directory to make room for the
      new entry. If the attempted expansion fails fsck prints the
      message:

```
SORRY. NO SPACE IN lost+found DIRECTORY
```

      and aborts the attempt to link up the lost inode. This in turn
      generates the UNREF error message in Phase 4. Clear out
      unnecessary entries in the lost+found directory. This error
      is fatal if the file system is being preened.

NO    Abort the attempt to link up the lost inode. This generates the
      UNREF error message in Phase 4.

```
DIR I=I1 CONNECTED. PARENT WAS I=I2
```

This is an advisory message indicating that a directory inode *I1* was successfully connected to the `lost+found` directory. The parent inode *I2* of the directory inode *I1* is replaced by the inode number of the `lost+found` directory.

```
DIRECTORY F LENGTH S NOT MULTIPLE OF B (ADJUST)
```

A directory *F* has been found with size *S* that is not a multiple of the directory block size *B*. (Note that this may reoccur in Phase 3 if the error condition is not corrected in Phase 2).

Possible responses to the `ADJUST` prompt are:

YES　　Round up the length to the appropriate block size. When preening the file system only a warning is printed and the directory is adjusted.

NO　　Ignore the error condition.

```
BAD INODE S TO DESCEND
```

An internal error has caused an impossible state *S* to be passed to the routine that descends the file system directory structure. `fsck` exits. If this occurs, contact your service representative or another qualified person.

# ❏ Phase 4: Check Reference Counts

This phase checks the link count information obtained in Phases 2 and 3. It reports error conditions resulting from:

▲　unreferenced files

▲　missing or full `lost+found` directory

▲ incorrect link counts for files, directories, symbolic links, or special files

▲ unreferenced files, symbolic links, and directories

▲ bad or duplicate blocks in files, symbolic links, and directories

All errors in this phase (except running out of space in the `lost+found` directory) are correctable if the file system is being preened.

## Phase 4 Messages

```
UNREF DIR I=I OWNER=O MODE=M SIZE=S MTIME=T (RECONNECT)
```

Inode *I* was not connected to a directory entry when the file system was traversed. The owner *O*, mode *M*, size *S*, and modify time *T* of inode *I* are printed. When preening the file is cleared if either its size or its link count is zero; otherwise it is reconnected.

Possible responses to the `RECONNECT` prompt are:

YES  Reconnect inode *I* to the file system in the directory for lost files (usually the `lost+found` directory). This may generate the `lost+found` error message in Phase 4 if there are problems connecting inode *I* to the `lost+found` directory.

NO  Ignore this error condition. This will always invoke the `CLEAR` error condition in Phase 4.

```
(CLEAR)
```

The inode mentioned in the error message immediately preceding cannot be reconnected. This message cannot appear if the file system is being preened, because lack of space to reconnect files is a fatal error.

Possible responses to the `CLEAR` prompt are:

YES  De-allocate the inode by zeroing out its contents.

NO  Ignore this error condition.

```
NO lost+found DIRECTORY (CREATE)
```

There is no `lost+found` directory in the root directory of the file system; when preening `fsck` tries to create a `lost+found` directory.

Possible responses to the CREATE prompt are:

YES    Create a `lost+found` directory in the root of the file system. This may generate the message:

```
NO SPACE LEFT IN / (EXPAND)
```

See below for the possible responses. Inability to create a `lost+found` directory generates the message:

```
SORRY. CANNOT CREATE lost+found DIRECTORY
```

and aborts the attempt to link up the lost inode. This in turn generates the UNREF error message in Phase 4.

NO    Abort the attempt to link up the lost inode. This generates the UNREF error message in Phase 4.

```
lost+found IS NOT A DIRECTORY (REALLOCATE)
```

The entry for `lost+found` is not a directory.

Possible responses to the REALLOCATE prompt are:

YES    Allocate a directory inode and change the `lost+found` directory to reference it. The previous inode reference by the `lost+found` directory is not cleared. Thus it will either be reclaimed as an UNREF'ed inode or have its link count ADJUST'ed later in this phase. Inability to create a `lost+-found` directory generates the message:

```
SORRY. CANNOT CREATE lost+found DIRECTORY
```

and aborts the attempt to link up the lost inode. This generates the UNREF error message in Phase 4.

NO  Abort the attempt to link up the lost inode. This generates the UNREF error message in Phase 4.

```
NO SPACE LEFT IN /lost+found (EXPAND)
```

There is no space to add another entry to the lost+found directory in the root directory of the file system. When preening the lost+found directory is expanded.

Possible responses to the EXPAND prompt are:

YES Expand the lost+found directory to make room for the new entry. If the attempted expansion fails fsck prints the message:

```
SORRY. NO SPACE IN lost+found DIRECTORY
```

and aborts the attempt to link up the lost inode. This generates the UNREF error message in Phase 4. Clear out unnecessary entries in the lost+found directory. This error is fatal if the file system is being preened.

NO  Abort the attempt to link up the lost inode. This generates the UNREF error message in Phase 4.

```
LINK COUNT TYPE I=I OWNER=O MODE=M SIZE=S MTIME=T COUNT=X SHOULD BE Y (ADJUST)
```

The link count for inode $I$ is $X$ but should be $Y$. The owner $O$, mode $M$, size $S$, and modify time $T$ are printed. When preening the link count is adjusted unless the number of references is increasing, a condition that should never occur unless precipitated by a hardware failure. When the number of references is increasing during preening, fsck exits with the message:

```
LINK COUNT INCREASING
```

Possible responses to the ADJUST prompt are:

YES  Replace the link count of file inode $I$ by $Y$.

NO      Ignore this error condition.

> UNREF TYPE I=*I* OWNER=*O* MODE=*M* SIZE=*S* MTIME=*T* (CLEAR)

Inode *I* was not connected to a directory entry when the file system was traversed. The owner *O*, mode *M*, size *S*, and modify time *T* of inode *I* are printed. Since this is a file that was not connected because its size or link count was zero, it is cleared during preening.

Possible responses to the CLEAR prompt are:

YES     De-allocate inode *I* by zeroing out its contents.

NO      Ignore this error condition.

> BAD/DUP TYPE I=*I* OWNER=*O* MODE=*M* SIZE=*S* MTIME=*T* (CLEAR)

Phase 1 or Phase 1B has found duplicate blocks or bad blocks associated with inode *I*. The owner *O*, mode *M*, size *S*, and modify time *T* of inode *I* are printed. This message cannot appear when the file system is being preened, because it would have caused a fatal error earlier.

Possible responses to the CLEAR prompt are:

YES     De-allocate inode *I* by zeroing out its contents.

NO      Ignore this error condition.

# ❑ Phase 5: Check Cylinder Groups

This phase checks the free block and used inode maps. It reports error conditions resulting from:

▲ allocated blocks in the free block maps

▲ free blocks missing from free block maps

▲ incorrect total free block count

▲ free inodes in the used inode maps

▲   allocated inodes missing from used inode maps

▲   incorrect total used inode count

## Phase 5 Messages

```
OG C: BAD MAGIC NUMBER
```

The magic number of cylinder group C is wrong. This usually indicates that the cylinder group maps have been destroyed. When running interactively, the cylinder group map is marked as needing reconstruction. This error is fatal if the file system is being preened.

```
BLK(S) MISSING IN BIT MAPS (SALVAGE)
```

A cylinder group block is missing some free blocks. The maps are reconstructed during preening.

Possible responses to the SALVAGE prompt are:

YES     Reconstruct the free block map.

NO      Ignore this error condition.

```
SUMMARY INFORMATION BAD (SALBAGE)
```

The summary information was found to be incorrect. The summary information is recomputed during preening.

Possible responses to the SALVAGE prompt are:

YES     Reconstruct the summary information.

NO      Ignore this error condition.

```
FREE BLK COUNT(S) WRONG IN SUPERBLOCK (SALVAGE)
```

The superblock free block information was found to be incorrect. The superblock free block information is recomputed during preening.

Possible responses to the SALVAGE prompt are:

YES     Reconstruct the superblock free block information.

NO      Ignore this error condition.

# ❏ Cleanup Phase

After a file system has been checked, a few cleanup functions are performs. The cleanup phase displays advisory messages about the status of the file system.

```
V files, W used, X free (Y frags, Z blocks)
```

This is an advisory message indicating that the file system contains *V* files using *W* fragment-sized blocks, and that there are *X* fragment-sized blocks free in the file system. The numbers in parentheses break the free count down into *Y* free fragments and *Z* free full-sized blocks.

```
***** FILE SYSTEM WAS MODIFIES *****
```

This is an advisory message indicating that the file system was modified by fsck. If this file system is mounted, you may need to unmount it and run fsck again; otherwise the work done by fsck may be undone by the in-core copies of tables.

# Glossary

**application**  The software designed to perform a specific task. For example, you use a spreadsheet application to manipulate columns and rows of numbers and a word processing application to create, edit, and format printed pages.

**automounter**  A daemon that automatically and transparently mounts an NFS file system as needed. See `automount`(1).

**bad block**  A disk sector that does not store data reliably.

**block**  The basic unit of buffering in the kernel. See also *indirect block*, *logical block*, and *physical block*.

**block device**  A device upon which a file system can be mounted, like a hard disk drive. Data transfers occur in blocks.

**boot**  To start the operating system. The kernel bootstraps itself from secondary storage into an empty machine.

**boot block**  the first block of a file system. It contains a bootstrap program in bootable file system, and is reserved but unused otherwise.

**boot program**  A program that loads the operating system into memory.

**buffers**  A staging area for input and output where arbitrary-length transactions are collected into blocks before being read or written.

**buffer pool**  A region of memory available to the file system for holding blocks of data.

**character device**
  A device on which a files system cannot be mounted, such as a terminal or the null device.

*child process*     See *fork*.

*client*     A compute that mounts a resource that has been shared by a server.

*client caching*     The ability of an RFS client to store remote data blocks in its local buffer pools. This technique improves RFS performance by reducing the number of times data must be read across the network.

*clock tick*     The system clock ticks HZ times per second, where HZ is a hardware-dependent constant defined in the `param.h` header file.

*command*     An instruction that tells a computer to perform a specific function or to carry out a specific activity.

*crash*     If a hardware or software error condition develops that the system cannot recover from, it crashes. Possible fatal error conditions occur when the system cannot allocate resources, manage processes, respond to requests for system functions, or when the electrical power is unstable.

*cron*     A command that creates a daemon that invokes commands at specified dates and times.

*current name server*
     When a domain is established, a primary name server and option secondary name servers are assigned. Only one of these machines is actually handling domain name server responsibilities at a time. That machine is called the *current name server*. See also *domain name server, primary name server, secondary name server*.

*cylinder*     The set of all tracks on a disk that are the same distance from the axis about which the disk rotates.

*cylinder group*     A contiguous band of cylinders that are treated as a unit in a `ufs` file system.

*cylinder group map*
> The data structure that keeps track of allocated and free blocks in a cylinder group.

*daemon*
> A program that runs as an autonomous background process to handle UNIX system activities. Examples are the LP print service scheduler `lpsched`, `crontab`, the electronic mail service, and the BNU server `uucico`.

*default*
> The value that is used if no value is specified.

*device*
> A physical I/O unit, or the special file that represents it to UNIX.

*device driver*
> A Stream component whose principle functions are handling an associated physical device and transforming data and information between the external interface and the Stream.

*directory*
> A file that holds a list of filenames and associated i-numbers. A directory hierarchy is created by having one directory contain an entry for another directory.

*domain*
> A logical grouping of hosts in a Remote File Sharing environment. Each host in a domain relies on the same domain name server(s) for certain resource sharing and security services. Each domain has one primary and zero or more secondary domain name servers.

*domain name server*
> A computer that creates and maintains the following information for hosts in a Remote Files Sharing domain: advertised resources, host names and passwords, names and addresses for name servers of other domains, and host user and group information used for ID mapping. See also *current name server*, *primary name server*, and *secondary name server*.

*downstream*
> A direction of data flow going from Stream head towards a driver. Also called *write-side* and *output side*.

*driver*            A module that forms the Stream end. It can be a device driver or a pseudo-device driver, and is a required component in STREAMS, except in STREAM-based pipes. It typically handles data transfer between the kernel and a device and little or no processing of the data.

*error message*     A response from a program indicating that a problem has arisen or that something unexpected has happened that requires your attention.

*FIFO*              A named permanent pipe that allows two unrelated processes to exchange information using a pipe connection.

*file*              A potential source of input or destination for output. A file has an inode and/or associated contents. There are plain files, special files, and directories in a file system.

*filename*          A pathname, or the last component of a pathname.

*file system*       A collection of files that can be mounted on a block device. Each files appears exactly once in the i-list of the file system and is accessible via some path from the root directory of the file system.

*filter*            A program that processes the data in a file before it is printed.

*flow control*      A mechanism that regulates the rate of message transfer wiling a Stream and from user space into a Stream.

*fork*              To split one process into two, the parent process and the child process, with separate but initially identical text, data, and stack segments.

*formatting*        The process of imposing an addressing scheme on a disk, including establishing a VTOC and mapping both sides of the disk into tracks and sectors.

*free list*         File system blocks that are not occupied by data.

*i-list*            The index to a file system, listing all the inodes of the file system.

*ID mapping*        To define the permissions remote users and groups have to your shared resources. The tools available for mapping let you set permissions on a per-computer basis and on a global basis. You can then map individual users or groups by ID name or number. When you map IDs for RFS, it is easiest to do so with ID numbers, since mapping by name requires that you have copies of the remote computer's `/etc/passwd` and `/etc/group` files.

*indirect blocks*  Data blocks that are not directly referenced by an inode (because the file is larger that 10 logical blocks).

*init*              A general process spawner that is invoked as the last step in the boot procedure. It regularly checks a table that defines which processes should run at what run level.

*inode*             An element of a file system. An inode specifies all the properties of a particular file and locates the file's contents, if any.

*inode number, i-number*
                   The position of an inode in the i-list of a file system.

*interrupt*         A signal generated by a hardware condition or peripheral device. For example, typing a break character on a terminal will generate an interrupt that will terminate the user process connected to the terminal.

*IPC*               An acronym for interprocess communication.

*kernel*            The UNIX system proper: resident code that implements the system calls.

*kernel address space*
                   A portion of memory used for data and code addressable only by the kernel.

*line discipline*   A STREAMS module that performs `termio`(7) canonical and non-canonical processing. It shares some termio processing with a driver in a STREAMS terminal subsystem.

*local resource*   A directory that resides on your machine that you have made available to other computers. If a remote machine mounts the resource, it will have access to all subdirectories, files, named pipes, and devices within the directory, depending on file permissions.

*log files*   Files that record transactions and events that occur on the system. For example, the BNU package maintains eight log files, including lists of all errors, all connections to remote computers, and all file transfers.

*logical block*   A unit of data as it is handled by the system. UNIX uses a logical block size of 1024 bytes.

*message*   One or more linked message blocks. A message is referenced by its first message block and its type is defined by the message type of that block.

*message block*   A triplet consisting of a data buffer and associated control structures, a `msgb` structure and a `datab` structure. It carries data or information, as identified by its message type, in a Stream.

*message queue*   A linked list of zero or more messages connected together.

*modem*   A device that modulates and demodulates data transmitted over communication lines.

*module*   a defined set of kernel-level routines and data structures used to process data, status, and control information on a Stream. It is an optional element, but there can be many modules in one Stream. It consists of a pair of queues (read queue and write queue) and it communicates to other components in a Stream by passing messages.

*mount*          The action a client performs to access files in a server's shared directories. When a client mounts a resource, it does not copy that resource, but rather transparently accesses the resource as if it were local.

*mount point*    The location within the directory tree though which a machine accesses a mounted resource. The mount point for a resource is usually an empty directory.

*named Stream*   A Stream, typically a pipe, with a name associated with it via a call to `fattach`(3C). This is different from a named pipe (FIFO) in two ways:

- a named pipe is unidirectional while a named Stream is bidirectional

- a named Stream does not have to refer to a pipe; it can be any type of Stream.

*network*        The hardware and software that constitute the interconnections between computer systems, permitting electronic communications between the systems and associated peripherals.

*network listener*
                 The process used by a transport provider to wait for any type of incoming requests from the network. Once a request comes in, the listener directs it to one of the processes registered with the listener. The process represents a service, such as `uucp` (BNU), or RFS.

*Network File System (NFS)*
                 a file system type that provide file sharing across networks.

*networking*     Sending data from one system to another over some communication medium (coaxial cable, telephone lines, etc.). Common network services include file transfer, remote login, and remote execution.

*node name*      The name you assign to your computer for communications needs. Networking software such as BNU, RFS, and NFS, use this name to identify your machine.

**operating system**

> The program that manages the resources of the computer system. It handles I/O, process scheduling, and the file system.

**option**

> An addition to a command to improve or enhance the function. The option is usually indicated by a – followed by a key letter and arguments, if any.

**page**

> A fixed length, 1024-byte block that has a virtual address and that can be transferred between main and secondary storage.

**paging**

> The process by which programs are broken into pages and transferred between main and secondary storage by the paging daemon.

**parent process**  See *fork*.

**partitions**

> Units of storage space on a disk.

**pathname**

> The path through the file system tree that is specified to identify a file. An *absolute pathname* starts from the root directory /. A *relative pathname* starts from the current directory.

**physical block**  A unit of data as it is actually stored and manipulated. UNIX uses 1024-byte physical blocks.

**PID**

> A process ID, an integer that identifies a process.

**pipeline**

> Two or more commands connected with the pipe operator |. The standard output of the first command becomes the standard input of the next command, and so on. Pipelines are uni-directional.

**polling**

> The interrogation of devices by operating systems to avoid contention, determine status, or ascertain readiness to send or receive data.

**primary name server**
The computer that is assigned to provide a central location for the addressing and information collection for an RFS domain. Information includes a list of domain members, resources offered by domain members, and optional user ID mapping information. Secondary name servers can be assigned to continue limited name service when the primary is down. See also *current name server, domain name server, secondary name server.*

**process**
A connected sequence of computation. A process has a core image with an instruction counter, a current directory, a set of open files, a controlling terminal, a userid, and a groupid.

**process id**
An integer that identifies a process.

**profile**
An optional shell script `.profile` that is executed when a user logs in to establish an environment and other working conditions tailored the that particular user.

**profiler**
A tool that collects statistics about the execution flow of a process.

**pseudo-device driver**
A software driver, not directly associated with a physical device, that performs functions internal to a Stream, such as a multiplexor or a log driver.

**raw device**
A block device with unbuffered read and write operations that are synchronized to natural records of the physical device.

**reboot**
See *boot.*

**Remote File Sharing (RFS)**
a file system type that provide file sharing across networks.

*remote resource* A directory that resides on a remote machine that is available for you to connect to. You must mount the resource to make it available to users on your system. Once you mount the remote resource, your users can access all subdirectories, files, named pipes, and devices in the resource, depending on the files permissions established by the server.

*resource*          See *local resource* and *remote resource*.

*root*              The origin of the directory hierarchy in a file system, called '/' by convention.

*rotational gap*    The gap between actual disk locations of blocks of data of the same file The rotational gap compensates for the continuous high-speed rotation of the disk so that when the controller is ready to reference the next physical block, the read/write head is positioned correctly at the beginning of that block.

*run level*         A software configuration of the system that allows a particular group of processes to exit. Also called a *run state*.

*schedule*          To assign resources to processes.

*search path*       An ordered list of directory pathnames that will be prefixed to command names until the pathname of an executable file results. The search path is specified in the PATH environment variable.

*secondary name server*
                    A computer designated to take over name server responsibilities temporarily should the primary domain name server fail. The secondary cannot change any domain information. See also *current name server, domain name server, primary name server*.

*sector*            A 512-byte portion of a track that can be accessed by the disk heads in the course of a predetermined rotational displacement of the storage device.

*segment*  A contiguous range of address space of a process with consistent storage access capabilities. The four segments are:

- the *text segment*, containing executable code

- the *data segment*, containing static data that is specifically initialized

- the *bss segment*, containing static data that is initialized by default to zero values

- the *stack segment*, contain automatic data.

Sometimes the data segment, bss segment, and stack segment are collectively called the data segment.

*semaphore*  An IPC facility that allows two or more processes to be synchronized.

*server*  A machine that shares file systems or portions of file systems, allowing remote machines to mount these resources

*share*  The action a server performs to allow some or all of its file system to become available to other machines. See `share`(1).

*shared memory*  An IPC facility that allows two or more processes to share the same data space.

*shared resource*
          a directory tree that can be accessed by users on remote computers using the RFS or NFS file sharing systems. See also *local resource, remote resource*.

*signal*  An exceptional occurrence that causes a process to terminate or divert from the normal flow of control. See *interrupt* and *trap*.

*special file*  an inode that designates a device.

*Stream*  A kernel aggregate created by connecting STREAMS components together. The primary components are the Stream head, the driver, and zero or more pushable modules between the Stream head and driver.

**Stream-based pipe**

A mechanism used for bidirectional data transfer implemented using STREAMS and sharing the properties of STREAMS-based devices.

**Stream end**

The Stream component furthest from the user process, containing a driver.

**Stream head**

The Stream component closest to the user process. It provides the interface between the Stream and the user process.

**STREAMS**

A kernel mechanism that provides the framework for network services and data communications. It defines interface standards for character input/output within the kernel, and between the kernel and user level.

The STREAMS mechanism consists of integral functions, utility routines, kernel facilities, and a set of structures.

**super block**

The second block in a file system, containing the block allocation information. See also *boot block*.

**swap**

To move the core image of an executing program between main memory and secondary storage to make room for other processes.

**swap area**

The part of secondary storage to which core images are swapped. The area is disjoint from the files system.

**system calls**

The set of system primitive functions though which all system operations are allocated, initiated, monitored, manipulated, and terminated. Some of them can be invoked by user processes to accomplish system-dependent functions like I/O, process creation, system data structure initialization or interrogation, etc.

**system name**

The value of the SYS parameter, up to six characters long.

*track*  An addressable ring of sectors on a disk or diskette. Each disk or diskette has a predefined number of concentric tracks, information the read/write head uses to properly position itself to access sectors of data. See also *cylinder, sector.*

*trap*  A method of detecting and interpreting certain hardware and software conditions via software. A trap is set to catch a signal or interrupt and determine what course of action to take.

*tunable parameter*

variables used to set the sizes and thresholds of the various control structures of the operating system.

*tuning*  Modifying the tunable parameters of an operating system to improve system performance.

*UID*  User identification number. See *userid/groupid.*

*upstream*  A direction of data flow going from a driver towards the Stream head. Also called *read-side* and *input side.*

*user/group name*

The names associated with each local user and group that is allowed access to your computer. This information can be found in the first field of the /etc/passwd or /etc/group files, respectively. Remote users and groups can be assigned the same permissions as the local users and groups by using RFS ID mapping. See *ID mapping.*

*userid/groupid*

Every user and group name has corresponding number that is used by the UNIX operation system to handle permissions to files, directories, devices, etc. These numbers are defined in the third field of the /etc/passwd or /etc/group files, respectively. Remote users and groups can be assigned the same permissions as the local users and groups by using RFS ID mapping. See *ID mapping.*

*virtual memory*

A mechanism that permits programs to treat disk storage as an extension of main memory.

*VTOC*

Volume Table of Contents, the section of a disk which shows how the partitions on the disk are allocated.

# Index

## Files

`$HOME/.profile`  16

`$PATH`, *see* PATH variable

`.profile`  6, 18, 83

`/boot`  36, 101, 246

`/dev`  97, 99

`/dev/log`  271

`/etc/acct/holidays`  45, 47, 285

`/etc/boot_tab`  131

`/etc/conf/pack.d/rfs/space.c`  278

`/etc/device.tab`  132

`/etc/dfs/dfstab`  176, 182

`/etc/dfs/sharetab`  182

`/etc/dgroup.tab`  141

`/etc/group`  337, 345

`/etc/inittab`  22

`/etc/master.d`  29, 246, 254

`/etc/master.d/arp`  257

`/etc/master.d/hrt`  260, 272

`/etc/master.d/ip`  257

**`/etc/master.d/kernel`**  265

`/etc/master.d/kernel`  6, 30, 249, 250, 258–260, 262, 264, 266, 270, 271, 272, 274

`/etc/master.d/llcloop`  257

`/etc/master.d/log`  260, 271

`/etc/master.d/msg`  256, 261, 275

`/etc/master.d/nfs`  257

`/etc/master.d/port`  273

`/etc/master.d/ports`  260

`/etc/master.d/prf`  234, 256, 260, 275

`/etc/master.d/README`  99

`/etc/master.d/rfs`  257, 262

`/etc/master.d/RT`  36

`/etc/master.d/rt`  30, 34, 40

`/etc/master.d/s5`  6, 260, 273

`/etc/master.d/sad`  260, 271

`/etc/master.d/sem`  249, 250, 257, 261, 276

`/etc/master.d/shm`  257, 261, 277

`/etc/master.d/tcp`  257

`/etc/master.d/ts`  30, 31, 40, 260, 273

`/etc/master.d/udp`  257

`/etc/master.d/ufs`  256, 260, 274

`/etc/master.d/xnamfs`  257

`/etc/mnttab`  177

`/etc/motd`  16

`/etc/passwd`  337, 345

`/etc/profile`  16–18

`/etc/skel`  18

`/etc/skel/.profile`  19

`/etc/system`  35, 36

`/etc/uucp`  152, 155

`/etc/vfstab`  75–76, 82, 83, 85, 87, 122, 123, 131, 181, 183, 185, 282, 306

`/home`  8, 79, 117

`/sbin/init`  110, 263

`/sbin/init.d/nfs`  178

`/sbin/init.d/perf`  190, 233

`/sbin/inittab`  124

`/sbin/mount`  239

`/sbin/rc2.d/S21perf`  190

`/stand`  101, 117, 127

`/stand/mini_system`  255

`/stand/mUNIX`  253, 255

`/stand/system`  120, 246

`/stand/unix`  119, 120, 129, 131, 243, 245, 249, 253

`/tmp`  8, 79, 103

`/usr`  8, 79, 103, 117

`/usr/include/sys/fs/ufs_quota.h`  82

`/usr/lib/acct`  45

`/usr/lib/acct/startup`  45

`/usr/src/cmd/acct`  45

`/var`  8, 79, 117

`/var/adm/pacct`  45

`/var/adm/sulog`  77

`/var/adm/wtmp`  46, 77

`/var/cron/log`  77

`/var/help/HELPLOG`  77

`/var/mail`  9

`/var/spell/spellhist`  77

`/var/spool/cron/crontab/sys`  191
`/var/spool/cron/crontabs`  7
`/var/spool/cron/crontabs/sys`  190, 191
`/var/spool/uucp`  80
`/var/spool/uucp/.Admin/command`  157
`/var/spool/uucp/.Admin/errors`  158
`/var/spool/uucp/.Admin/perflog`  158
`/var/tmp`  103, 118

## A

accounting  16, 23
    daily command summary  48–51
    daily usage report  47–48
    monthly reports  52
    process  44–51
    programs  45
accounting, process  230
`acctcom`  45, 50
`acctcon`  46, 282
`accton`  45
`acctsh`  48
application  333
application tuning  2
`ARCHITECTURE` parameter  258, 264
`ARG_MAX` parameter  258
`at`  7
`automount`  184–188, 333
automounter  184–188, 333
    debugging  185–188

## B

`backup`  119
bad block  333
    detecting  105, 106–107
    firmware error message  112
    handling  101, 104–116
    logging  109–111
    recovery  107–116
    system panic  113–114
bad terminal lines  225
Basic Network Utilities, *see* BNU
`batch`  7, 285
`biod`  176, 178, 184
block  333
block device, *see* device, block
block size
    choosing  69
    converting  72
    impact  66
    s5  66, 70, 71–72
    ufs  60, 63, 66, 73, 73–74
BNU  10, 152–160, 339
    administering  152
    checking status  152
    command log  157
    `Config` file  155, 156
    data base files  152, 153
    database files  152, 155–156
    detecting problems  160
    error log  158
    file transfer  152
    `Limits` file  155, 156
    log files  152, 157–159, 338
    network daemons  152, 339
    performance log  158–159
    remote command execution  152, 153
    remote login  152
    `uucico` daemon  156, 160, 335
    `uusched` daemon  156
    `uuxqt` daemon  156
boot  333
boot block  333
    s5  57
    ufs  61
boot file system  121
`boot` partition  101, 102, 118, 119–124
    operations on  120–121
boot program  117, 119, 120, 128, 333

boot, default parameters    125–127
bootable disk    127–132
bootable  operating  system,  configuring
        245–255
brk    268, 269
buffer pool    333
buffer size    3, 4
buffer usage    189
buffers    333
BUFHWM parameter    224, 258, 265
buildsys    124

# C

cd    20, 81, 82, 131, 281, 284
CDPATH variable    20
character device, *see* device, character
chargefee    48
child process    334
chmod    17, 81, 281
ckpacct    45
client    334
client caching    10, 334
clock tick    334
command    334, 340
compaction
    bfs    65, 96
compute-bound    32
configuration, system    245–255
configuring unix    245–255
core dumps    227
CORLIM parameter    269
cpio    72, 74, 80, 281, 284
CPU usage, monitoring    44
CPU utilization    189
crash    334
crash    243
CRC, *see* Cyclic Redundancy Check
cron    7, 45, 190, 192, 334
crontab    335
ct    152
cu    152, 160
cunix    249, 254–255
curses    21
Cyclic Redundancy Check    108

cylinder    334
cylinder group map, ufs    61, 331, 335
cylinder group, ufs    60, 61, 67, 73, 331, 334

# D

daemon    335
    biod    184
    disk error    110, 111, 113
    mountd    177, 181
    network    176, 177, 178, 181, 182, 183, 184
    nfsd    183
daemons
    mountd    178
data section    21
daytacct    48
dcopy    281
dd    72, 74
default    335
default configuration    2
demand paging, *see* paging
deny list    336
devattr    138–139
devfree    146
device    335
    alias    101–102, 132–133, 135
    attribute    101, 102, 132–140
    block    99, 100, 128, 333
    character    99, 100, 128, 333
    characteristics    97–101
    driver    102, 335
    group    101, 102, 140–145
    major number    97, 98–100, 108, 109
    minor number    97, 98–100, 108, 109
    partition *see* disk, partitioning
    reservation    101, 102, 145–147
devreserv    146, 147
df    11, 77, 284
dfmounts    173, 174–175, 283
dfshares    171, 173, 173–174, 181, 283
dgmon    122

diagnostics
    automounter problems   185–188
    NFS mounting problems   180–182
    s5 file system consistency   288–304
    ufs file system consistency   305–332
directory   335
    compressing   81, 281
    definition   53
    large   9–10, 55, 80–81, 281, 282
    lost+found   69, 72
    moving   284
    root   63, 69, 71, 72
    skeletal   18
directory block
    s5   91–92
    ufs   95
directory file,s5   60
directory size, controlling   9–10, 80–81
directory tree   53, 56
disk
    bootable   101, 127–132
    data loss   116
    defective block *see* bad block
    formatting   67, 101, 104, 282, 336
    free space   284
    hard   97
    manufacturing defects   107
    non-mapped blocks   106
    partition, definition   67
    partitioning   8, 67, 72, 75, 101, 104, 116–119, 284
    quotas   8, 55, 82–83, 282
    read/write errors *see* bad block
    repartitioning   101, 103, 118–119
    sector, definition   67
    seek distance   236–239
    slowdown   224
    space   3, 8
    usage   4

    balancing   3, 4, 8, 54, 79–80
    monitoring   54, 76, 77–79
disk block addressing
    bfs   65
    s5   58–59
    ufs   62
disk drives   7
diskette
    bootable   114
    floppy   98, 114
    formatting   282
dispadmin   35, 37–40, 283, 284
distributed printing configuration   336
domain   335
downstream   335
driver   336, 343, 344
driver, pseudo-device   341
drvinstall   99
du   2, 11, 78–79, 285

**E**

echo   18
edquota   82, 83, 282
environment variable   16, 19–21
errdump   227, 240–241, 285
error message   336
exec   22
execution stack   21
exit   45

**F**

fattach   339
ff   76
FIFO   336, 339
file   336
    definition   53
    inactive   54, 76, 78
file sharing   170
file size, and block size   9
file system   2, 3, 7, 336
    bfs   57, 121

bootable   74

checking   8, 282

compressing   81, 281

consistency   84–96, 287–304, 305–332

creating   8, 67–75, 281

definition   53

maintaining   76–79

mounting   8, 55, 56, 75, 76, 82, 103

performance   79–81

repair   8

root   55, 69, 84

s5   56, 57–60

size, bfs   64

start-of-day counts   8

ufs   57, 60–63

used space in   11

usr   69

file system inconsistencies   282

file system type   3, 8, 9

bfs   54, 63–65, 68, 74–75, 95–96, 121, 122, 128, 281

nfs   54

rfs   54

s5   54, 60, 66, 67, 68, 69, 69–72, 75, 86–92, 281, 287–304

selecting   66–67, 284

ufs   54, 60–63, 66, 67, 68, 69, 72–74, 75, 92–95, 281, 305–332

filename   336

files

inactive   282

filters

definition of   336

find   9, 78–79, 80, 80–81, 131, 281, 282, 284

firmware mode   122–124, 125–127, 128, 129, 131, 242

FLCKREC parameter   258

floppy diskette   114

flow control   336

fltboot   125, 126

fmtflop   104, 282

fmthard   67, 104, 116, 118, 122, 130

fmthd   284

fork   336

fork   22, 23, 24, 263

format   104, 282

formatting a disk   67

formatting, see disk, formatting

fragment, ufs   60, 67, 73

free block map, ufs   330–332

free disk space

ufs   73

free list   336

consistency checking   300–303

fsba   72

fsck   8, 76, 84–96, 121, 224, 282, 287–304, 305–332

example   86

options   86–87

FSFLUSHR parameter   259, 266

FSType, see file system type

fusage   213, 227, 231–232, 284

## G

getdev   135–138

getdgrp   141–143

getgroups   269

getrlimit   267, 268

getty   22

GPGSLO parameter   259, 267

grep   184

group ID number   345

group name   345

## H

HCORLIM parameter   259

HCPULIM parameter   259, 268

HDATLIM parameter   259, 268

hdeadd   112, 114

hdefix   112, 115, 115–116

hdelog   110

hdelogger   105, 110, 111, 114

HFNOLIM parameter    259
HFSZLIM parameter    259, 268
hog factor    230
HOME variable    19
HRTIME parameter    260, 272
HRVTIME parameter    260, 272
HSTKLIM parameter    259, 268
HVMMLIM parameter    259, 269
HW_PROVIDER parameter    258, 265
HW_SERIAL parameter    258, 265

# I

I/O completion    4
ID mapping    337, 345
i-list    337
i-list, s5    57
indirect addressing
    s5    59
    ufs    62
indirect block, s5    91
indirect blocks    337
init    337
init    22, 36, 124
INITCLASS parameter    30, 33, 260, 272
INITCLASS variable    35, 36
initdefault    124
inittab    120, 124
inode    10, 337
    bfs    64, 64–65, 74, 130
    consistency checking    289–292, 311–323
    maximum number    66
    number    10, 337
    quota    82, 83
    s5    57, 58–60, 66, 89–91
    shortage    3, 4
    table    5
    ufs    61–63, 66, 93–95, 311–323
input side    345
interprocess communication    189, 337
inter-record gap    87, 117
interrupt    337, 345
interrupt handling    23

i-number    337
    bfs    64
    s5    58
ioctl    271
IPC    337

# K

kernel    337
kernel address space    337
Kernel Memory Allocation (KMA)    189
kernel mode    23, 24
kernel profiling    227, 232–235, 281, 282
kernel size    5
kernel table usage    189
kernel tunable parameters    264
kernel tuning    12
kill    7, 184, 285

# L

labelit    72, 73, 74, 134
large directories    3, 8
large jobs    3, 4, 5, 7
least-recently used (LRU) algorithm    41, 266
letter quality    338
line discipline    338
listdgrp    144
locality of reference    41
log driver tunable parameters    271
log files    338
logical block    9, 338
logical block size    9
logical blocks    67
login    22
LOGNAME variable    20
lost+found    296, 298
lost+found    92, 95, 323, 324, 325, 327, 328, 329
    s5    69
    ufs    72
lp    240
lpsched    335
ls    22, 99, 100, 103, 181, 182

# M

magic number, bfs   64
maintenance   3, 8
master files   246
MAXCLSYSPRI parameter   30, 33, 260, 271
MAXGDP parameter   262, 280
maximum file size
    s5   60
    ufs   63
MAXPMEM parameter   259, 267
MAXSERVE parameter   220–221, 225, 262
MAXUP parameter   258, 263
mboot   119
measuring
    disk activity   227
media-specific data area   105
memory dump   285
memory dumps   227
memory shortage   3
memory size   4, 5, 16, 29, 41, 43
message   338
message block   338
message of the day   16
message queue   338
message tunable parameters   275–276
messages   204
MINARMEM parameter   259, 267
MINASMEM parameter   259, 267
mini_system   120
MINSERVE parameter   220–221, 225, 262, 279
mkboot   246, 249
mkdir   81, 171, 281
mkfs   67, 68–75, 121, 130, 281, 303
mmap   269
modem   338
modem interrupts   3, 4, 10, 46
module   338
monacct   45, 51
monitoring   11
    buffer activity   193, 195–196, 283
    command execution   282
    CPU utilization   193, 208–209, 283
    disk access   236–239, 284

disk activity   193, 199–200, 283
disk seek distance   284
file access   194, 283
file access operations   193
free memory   207
interprocess communication   193, 204, 283
kernel memory   193, 202–203
kernel memory allocation   283
KMA, see monitoring, kernel memory
memory freeing   201–202
memory freeing activity   193
memory usage   283, 284
overall system performance   193, 214–218, 283
page fault activity   193
page faults   205–206, 283
page-in   193, 205–206
page-out   193, 201–202
paging   283
queue activity   283
remote buffer usage   193, 283
remote CPU utilization   193, 209–210, 283
remote system calls   193, 283
remote use of resources   231–232
RFS buffer activity   195–196
RFS client caching   193, 218–220, 283
RFS operations   193, 212–213
RFS server activity   220–221
RFS server availability   193, 284
RFS system calls   197–198
scheduling queue activity   193, 206–207
shared resource usage   284
swap space   193, 207, 284
swapping   211–212
switching   211–212
system calls   193, 196–198, 284

system tables    193, 210–211, 284

terminal activity    284

terminal line activity    193, 213–214

unused memory    193

monitoring system activity    281

mount    339

mount    76, 121, 131, 171, 176, 176–177, 179, 180–182, 183, 185, 219, 239, 284

mount point    339

mount system call    177

mountall    76

mountd    176, 177, 178, 181

MSGMAP parameter    261, 275

MSGMAX parameter    261, 275

MSGMNB parameter    261, 275

MSGMNI parameter    261, 275

MSGSEG parameter    261, 276

MSGSSZ parameter    261, 275

MSGTQL parameter    261, 276

mUNIX    120, 124

mv    77, 81, 172, 281, 283

**N**

name server, current    334

name server, domain    335

name server, primary    341

named Stream    339

NAMERT parameter    30

NAMETS parameter    30

NAUTOPUSH parameter    260, 271

NAUTOUP parameter    259, 266

NBPW parameter    261, 276

NBUF parameter    224, 258, 265

NCALL parameter    258, 263

ncheck    76

NCLIST parameter    258, 263

NDQUOT parameter    260, 274

netstat    184

network    339

network daemons

uusched    152

uuscico    152

uuxqt    152

Network File System    10, 339

network host

down    10

network listener    339

network server

dead    10

inappropriate    10

networking    2, 339

newboot    121, 131

NFS    170–188, 339, 343

administering    172–173

automounting    184–188

biod daemon    176, 178, 184

browsing available resources    173–174

clearing client problems    180–182

clearing server problems    179–180

client    172

error messages    181–182

fixing hung programs    182–183

hard mounts    179

improving access time    184

monitoring usage    173–175

mountd daemon    176, 177, 178, 181

mounting a resource    173, 176–177

nfsd daemon    176, 177, 178, 182, 183

server    172

sharing resources    170–172, 173, 283

soft mounts    179, 183

starting and stopping    173

troubleshooting    175–184

NFS resources, defined    171

NFS resources, hard mounted    179

NFS, *see* Network File System

NFS_GETFH system call    177

nfsd    176, 177, 178, 182, 183

nfsd(1M)    183

NGROUPS_MAX parameter    259, 269

NHBUF parameter    258, 265

nice    7, 273, 285

NINODE parameter    260, 274

NINODES parameter    6, 224

`NLOG` parameter    260, 271
node name    339
`NODE` parameter    258, 264
noisy terminal line    46
Non-Volatile RAM (NVRAM)    122, 125, 129
`NPBUF` parameter    258, 265
`NPRIME`    47
`NPROC` parameter    6, 224, 258, 262, 263
`NRCVD` parameter    262, 279, 280
`NRDUSER` parameter    262
`nroff`    7
`NSNDD` parameter    262, 280
`NSRMOUNT` parameter    262, 280
`NSTRPHASH` parameter    260, 271
`NSTRPUSH` parameter    260, 270

## O

off-peak hours    4, 5, 7
    setting up    45–46, 285
operating system    340
option    340
output side, see downstream

## P

page    340
page fault    42
page faults    5
`pageout`    42
`PAGES_UNLOCK` parameter    267
paging    5, 16, 41–44, 189, 282, 340
paging behavior    4, 5
    monitoring    43–44
paging daemon    27, 29
paging parameter
    low-water mark    42–43
    memory    42
paging tunable parameters    266–267
parameters
    tunable    29
parent process    340
partition
    `boot`    119–124

definition    67
    `stand`    119–124
partitioning a disk    67, 72, 75
partitions    340
`PATH` variable    5, 6, 17, 19, 20, 224, 282
pathname    340
performance monitoring tools    2
performance, kernel    232–235
physical block    340
PID    340
pipe    22, 78
polling    340
`pr`    240
`prdaily`    45
preemption    24
preening, `ufs` file systems    305, 311, 314, 315,
      319, 322, 323, 324, 325, 326, 327, 329,
      330, 331
`prf` profiler commands    232–235
`prfdc`    13, 227, 233, 234–235, 281, 282
`prfld`    13, 227, 233, 233–234, 275, 282
`PRFMAX` parameter    234, 260, 275
`prfpr`    13, 227, 233, 235, 282
`prfsnap`    13, 227, 233, 281, 282
`prfstat`    13, 227, 233, 234, 282
`PRIME`    47
`priocntl`    28, 272
priorities
    fixed    25
priority
    global    27, 29
    of a sleeping process    33
    real-time    26
priority, process *see* process priority
process    341
    classes of    25
    daemon    23
    kernel    23, 27
    priority    25
    queues    25
    real-time    25, 26, 28, 35
    runaway    3, 5, 7, 35, 282, 285

system   25, 26
time-sharing   26
user   23, 27
process accounting   230
process handling   2
process ID   22
process id   341
process number   341
process priority   25–28
global   29
real-time   34
process structure   5, 15
process switching   189
process table   5
profile   341
profiler   13, 341
profiler   232
profiling, kernel   232–235
prtvtoc   72, 75, 116, 119, 122, 130, 131, 239, 284
ps   2, 4, 7, 183, 184, 202, 282
PS1 variable   19
pseudo-device driver   341
PUTBFSZ parameter   258
PUTBUFSZ parameter   263
putdev   133, 135, 139–140
putdgrp   141, 144

## Q

quot   83
quota   83
quotacheck   83
quotaoff   83, 282
quotaon   83, 282
quotas   83
quotas, see disk, quotas

## R

raw device   341
RCACHETIME parameter   262
RCHACHETIME parameter   219
read system call   170

read-side   345
real-time
process priority   34
scheduler class   27
reboot   341
reconfiguring UNIX   2
REL parameter   258, 264
Remote File Sharing   10, 341
Remote File Sharing, see RFS
remote resource   342
re-partitioning a disk   72
repquota   83
resource   342
resource imbalance   4
resource, local   338
response time   2
RF_MAXMEM parameter   262
RFS   337, 339, 343
client caching   218–220, 283
heavy use of shared resources   225
monitoring performance   195–196, 197–198, 209–210, 218–221
not enough server processes   225
server   284
server activity   220–221
too many server processes   225
RFS, monitoring   189
RFS, see Remote File Sharing
rlogin   181
rm   81, 172, 281, 284
root   342
root   16, 117
root directory   72
ROOTFSTYPE parameter   258, 263
rotational gap   342
rpcbind   177, 180, 181
RSTCHOWN parameter   259, 269
rt_dptbl   34, 35, 38, 40
run level   342
run state   342
runacct   45
runaway process   282
runaway process, see process, runaway

# S

s5   9
sa1   13, 190, 190–191, 192, 285
sa2   13, 190, 191–192, 285
sadc   13, 190, 281
sadc sampling command   190
sadp   13, 224, 227, 236–239, 284
sag   13, 221–223
sanity words, bfs   64, 96
sar   2, 4, 5, 6, 13, 43–44, 67, 190, 192–225, 281
sar -A   193, 214–218, 229, 283
sar -a   193, 194, 283
sar -b   193, 195–196, 224, 265, 283
sar -C   193, 218–220, 283
sar -c   193, 196–198, 224, 282, 284
sar -d   193, 199–200, 283
sar -Db   193, 195–196, 224, 283
sar -Dc   193, 197–198, 209, 283
sar -Du   193, 209–210, 213, 225, 283
sar -g   193, 201–202, 206, 207, 224, 274, 282, 283
sar -k   193, 202–203, 224, 283
sar -m   193, 204, 283
sar -p   193, 205–206, 207, 224, 282, 283
sar- p   202
sar -q   193, 206–207, 224, 283
sar -r   193, 207, 282, 284
sar- r   202, 206
sar -S   193, 213, 220–221, 225, 279, 284
sar -u   193, 206, 208–209, 224, 282, 283
sar- u   202
sar -v   193, 210–211, 224, 274, 284
sar -w   193, 206, 211–212, 224, 282, 284
sar- w   202
sar -x   193, 212–213, 225
sar -y   193, 213–214, 225, 282, 284
SAVEXP parameter   260, 273
schedule   342
scheduler   2
    configuration   28–36
    configuring   284
    parameter tables   31–33
    real-time policy   27
    time-sharing policy   26
    tunable parameters   29–30
scheduler class   26, 29
    installing   36
    listing   283
    real-time   27, 38
    removing   35–36
    system   27
    time-sharing   26, 27, 38
scheduler classes
    listing   37
scheduler parameters   15, 26, 37
    kernel class   33
    listing   283
    real-time   34–35
    time-sharing   31–33
scheduling algorithm   5, 15
    round-robin   27
scheduling parameters   5
scheduling policy   25
scheduling queue activity   189
SCORLIM parameter   259, 268
SCPULIM parameter   259, 268
SCSI   98, 102
SDATLIM parameter   259, 268
search path   6, 342
search paths   3
secondary name server   342
sector   67, 73, 104, 117, 342
    definition   67
segment   343
SEMAEM parameter   261, 277
semaphore   343
semaphore, tunable parameters   276–277
semaphores   204
SEMMAP parameter   261, 276
SEMMNI parameter   261, 276
SEMMNS parameter   261, 276
SEMMNU parameter   261, 276
SEMMSL parameter   261, 276
SEMOPM parameter   261, 276
SEMUME parameter   261, 276

SEMVMX parameter    261, 277
server    343
setrlimit    267
SFNOLIM parameter    259, 269
SFSZLIM parameter    259, 268
sh    22, 50, 131
share    171, 173, 174, 176, 177, 285
shared memory    343
shared memory table    5
shared memory, tunable parameters    277
shared resource    10, 283, 285, 343
    mounting    284
shared resources    3
    monitoring usage    231–232
SHLBMAX parameter    259, 267
shmat    269
SHMMAX parameter    261, 277
SHMMIN parameter    261, 277
SHMMNI parameter    261, 277
SHMSEG parameter    261, 277
shutdown    108, 113, 124, 127, 129, 247
signal    343, 345
signalstack    268
soft mounts    179
SPAU tools    11, 13, 189–225, 227, 228–230,
    232–235, 236–239
special file    75, 87, 98–100, 101, 128, 343
spell    77
SPTMAP parameter    259, 266
SRPC_DOMAIN parameter    258, 264
SSTKLIM parameter    259, 262, 268
stand partition    101, 119–124
    operations on    121–124
stand partitions
    multiple    122
start-of-day counts    8, 79
state
    kernel    24
    ready to run    23, 24, 25
    sleep    24, 33
    swapped    24
    user    24
    zombie    23, 24

statfs system call    177
stdin    22
stdout    22
STIME    7
storage block
    bfs    64
    s5    58, 60, 92
    ufs    63
storage devices    2
STRCTLSZ parameter    260, 270
Stream    335, 336, 338, 339, 341, 343, 344
Stream end    336, 344
Stream head    343, 344
Stream-based pipe    344
STREAMS    203, 336, 338, 343, 344
Streams    344
STREAMS tunable parameters    270
STRMSGSZ parameter    260, 270
STRTHRESH parameter    260, 270
su    77
summary information block
    ufs    61, 67
super block    344
superblock
    bfs    63–64, 96
    s5    57, 88–89, 298, 300, 301, 302
    ufs    60–61, 92–93, 307, 308, 331
super-user    50
superuser    179
super-user root    40, 82
superuser root    240, 267
surrogate image region    105, 107, 115
SVMMLIM parameter    259, 269
swap    344
swap area    344
swap partition    102, 118
swap space    41, 112, 117, 118, 189
swapper    22, 29
swapping    41
swapping behavior, monitoring    44
SYS    344
SYS parameter    258, 264
SYS_NAME parameter    30, 260, 271
sysadm    119, 155

sysdef    12, 275, 276, 277
sysdump    227, 242–244, 285
system    120, 124, 246, 255
system boot    111, 116
system call activity    189
system calls    344
system configuration    2, 3, 11, 12, 245–255
system dump    242–244, 285
system files    246
system load    7
system maintenance    2
system mask    17
system monitoring    11
system name    344
system panic    112, 113
system parameters    11, 12
System Performance Analysis Utilities, *see*
        SPAU tools
system profile    16, 16–18, 19
system reconfiguration    248
system reconfiguration, sample    250
system resources    7, 15
system state 1 (single-user)    111, 115
system state 2 (multi-user)    107, 243
system state 5 (firmware)    111, 242
system state 6 (reboot)    111
system tables
        too large    224
        too small    224
system tuning    11

thrashing    4, 16, 43
tic    21
TIME    7
time slice    23, 27, 28, 32, 38
time-sharing
        process priority    33
        scheduler class    26
timex    13, 227, 228–230, 282
TMPDIR variable    103
touch    249, 285
track    345
trap    345
troff    7
ts_dptbl    31, 35, 38, 40
ts_kmdpris    33, 35
TSMAXUPRI parameter    30, 273
tunable parameters    29, 256–277, 345
        kernel    264
        log driver    271
        message    275–276
        modifying    249
        paging    266–267
        scheduler    29–30
        semaphores    276–277
        shared memory    277
        STREAMS    270
tunefs    307, 308
tuning    345
TXMAXUPRI parameter    260

# T

table overflow    4, 6
table size    3, 4
tail    77, 283
tape drive    98
term    21
TERM variable    21
terminal line, noisy    282
terminfo    21
TERMINFO variable    20
termio    338
text section    21

# U

ufs    9
UFSNINODE parameter    260, 274
UID    345
umask    19
umount    121, 131, 185
umountall    115
unbootable operating system recovery    253
unix    119–124
unix, configuring    245–255
upstream    345
usage reports    1

daily   16
monthly   16
user ID number   345
user mask
default   16
user mode   24
user name   345
user process   5
user profile   16, 18–19, 83
user training   2
useradd   18
uucheck   152, 160
uucico   152, 154, 158, 160, 335
uucleanup   152
uucp   152, 155, 339
uudecode   152
uuencode   152
uugetty   152
uuglist   152
uulog   152, 160
uuname   152, 160
uupick   152
uusched   152
uustat   152, 160
uuto   152
uutry   152, 160
uux   152
uuxqt   152, 153, 154

**W**

wasted space   9
wc   18, 22
who   18, 181, 183
working set   41
write system call   170
write-side, see downstream

**X**

XENIX, shared data   272
XSDSEGS parameter   260, 272
XSDSLOTS parameter   260, 272

**V**

VER parameter   258, 264
vfstab   68, 75–76, 83, 85, 87, 176, 181, 183, 185
virtual address   41
virtual memory   346
vnode table   108
volcopy   72, 74
Volume Table of Contents   104
VTOC   284, 346
VTOC, *see* Volume Table of Contents

# Notes

# Notes

# Notes

# Notes

# Notes

# Notes

# Notes

# Notes